A GAME OF MOLES

A GAME OF MOLES

The Deceptions of an MI6 Officer

Desmond Bristow
with
Bill Bristow

LITTLE, BROWN AND COMPANY

A *Little, Brown* Book

First published in Great Britain in 1993
by Little, Brown and Company

Copyright (c) Desmond Bristow with Bill Bristow 1993

The moral right of the authors has been asserted.

*Certain individuals mentioned in this publication
have been supplied with pseudonyms to protect their
identity.*

A CIP catalogue record for this book
is available from the British Library.

ISBN 0 316 90335 3

Typeset by Hewer Text Composition Services, Edinburgh
Printed in England by Clays Ltd, St Ives plc

Little, Brown and Company (UK) Limited
165 Great Dover Street
London SE1 4YA

For Betty, Rosanne, and John Desmond

I dedicate this simple story to all those Spanish and Portuguese collaborators who quietly, secretly, and invariably dangerously, helped the Allied cause and received no thanks nor commendations.

They were, and are, amongst all those hundreds of unsung heroes. We should have remembered them.

Contents

Acknowledgements

My thanks go to those who encouraged me to write – a few ex-MI6 colleagues also wished me well; some thought that I should not proceed.

Gratitude I offer my son Bill, for the long hours he spent compelling me to elaborate upon details which I had forgotten, or thought not to be relevant to my own manuscript. In this he was helped by my wife Betty. But for her support and tireless proddings, what follows would never have appeared. To her I offer my thanks for her infinite tolerance. I owe deep acknowledgement to Drew Launay and Tim McGirk, at present the *Independent*'s correspondent in India, through whose introduction the 'Molegame' was taken up by Alan Samson, editorial director of my supportive publishers, Little, Brown. Alan has been of enormous help, patient and generous in encouragement and advice.

Special thanks to the late Kenneth Mills, who not only worked with me in Spain as Defence Security Officer in Gibraltar but became a very close friend.

Thanks also to Austin Baillon, whose contributions have added a spark of fun as well as inspiration.

Finally I thank all those friends and colleagues, no longer with us, whose friendship contributed to 'the best days of my life'. Those still living know who they are.

Author's Note

For a long time after the war my family was not aware of what 'Daddy' had been doing between 1940 and 1945.

Perhaps I had been so cagey that they were not even interested. Then, at the age of ten, our youngest son William began asking odd questions. This was in 1965. He had seen some French decorations and questioned my wife Betty about them. Betty invariably told Bill to ask me. I cannot recall how I replied to his enquiry. Later when he became more enlightened he pressed me to write my memoirs, such as they were. Reluctantly I began to do jottings.

By then, 1967, my erstwhile friend and sometime department boss, Kim Philby, had become a notorious figure as a prime traitor. Since his take-off to Moscow from Beirut in 1963, I had sometimes argued that he must be an MI6 double agent run by a most secret section that was not to be found in either 54, Broadway (the then MI6 headquarters) or at Leconfield House where MI5 was much more comfortably accommodated. I thought for a time that the powers-that-be must have taken Malcolm Muggeridge's advice and closed both outfits and had started up in an unknown place with new staff.

Alas, this was not so and I concluded that my former friend deserved his traitorous notoriety. My first jottings became some pages in which I briefly recorded my association with him. By 1983, I began to appreciate that not only Philby but also the double agent Garbo deserved some attention. Within a year these pages had become detailed reflections and notes on discussions with friends, in particular with Ken Mills with whom 'moles' never bored! It was then that I finally decided that I would seriously put pen to paper.

In the first place it was clear that the 'moles' had blackened the reputation not only of MI5 but MI6 also. No one then, nor any official body, had seen fit to issue a counterblast. It was not fair, I felt, to allow these traitorous characters and a few others to cast their miserable shadows over everyone who had been involved in MI5 and MI6 and other secret Government departments. It was not amusing to be asked what my KGB connections had been.

By 1989, two willing co-authors had become otherwise engaged and it was then that my son, Bill, who had been in Los Angeles for ten years and involved in making film documentaries and general television work, suggested that he would come to Spain for a father-and-son co-operative effort. This book is a result of that collaboration, mostly of a straightforward nature but sometimes beset by acrimonious moments.

1

Childhood to College

Mountains, olive trees, small steam engines whistling and puffing around mining pits, dust, goats, donkeys and freedom. I am the second son of an English mining engineer in south-west Spain.

It was 1919 and I was two years old when my father, the director and engineer of the copper mine at Santa Rosa, was given the added responsibility of the neighbouring mine at Sotiel Coronada. This meant moving, since the workload at Sotiel Coronada was much more demanding than at Santa Rosa, or that is what I was told later. The house staff of Santa Rosa packed our belongings onto one of the little mining trains, we said our goodbyes, climbed into the passenger carriage at the rear of the train trucks and shunted off to Sotiel, where I spent the next five years of a blissfully free-spirited life.

The village, in a bowl-shaped valley with craggy mountains to the north, south, east and west, was quite beautiful compared to the image one usually has of mining towns. Crusty old men with clear memories and long stories; eager young men with wives and children; goats, donkeys, cats, dogs and a lot of malaria walked the dirt streets and lived in the whitewashed, red-roofed houses, which were situated some two kilometres from the mining pits.

My father set about the very serious malaria problem by planting hundreds of eucalyptus trees in the low-lying land around the mine to soak up the excess water. When they had grown enough he burnt the strong-scented leaves of these wonderful trees, the smoke being a deterrent to the disease-carrying mosquitoes. The women fetched water from various distribution points, carrying it in pitchers on their heads; they often kept an extra supply outside their houses in open butts. These butts were a major breeding place for mosquitoes, so my father would accompany the nightwatchman around Sotiel turning over offending containers, until the people learnt that it was pointless to keep water in them. All garbage had to be placed in specially built concrete bins at the end of each day. As a result of his relentless efforts, in a relatively short period of time the area was rid of malaria and its deadly trail for good.

Our whitewashed house, quite modern and large, sat on a knoll in the centre of the eight-hundred-strong community. The citrus garden in the front had steps leading to a large patio bounded by the washhouse, home bakery, workshop and cellars. On the next level down, a fountain and palm tree made a cool place to sit; not that I was very good at sitting with so many wondrous adventures to be had. I remember being taken by Mum and Maria, my nanny, to our large fruit and vegetable garden, riding my brother's donkey around, having picnics by the garden hut followed by walks to the tennis court (not often used for tennis), and picking gourds of many shapes and sizes from the rusty link fencing.

Being the chief engineer, my father was kept very busy building bridges, canals, railway lines and mine shafts, and supervising the mechanical maintenance of the machinery. As director, he was also responsible for the domestic side of community life; my mother helped, often looking after the school, the emergency clinic, food and water supplies.

My father did not believe in overworking the labourers; shifts on the mines started at 7 am and finished at 2 pm. With their afternoons free, the more industrious labourers took up land allotments offered by my father and worked the soil. My parents created a co-operative where the community would buy and sell their fruit and vegetables.

It was a very hot day, and my father was at the breakfast table which is perhaps why I remember it so well since he was very rarely around the house and seemed a rather remote figure. We had churros, and I think it was the first time I had coffee, a very grown-up drink, instead of the usual milk. When breakfast was over, my father asked me to follow him into the front room, followed by my brother and mother.

'Happy fourth birthday, Derry,' they cheered. My father walked over to a tray with four candles on, and lit them. I remember being very concerned as I looked from my brother, to my mother, to my father and around the room; there were no presents to be seen. I eagerly blew out the candles, closed my eyes and made a wish. When I opened them I watched the smoke from the wicks float lazily in and out of the sunbeams, hoping my presents were going to appear.

Taking me by the hands my parents took me outside where I came face to face with Juana. Oh what joy, my very own donkey! Father lifted me into the pack saddle, smiled and patted the donkey on the rump. 'There you are, young man, off you go.'

I was full of pride as I rode down the track on my donkey.

I put my arms around Juana's neck and looked down to see little clouds of dust swirl gently around where her hooves landed on the dirt surface, and listened to the thud, thud, thud echo through the narrow street as we went on our first trip together. We said 'ola' to my friends, and I waved to everyone in the village. As we trotted back to the house a new sense of freedom came over me. When my trusty new companion came to a halt by the front door, I leapt down and gave my parents a big hug each.

'Gracias; muchisimas gracias,' I exclaimed; Spanish was my first language. After calming down a little I noticed my brother Martin, older than me by three years, loading picnic baskets onto his donkey Catalina. I could hardly contain myself – it meant a picnic up by the dam. Of course, whatever Martin's donkey could carry, Juana could carry more. Since his had the baskets, Mother was to go on mine. Off we went; through the village, up the little track by the stream, around the basin of the open mine, and on.

My father had headed the team which completed the dam in 1908. The collected water spread over the valleys forming a beautiful lake, bordered by pine trees and gloriously sticky Jarra trees, their soft white flowers so enjoyed by the bees.

'Derry, let me down please, I want to walk with Father; you should be riding your donkey, today of all days.' No sooner was my mother on the ground than I was up and off . . .

'Race to the rowboat,' yelled Martin as he put Catalina into a furious donkey trot. I kicked, and cried, 'Arre burra, arre.' Juana responded, launching me into the fastest pace I had ever been on a donkey. I felt the wind, the sun and the shadows on my face as we wove in and out of the pine trees.

'Well done, Derry,' my father's voice boomed out as I crossed the finishing line first. Of course Martin was too busy holding onto the picnic supplies to be able to realise his donkey's full potential. No sooner had my brother and I tethered our trusty steeds than off came our clothes and we dived into the crisp water for a swim.

Jamon serrano, cheese, fresh bread, tomatoes, cucumber sandwiches, asparagus, oh, and sausage rolls, and of course the cake. A feast fit for a king had been set out on the thick Spanish blankets. With the swimming, riding and walking, my appetite inspired me to grab a sausage roll, which normally I would have been severely reprimanded for; this seemed to go unnoticed this day. Eating, lazing in the sun, more riding and swimming, the bees buzzed and the birds flew and sang all around us.

'Derry, how about you and Martin rowing us around the island and back again?' Father asked as he helped Mother into the boat. Perched on top of the island was our Robinson Crusoe hut, housing chairs, a table and a coke-fed cooker made out of an old two-gallon petrol can. Many days other than birthdays were spent rowing, fishing and picnicking on the lake and island.

Following my birthday I spent most of my time with Juana, wandering around the countryside, often taking a packed lunch. There were days with José and his goatherd, listening to his stories and the goats' bells. I learnt that from May until July some unwary goats were killed by vipers that stayed up in the scrub areas. Once José built a small circle of fire with twigs, picked up a scorpion and put it in the middle of the flames. I watched in amazement as the creature danced around trying to find a way out, then finally committed suicide by stinging itself in the back of the head.

Other days, after a morning jaunt around the mines, Juana and I would follow the red, mineral-coloured River Odiel down to the old flour mill by the Roman bridge. There, I would climb up to the top floor and watch the light shine through small holes in the roof and create sunbeam patterns in the dust floating up from the milling area below. I listened to the water turning the wheel as I watched the grain being crushed by the stones. Antonio, the miller, always made a fuss of me and would put a sack of flour on Juana for the cook, who would make wonderful bread and cakes.

On one of these jaunts I ended up trading Juana with the head gipsy of the group that passed through the village every year. He wanted Juana and I wanted the horse with white socks on his front legs and a white blaze on his nose. I sat on my new horse and watched Juana and the gipsies, with their beautifully painted caravans, disappear over the brow of the hill. I took many long journeys on Rozinante, named after Don Quixote's horse. We would climb up into the mountains, often starting very early in the morning and not returning until sunset. When I think about some of the mountain paths we walked along, with sheer drops on one side and the steep slope of the mountain rising on the other, I feel funny. That is old age creeping in, I suppose.

Lessons, such as English, which always seemed too long, in reality took up only a few hours a week. Mum sat me down. 'The cat sat on the mat. Repeat after me, Derry.' Cows jumped over the moon, I always imagined that Humpty Dumpty's great fall was off our squash court wall.

It was by the squash court, when I was six years old, that Francisco the chauffeur bravely gave me my first driving lesson in our Model T Ford. After a few times with me sitting on his knee, we would pile cushions behind me and I would drive solo to the mine and back again.

Every summer, to escape the intense heat, two maids, chickens, a goat or two, fruit, vegetables and us climbed aboard the train for Huelva, then took a ferry to the coast town of Punta Umbria where we had a summer house right on the beach. Hard golden sands, fresh fish brought to us by the fishermen; cockles and mussels, sandcastles and English friends – for this was a community built by the English mining companies in that area. Every weekend we walked along the hot wooden planks spread over the sand dunes to the pier on the river side of the peninsula to meet the little ferry from Huelva. My father would step off the ferry with a bag of fruit and vegetables from the garden at the mines. Monday morning we would all walk back to the pier to see him off to work.

In the autumn of 1925 I made my first trip to England as a schoolboy at Dulwich Preparatory School. I had heard a lot about school and England from my brother. England was very green compared to Spain and the magnificent buildings around the school and in London were quite a change. Prep school was very much the same for me as for anyone else who went to one. Not speaking very good English created some extra problems for me, but being athletic helped overcome that barrier. The staff were wonderfully understanding and helped me and many other foreign-speaking children to adapt to English boarding-school life. Rugby, cricket, swimming and of course languages were my interests. I would sit with friends, mostly either colony children or foreign children, on the fire escape at night and watch the numerous firework displays at Crystal Palace. The restrictions on my freedom took a little getting used to after the very free life on the mine, but having so many children around of my age alleviated the problem to a certain extent. In 1931 I went on to Dulwich College, where life was fairly similar to prep school, just freer in some ways and stricter in others, because one was older. I managed to do well in sports and relatively well academically, winning a place at Magdalene College Cambridge.

Rowing (I became captain), reading French and Spanish, drinking certain amounts of port and other college activities made up three of the most enjoyable years of my life. The college buildings were beautiful, and lush green lawns gently sloped down to the river, where chaps wearing boaters and highly coloured blazers could be found punting up and down trying to find picnic spots for their girlfriends. Cambridge inspired good-spirited bad behaviour. One year, in an effort to raise money for Poppy Day, a friend poured petrol over me, struck a match, and all ablaze I dived off a bridge into the river Cam where the flames sizzled out before doing any damage.

José Muñoz Rojas, one of my Spanish lecturers who left Spain because of the Civil War, is still a close friend. I quote his words: 'You, Desmond, are my very worst pupil.' This has remained a joke between us ever since. Cambridge was interspersed with train and boat trips to the Iberian peninsula for holidays on the mines or at Punta Umbria with my parents. These trips, made between 1936 and 1939, were always tense and nervous due to the Spanish Civil War.

2

Spain; to St Albans with Philby

The Spanish Civil War ground to a bloody halt in March 1939. I left Cambridge in May and spent the early part of the summer rowing at Henley. After participating in the Regatta I sailed to Spanish shores for the summer holidays while waiting for a job in Chile or Canada as a trainee timber company manager. When the inevitable World War was declared, I realised it was not going to be a job in Chile or Canada. I wanted to join up, but the bureaucratic blockade characteristic of a dictatorial state after a civil war delayed my being permitted to leave the country, so I lost my place for an immediate commission.

Permission to leave was eventually granted and I was invited to escort three middle-aged English ladies from Madrid on the train journey through Spain and France on to England; reluctantly I agreed. I left the house in Sotiel Coronada on October 3rd, never to see it again as my beloved home. Francisco drove us to Seville, the bustling beautiful station echoing with childhood memories of schooltrips. Again the painful goodbye to my parents on the ironworked platform and the fateful steps onto the night train to Madrid; this time I was going to war. Steam and whistles filled the air, my train pulled slowly out. The ten-hour journey brought us under the glass dome of Madrid's Atocha station, which had been shattered in the Civil War. Madrid was a shell of its former glory; there were food shortages, no cars or horse carriages, very few people in the streets; hotels were glad for any business.

After a regal reception at the sumptuous Hotel National, I met the three ladies for breakfast and escorted them onto the train taking us to the border town of Irun. I have to admit that in their own very English way they kept me amused and somewhat alleviated my depression.

The countryside north of Madrid was pockmarked by shell holes; the empty trenches wound their snakelike courses, twisted tanks and trucks lay around, all presenting a scene which not only saddened me, but gave me nervous twinges. This, I thought, is what I'm heading for. As we slowly rattled northwards, the dangling power lines, broken telegraph poles, bomb-shattered and machine-gun bullet-marked walls, really awakened me to the destructive elements of war. The arrival at the French frontier thankfully gave me something to do, bringing me out of my gloom.

Shepherding the ladies from one country to another was no problem, but the luggage was a different story; there were no porters or trolleys. The scene presented a sort of climax. There we were with piles of luggage, leaving one country ravaged by civil war, setting foot in another which was already the stage of the Second World War.

Hendaye on the French side was bustling, organised and almost felt normal, except for the hordes of young men in uniform carrying guns. I enjoyed the buffet goodies of French pastries and coffee during our short wait at that lovely little frontier town.

The train, twice its normal length, smelt of sweat, and though full to the brim was very quiet. One could sense the anxiety and fear and the hundreds of different stories being told by hundreds of strangers' eyes, all brought together under circumstances playing havoc with our lives and imaginations.

We drew away from Hendaye at 2 am. The crisp morning air of that 5th of October helped ease the cramped conditions; the frequent stops to pick up conscripted *poilus*, in uniform and armed, heading north to the front, made me feel more and more like a Spanish sardine and confident the war would be over by Christmas.

Food was a problem. At Angoulême, having managed to acquire six croissants, a kilo of bananas and a bottle of water from the packed station buffet, I saw my train starting to pull out. Panic struck; holding onto the supplies I made a run for it, only to have my path cut by a goods train. Without thinking, I jumped onto the buffers between two of the moving wagons across the couplings and down on the other side; as I made a grab for the handrail of the last carriage on my train it stopped, almost making me fall over. It remained in the station for another hour, which gave me a chance to find the ladies without having to wade through the packed carriages, not an easy task with all the supplies I was carrying.

In Paris, where the can-can was still kicking, restaurants still cooking, the café au lait flowing and the people full of joie de vivre, we transferred to the boat train and finally arrived at Victoria Station, London. Although we were across the Channel, London, where I stayed for one night, was not full of joie de vivre. Cars had headlight blinkers on for the blackout, sandbags were in evidence and people generally were very serious. The following morning I caught the train to Cambridge and went to the university recruiting office. It really seemed that I had lost my place, having been delayed from leaving Spain; there were no vacancies for me in the war, and I was instructed to come back every two or three days. Strange, thinking of it now, that I had to wait to join in the war. To fill in time and save money I coached rowing and lived at Magdalene College for three weeks. At the end of the third week, having been rejected again and again, I decided to go and see my girlfriend Betty who lived near Worcester, where I secured lodgings and drove tractors through the winter of 1939–1940.

On February 27th 1940 I trudged through the snow to Worcester station and caught the train to London, took the underground train to Westminster, walked to the War Office, wended my way through security checks and piled-up sandbags and approached the Colour-Sergeant in charge of volunteers. I explained about missing my commission due to the hold-ups in Spain, and then my waiting in Cambridge.

He looked me straight in the face and asked, 'What do you want me to do about it, young man?'

'Well, I'm bored, I'm broke and I want to join up, and I was wondering if you might have any vacancies in this war?' I replied.

Two weeks later I was marching in the ranks of the Oxfordshire and Buckinghamshire Light Infantry as a private. Having done a lot of basic training at school, drill was very tedious especially with Oxfordshire and Buckinghamshire lads who did not know their left foot from their right. There were four of us with a university education in my barracks and we quickly became caretakers. Writing letters to parents and girlfriends was often an enjoyable benefit of being educated. One individual would compose letters of incredible passion to his girlfriend in Banbury. Darning socks and sewing buttons on tunics was one of the drawbacks. Promotion to corporal was soon followed by my transfer to Bloody Bulford officers' training camp.

Sergeant Davis was not the bullying sergeant I had expected; on the contrary he was a fairly soft-spoken man whose main duty was to get us fit, which he did. At Bloody Bulford I became the friend and chess opponent of Leo Long, who nearly always beat me. Leo Long has become famous for being the Russian agent who was a G2 officer to General Montgomery after D-Day.

Again I was subjected to drill training, part of the price of being in the infantry. After a week of intensive drill and field exercises I took some leave to see Betty. I had to change trains at Oxford and was standing on the platform when a hospital train with wounded from Dunkirk pulled in. I watched in horror as hundreds of young men like myself limped, hobbled on crutches, or were carried on stretchers, with arms or legs missing and bloody bandages around their faces and eyes. Many who could walk but not see would help those who could see but not walk. Slowly they moved down the platform as nurses helped and guided them to the waiting ambulances. Suddenly the idea of being an infantryman lost its appeal.

Thankfully, on my return I was asked to attend an interview. Several interviews later I became a lieutenant in the British Intelligence Corps. My training at Oxford was only interrupted by trips on my Matchless 500 motorcycle to see Betty.

Training consisted of learning all about enemy uniforms, hand weapons, tanks, airplanes, ships, habits and the German way of life. We also learnt the true art of discretion. I translated many military slogans and technical terms from the Spanish army into English, and many English military terms into Spanish. In April 1941 my appointment as an instructor on the Spanish and Portuguese armies bewildered me since I thought I was only slightly less ignorant on the subject than the rest of our defence establishment. The concern at the time was that the Spanish might decide to help Hitler since he had helped Franco during the Civil War.

I was stationed in Cambridge where I felt quite at home. The work was rather boring and office bound, but the security of the job encouraged me to propose. On May 18th, 1941, Betty and I were married, and I am glad to be able to say we are still married today despite the complications caused by the war and my work.

After a few more months of lecturing, despite my promotion to captain I started to get very bored. There was only so much one could say about the Spanish and Portuguese armies – they were under-equipped and not very fit. The Spanish suffered very badly during the Civil War and the Portuguese, well . . . they were Portuguese.

One day I was told that 'a gentleman from the War Office' had come to see me; this was Richard Broomham-White, who explained briefly about the need for Spanish-speaking officers, asked a couple of irrelevant questions, and generally chatted. We arranged for me to go to London, to the War Office, to meet Lieutenant Colonel Cowgill who wanted to interview me. Lieutenant Colonel Felix Cowgill, sitting behind his large oak desk, fired questions about my fluency in Spanish and my knowledge of the country. Sitting behind the Colonel was a pleasant-looking civilian taking notes and obviously studying me very carefully.

'How would you like to work on a rather secret project?' the Colonel asked.

'Anything to get my bum out of the seat in the office at Oxford,' I replied.

On 3rd September I found myself the passenger in a car going to St Albans, the driver being the pleasant-looking civilian. He immediately put me at my ease and offered me a cigarette. After some preliminary chit-chat about the traffic and Cambridge, he started to explain where we were going and what we would be doing. He had a slight stammer.

'The old mansion, Glenalmond, h-h-headquarters of S-s-section V is where you are going to be working with me in the Iberian sector of the Counter-Intelligence Department, MI6. There'll be about h-h-half a dozen of us collecting all the information we can about German movements in Spanish-speaking countries, including S-s-south America.'

As I watched the green countryside dashing by the car window, I thought to myself, I'm in the Secret Service. He continued talking while guiding the car through the curving country lanes. The sun shining through the hedgerows reminded me of the sunbeams in the old flour mill at home in Spain.

'By the way, my name is Desmond, Desmond Bristow,' I informally introduced myself as we arrived at St Albans. The driver, throwing his cigarette out of the window, looked at me and with his slight stutter replied, 'H-h-how do you do, Desmond. I'm Kim Philby.'

3

Snakepit for the Abwehr

After driving through the old Roman town of St Albans, we arrived at the private gravel driveway leading to Glenalmond, an Edwardian brick mansion tucked away behind large English hedgerows with a rather run-down garden. The reception officer greeted us and while waiting for our security clearance I couldn't help noticing the atmosphere of excited and nervous efficiency. New telephone lines were being installed, filing cabinets put in place, runners were carrying important-looking dossiers from room to room. Clearance granted, Philby and I made our way up the stairs and knocked at Colonel Cowgill's office.

Having said our formal salutations to Colonel Cowgill, we were ushered by his secretary downstairs to the Iberian sector office. Large french windows opened onto a small back lawn and a path which wound in between some chestnut trees, around an old lily pond full of green water and on down to a very overgrown rose garden. My desk, situated along the inner wall of the room, was thankfully near an old cast-iron stove. The few pictures on the walls were of naval officers who had once been connected with the Secret Service, and now appeared to be spying on us. The rest of the wall space was taken up by notice boards with constantly changing messages.

That evening Kim gave me a lift to my digs and waited outside while I dropped my luggage off. Mr and Mrs French provided bed and breakfast, and sandwiches or hot supper depending on what time I arrived back from work. They were the typical middle-aged English couple doing their bit for God and country, which was getting rent for housing chaps working on those 'ssshhh, very secret projects up at the old manor'. Kim honked the horn.

'Come on D-d-desmond, the pub will be out of b-b-beer if we don't go now.'

The King Harry on Harry Lane was to become our main relief centre, *pub*licly speaking. The smoke-stained beams, log fire, the smell of beer stored in barrels creeping up from the cellar, created an atmosphere conducive to conversation; the typical English pub. The evening was very pleasant; we told each other about our backgrounds, our families and various interests. I liked Kim Philby, my boss, and he seemed to like me; we got along very well, which made the prospect of my new work all the more exciting.

The first week was taken up establishing a routine and dividing the tasks between us. Our merry band of Iberian specialists were Kim Philby, Tim Milne from Oxford University, a bit older than myself, humourless and rather reserved, whose job was sorting through the pouch, choosing which of the intercepted Abwehr messages would come to us or go upstairs to the German, Dutch and French sections. (The Abwehr was the German intelligence service.) He and Kim were friends from before the War, having walked around Europe together. With hindsight, knowing now that Philby was working for the Russians even then, I can see it was bloody smart of him to manoeuvre Milne into that position, because Milne would have alerted Kim whenever anything important was snared by ISOS (Intelligence Service Oliver Strachey) and Philby would have been able to pass it on to the Russians. Trevor Wilson, in his mid-thirties older than the rest of us, had landed in the Iberian section for no obvious reason other than his knowledge of Morocco and perhaps his comedic abilities; he could always make us laugh, except Milne of course. Trevor had been a purchaser of skunk excrement in Abyssinia for the French perfume company Molyneux, and spoke the excellent French befitting a purveyor of skunk droppings, which proved useful in our North African spy operations.

Frank Hyde, a jovial character who enjoyed wearing his uniform, had been a liaison officer with the British navy in Barcelona at the outbreak of the Spanish Civil War. One day, while he was polishing his buttons, he told his sad tale about a Spanish Communist committee in his neighbourhood.

'They knocked on my door and as I opened it they put a gun in my face. "You have a fascist parrot," they said, and at that moment my parrot squawked, "I am a royal parrot and I'm for Spain and Portugal."' Frank started to crack a smile. 'My maid had taught the poor creature these dangerous words.' He then started to laugh. 'You'll never guess. These four anarchist Commie chaps took my feathered friend outside, gave him a trial, found him guilty, then shot him.' As you can imagine, we all burst out laughing.

Last but not least there was Jack Ivens who had been importing fruit from Portugal and Spain before the War, and whom I worked closely with in the beginning. I can't say much about Jack, other than that he was a soft-spoken family man who adored his Greek wife

'Anything to get my arse out of a chair,' I'd said at the interview, only to find myself boxed up in an old brick manor house hidden by tall hedgerows. I was chasing German and Italian spies all right, but in the most menial way possible. My job was cross-checking the hotel lists and airline passenger rosters being sent to us by our chaps in Madrid and Lisbon, looking for any likely suspects. There were plenty. Thousands, I'd say. Thanks to the geniuses at ISOS, a section of Ultra, we also received intercepted, decoded and decyphered messages being sent by agents of the Abwehr from Spain to Germany.

One Nazi wireless operator whose messages from La Coruna we intercepted possessed singularly bad luck and was often a target of our humour. One day Trevor gleefully reported, 'Hans Bugge has finally done it, poor bugger. His latest report to the Abwehr reads, and I quote, "I ran into an oxcart while riding my motorcycle, went over the cliff and broke my arm. Nothing else to report, signed Hans."'

Trevor's next antidote to the monotonous but tense days of roster-scanning was when he discovered a regular passenger from Istanbul to Madrid named Mustapha Kunt.

All this may seem ridiculous, reading it now, but there was a lot of tension, and roster-checking was as dull as it was important; silly humour often kept us going.

One foggy morning in late October the motorcycle courier brought over a batch of German messages from our men in ISOS. Tim Milne, scanning the intercepts, remarked, 'This sounds very odd.'

The room was icy cold as I had only just lit the fire. Kim was sitting by the bay window wearing the scarred leather jacket he had picked up in Spain during the Civil War. He glanced over and asked, 'What does it say?'

'Madrid's telling Berlin that their V-man, Arabel, has

reported the formation of a convoy in the bay of Caernarvon,' replied Milne.

Arabel? The name had never cropped up on the wires before.

Philby, not wasting a second, picked up his green phone, the scrambled line to MI5, and dialled the number for Herbert Hart who ran MI5's Abwehr research department.

'H-h-have you seen this message from M-m-madrid on the Caernarvon convoy, Hart?' asked Kim. This was the first time I noticed Kim clicking his fingers, which I soon realised was to help him fight his stammer. The rest of us in the room stopped what we were doing and listened intently. For me this Arabel was a welcome distraction. I was going through a battered Lisbon directory page by page, trying to match up a telephone number with a name and street address. It was obvious from Philby's conversation that MI5 had also received a copy of the message from ISOS and were extremely worried.

'Get Scotland Yard onto it,' Philby told Hart, clicking his fingers again, which obviously did help him stop his stammer. 'Ask them to see if any l-l-likely character in that area of North Wales fits the bill. We'll go on watching and see what comes of it. Bye for now.'

'So!' exclaimed Jack Ivens. 'It seems as though we have a Spaniard at large. Surely he must be a sailor off one of those merchant ships tied up in Liverpool?'

'Why should he or she be a Spaniard?' I asked. 'Arabel could be a Dutchman or woman, Swedish national or whatever.'

I sat playing with a cigarette, Trevor fiddled with his glasses, we were all looking at each other. I glanced over to Kim and asked, as though he would know the answer, 'I wonder what means of communication our mysterious Arabel used?'

Kim shook his head and, raising his eyebrows, said quietly to all of us, 'Listen, we must not get c-c-carried away on a guessing game, it wastes t-time, and if this character is important there will be another reference from ISOS soon enough.'

Without saying it, Philby had told us to get back to our routine work; but of course one could not help wondering about our Arabel.

At the beginning of the following day we received a written report from Commander Ewen Montague, MI5's liaison officer with the Admiralty. CONVOY. CAERNARVON. DOES NOT EXIST. The excitement of the previous day gave way to disappointing normality. The next report arrived a few days later from Commander Burt, MI5's controller of Scotland Yard's Special Branch. AFTER EXTENSIVE SEARCH. NORTH WALES AND LIVERPOOL. A NEGATIVE ON OUR SPANISH FRIEND ARABEL. But despite all the negative reports from our departments investigating Arabel, a second message from him to his German masters was picked up by ISOS a week later and immediately sent to our office. However, what he or she said only added to our perplexity. The cable bore the same code as the previous one used by the Germans working in Madrid. 60: ABWEHRSTELLE 1 BERLIN. ARABEL STATES CONVOY SAILED FOUR DAYS AGO IN SOUTHERLY DIRECTION.

'What's going on?' Kim asked with exasperation. 'We know there is no bloody convoy. Why and who is this Arabel and why is he so obviously lying?'

'Shouldn't we alert stations in Madrid and Lisbon?' asked Trevor.

'No; em-emphatically no,' replied Philby. 'That might blow ISOS. We can't let the Germans know we have cracked their c-c-codes. Either Arabel's a complete phoney, a r-r-ruse to catch us out – ' Kim stopped and then slowly added, 'H-he is still around for some reason. Five thinks he might be a member of the S-s-spanish mission in London.'

This made sense, as many of Franco's Falangist officers were rabidly pro-Nazi, and did not agree with his wish for Spain to remain neutral, therefore one of them might have infiltrated the London Embassy at the Germans' bidding. We figured this would also explain why Arabel was filing through Madrid. Then, with the strong Nazi support across the Irish sea, others in the section thought Arabel might have been in Ireland, not England at all.

The hordes of refugees then arriving in Britain were run past very tough interrogators who were set up at Wormwood Scrubs and at the Royal Victorian Patriotic School in Battersea. MI5, who ran these interrogators, checked and double-checked and none of the newcomers matched up with Arabel.

Having the distinct feeling that this Spanish mystery was going to become larger and our office very much busier in the near future, I decided now was as good a time as any to visit my pregnant wife in Worcester. Having cleared it with Kim Philby and Felix Cowgill, I set off on the train, still wondering who Arabel could be, and if the Germans were trying to catch us out. It was interesting sitting on the train with the other passengers; their uniforms very clearly explained who they were. Their conversation was all of horror and heroics; but at least they could *talk* about their activities. I had some cover story explaining my circumstances and why I was in St Albans – none of it true, of course. Mind you, just having a cover story made it all the more tempting to talk about work. Thank goodness Betty was pregnant and I could occupy my mind with that.

Not having seen Betty for over two months, my excitement as the train approached Worcester was hard to contain. As I stepped out of the carriage and saw her smiling face with that warm glow women seem to have when pregnant, I forgot all about being a Secret Service man. The village postman, who had given Betty a lift to Worcester, drove us back to Kerswell Green. The six-mile journey down the narrow winding lanes was over far too quickly, as was the whole weekend. Getting up very early the next morning to help feed and clean out the pigs, and generally lending my wife a hand with her Land Army duties, put me back in touch with a reality hard to maintain when working in a secret world. The cottage she shared with her mother was warm and comfortable. After cleaning out the second pigsty I washed my boots off, walked to the end of the garden and took the Matchless 500cc out of the shed. I pushed it up the garden path towards the road, and as I wheeled that lovely machine past the window, I asked, 'Betty, do you want to go for a spin up to the bluebell wood and back?' On seeing her hesitation I explained, 'I've decided to take the bike to St Albans with me and have managed to acquire a couple of extra petrol coupons.'

Oh what joy to feel her arms around my waist as we leaned in and out of the corners, the wind pushing me against my precious passenger and pulling at our hair. We stopped on a grass verge and went for a walk in the woods, making the most of the little time we had together. After our walk

I kick-started the motorbike into life and Betty climbed on to the pillion seat. Perhaps because of all the excitement on being with Betty and riding the bike again, or perhaps in my haste to get home before it started to rain, I managed to accelerate too fast, leaving Betty sitting on the verge which caused some concern for the expected baby. (I hasten to add, our daughter Rosanne was born healthy in January 1942.)

I left the next day, Sunday, in the pouring rain, and arrived at Mr and Mrs French's tired, wet and sad; yet somehow looking forward to the Monday morning in-tray, my mind again wondering about our Spanish German spy.

The office was not the hive of activity I had expected; Arabel had been quiet, it was still raining, and the most excitement was created by my motorbike. I was running my finger over names and addresses in the Lisbon directory when Kim turned to me.

'Desmond, we have three arrivals from Spain – H-h-huelva, to be more precise. They need to be interrogated. Since this is your domain you'd better get going.' I took the train to London and was met by Detective Inspector Reginald Spooner of Special Branch who gave me the background. These three Spanish longshoremen in Huelva had been given money by the Germans to load explosives on to English ships. They had consistently taken the money and dumped the explosives into the sea, thus saving British lives, ships and tons of supplies. The Germans became suspicious and the Three Charlies, as we called them, stowed themselves away on a British ship and arrived in England. I was rather tense for the first day, not being used to cross-questioning people, but with the help of Reginald Spooner, by the end of the third day I had become quite apt at cross-examining. Their stories checked out, and unbeknown to them they knew my father and the mines I had lived on as a child, which amused me no end. For their efforts the Three Charlies were given jobs in a very lowly group called the Pioneer Corps. It irks me today thinking of how little we British compensated such people.

I arrived back at HQ at 6.30 on Thursday evening, in time for a session in the glass conservatory at the back of Glenalmond, commonly called the snakepit. The dust and dead palm trees, the sound of glass clinking as the pink gins were stirred, set up the atmosphere for relaxed chatter about work. I quickly recounted my last few days as an interrogator and relayed my astonishment that the Three Charlies had successfully got away with their counter-sabotage activities.

Trevor peered over the top of his glass. 'Arabel has been at it again; even Kim the expert is at a loss.'

The Abwehr's trust in this creative liar grew with every fishy message. From Madrid we found out that Arabel's Abwehr contact Frederico was swallowing his agent's every tale. We could only suppose the Germans were either extremely gullible or they were setting a trap, as Philby had suggested. As the session drew to an end I stepped out of the back doorway into the dark autumn evening. A damp mist was hanging in the air as I emerged from the snakepit onto the lawn. I walked around the side of the mansion to the front driveway. I listened to the crunch of the gravel under my feet, zipped up my jacket, put on my tan pigskin gloves and started up my Matchless. The throb of the single-cylinder engine echoed as I wiped the evening dew off the seat. I felt a tap on my shoulder which made me jump a little. Philby was standing behind me, his collar pulled up around his neck. 'D-desmond, give me a lift and I'll stand you a Jameson's at King Harry's.' I took it slowly down the drive to the road as the bike needed warming up. Once at the gate I accelerated quite hard, skidding a little on the gravel as we entered the road. The headlight beam cut through the darkness and shone on the damp fallen leaves; the elm trees on either side created large dark shadows and intensified the loud throaty noise of the engine. My nose was running by the time we arrived. In the pub, the chill was soon relieved by the fire and the spirit of Mr Jameson's best Irish whiskey. Kim seemed a little anxious that night; I assumed it was due to the ever-growing pressure our sector was experiencing.

'Everything OK?' I asked.

'Yes, fine. Our section is becoming more important by the minute, and we're all doing very well, I'm glad to say.' He continued almost in the same breath and without his usual stutter, 'I was wondering what you think and feel about Franco?' I was somewhat taken aback by the question, as it seemed rather out of place.

'Well, he has both the British and Germans interested in what was once a totally divided country. I think he is good for Spain, and providing the Commies and anarchists don't regain strength, he will rebuild the country, turning it into a fairly wealthy nation. After all, it's very rich minerally and agriculturally,' I replied. Sipping on his whiskey he looked at me and pondered for a second. 'Yes, I think you could be right, I got that f-f-feeling when I was covering his Nationalist side as the *Times* correspondent during the Civil War. But actually I was wondering if you had any feelings about his leaning towards the Germans . . . or to our side?' He finished his whiskey and ordered two more.

'Kim, I don't know, but I find it hard to imagine him actually coming out and openly supporting either side;

Spain is far too unstable to fight. If I was him I would stay neutral.'

He leant back in his chair and unfastened his coat. 'Yes, I suppose you are right. H-h-how's Betty?' he suddenly asked, changing the subject. His stutter had returned.

Thinking back on it now he was obviously testing me as a potential partner in his work for the Russians.

We drank, and talked family and work. I dropped him off at his house late that night and picked him up early the following morning to take him to the garage where his car had been serviced. He was leaving for London after lunch as he was on night duty at Secret Service HQ, 54 Broadway, a chore we all unfortunately had to do at some point.

The Iberian section was by now a hive of nervous activity. We had an ever-increasing number of reports arriving from Madrid, Lisbon, Tangier, and Gibraltar. In Madrid, Lisbon and Tangier we (Section V) had our own stations from mid-1941; prior to this we accepted what the MI6 chaps reported. These stations would receive reports from consular representatives (agents). In Spain, the towns covered were Bilbao, San Sebastian, Vigo, Zaragoza and Seville. Lisbon drew information from Oporto. As a result of our newly formed organisation abroad, more and more information of a purely counter-espionage nature was reported by these consular posts, often naming Germans and Italians suspected of being secret agents. In early 1941 these reports had been a trickle, now (late 1941) they were a torrent. We had a big field of neutrality to operate in, enabling our agents to operate without too much danger despite the number of Germanophiles in both Spain and Portugal.

From late 1941 to spring 1942 our card index became a mammoth register of names, addresses, and telephone numbers, and we spent many evenings making and checking the relevant files and creating a cross-reference system.

I remember the feeling of gloom as I read ISOS messages and found one containing a solitary telephone number. That meant my Sunday visit to the pub with Kim or Jack, and my Sunday motorcycle ride had to be ditched in favour of the arduous task of matching a name and address with Madrid 27533. Have you ever tried reading a telephone directory backwards? I assure you it is not something one would do by choice. However, this tedious challenge gave me great satisfaction when I identified yet another enemy agent. Surprising as it may seem this work was all-absorbing, and would keep me up all night smoking and drinking cold coffee. On the day of revelation the excitement I felt walking into the office and the inevitable cheers and congratulations I received inspired me for the next dreaded bout.

The ever-increasing number of telegrams and letters from stations requiring urgent replies kept the seven of us and three secretaries busy for long periods without a break. By January 1942 we were working as a very close-coupled unit; our socialising in the pubs had to become less and less, and the clinking of glasses and rattling of tongues and brain cells in the snakepit happened more and more. Pubs were a dangerous place to talk and our secrets were becoming bigger. We had to condition ourselves not to talk shop anywhere, and since I found the work exciting and fascinating it was quite hard at first, especially with my wife. Somehow I found a way of switching off the work side of my life, perhaps helped by the fact I'm a Gemini. Jack Ivens and I often helped each other with our problems and our workloads.

Office procedure was as follows: at 8.30 am we would

peruse papers left over from the night before and clear any backlog. At 10.30 'the Bag' would arrive from Broadway, containing the correspondence from Section V stations, which had first been delivered to MI6 HQ from the Foreign Office. Since all mail came to England by diplomatic bag from Madrid, Tangiers, Lisbon and Gibraltar independently, it was anybody's guess which bag would arrive on any one day of the week. Once, having bet Trevor that the Madrid bag would arrive on Wednesday two weeks in a row, I received free pink gins for a week in the snakepit. Unfortunately betting did not go down all that well, so the opportunity to make the most of my lucky streak ended abruptly. Often mail would be preceded by a telegram, demanding an urgent response to a letter about to arrive. Some of this correspond-ence had to be sent to another station. I remember reading a letter from Madrid, dated December 23 1941: 'Herr Mueller arrived in Madrid on an official visit yesterday. Attended very discreet meeting with Sr Serano Suñer [Spanish Foreign Minister]. After lunch Mueller met with Johan Bernhardt [German Procurement Officer in Spain] for two hours. This morning left by Swiss Air flying to Berne.'

We alerted our head of station in Berne, who promptly had Herr Mueller watched. We found out he was one of Germany's top metallurgists, visiting Spain to secure the purchase of wolfram, the mineral used to harden steel. Our card index read: 'Herr Mueller no known connection with Abwehr; metallurgist, German arms company.' A letter sent and telephone call made to the Ministry of Economic Warfare promising to inform them of further developments was of no direct advantage to us, but made them realise the usefulness and co-operative attitude of the newly-formed band of merry men in the Iberian sector. The information we passed on enabled our purchasers in Spain to outbid the Germans; thus we gained, and our enemy lost, a supply of much needed wolfram. Besides the foreign correspondence, messages were constantly passing to and from other departments including the army, navy and air force.

Our picture of the Abwehr grew day by day, more names, activities and possible targets constantly being revealed.

Interludes seemed infrequent. One Friday morning just before Christmas, Kim walked into the office, came over to me and asked, without stuttering, 'Hey, Desmond! I was wondering if you wanted to come up to London for the weekend? I am staying with some good friends of mine, Tommy and Hilda Harris, who have a lot to do with Spain. He is a Spanish art collector and dealer, and lived in Spain for many years. She is great fun and a very good cook.'

I accepted willingly, and we left just after lunch. It was raining and very cold. I remember having to fix the lights on Kim's Vauxhall just before we arrived in London. When it started to get dark he turned them on and they fused.

Chesterfield Gardens was in a very beautiful part of London and meant that the Harrises were rich. Hilda Harris greeted us, Kim made the introductions, and Hilda took me up to my bedroom on the third floor. The wardrobe was a seventeenth-century cupboard with brass-studded lattice work on its doors; very Spanish, and very rare in England. I washed and changed; walking downstairs I could not help noticing the virtual museum pieces of furniture and art decorating the landings. After the inevitable drink, Kim excused himself and drove off, supposedly to see his mother. Hilda, Tommy and I walked around the corner to a little hole-in-the-wall restaurant and started an early supper.

Shortly before we were turned out of the restaurant Kim arrived and ordered a drink.

'Desmond, I am going to persuade Felix to employ my sister. She speaks a little French and is good with a typewriter.'

'Good idea, Kim,' I replied, a little surprised at his openness in front of the Harrises.

We returned to their house and sat up drinking, talking about the Civil War. Kim explained that Tommy was working for MI5 and was closely associated with many members of the Intelligence and the Secret Services.

The following day at breakfast we talked about the Spanish Embassy staff, and who amongst them was busy in the intelligence field. Tommy was then in the second week of interrogating a suspect Spanish journalist, who ended up not being an agent for the Abwehr although some of his articles had been sent to Berlin. We knew that Señor Alcaza de Velasco was running a small group of agents for the Spanish Foreign Minister, Senor Serrano Suñer. ISOS was showing that some, but not many, reports of very little significance were reaching the Abwehr in Madrid. Tommy was becoming MI5's Spanish expert.

We ate and drank very well. As Sunday afternoon rolled on, it started to snow. Kim and I drove back to St Albans, talking a little about the War, and a lot about the Harrises. Tommy was an enchantingly enigmatic character, who from this first meeting appeared to have many talents and a lot of energy.

I thanked Kim for what had been a marvellous break.

'OK, Desmond, just thought you would get on with Tommy and Hilda. See you in the morning – I'll pick you up at 7 am.'

Christmas passed by with a rapid clinking of glasses hud-
dled around the fireplace in the snakepit. Snow decorated
the hedgerows, and a few paper cutouts decorated the halls
and offices, thanks to the secretaries.

Despite the snow and ice, the Bag always arrived at 10.30
clutched in the arms of the often near-freezing motorcycle
dispatch rider, who would stop by the hall stove to remove
the icicles from his moustache. Personal mail was also very
efficient, despite the blizzards, and I received a telegram on
14th January from my wife's mother: 'Betty gave birth to
your daughter, January 13th. Congratulations.'

Five days later I arrived on leave at Yew Tree Cottage.
The baby was crying, Betty was smiling with pride. Betty's
mother had kept the Christmas tree up and lighted the fire.
Kim, before I left, had taken me to the pub for a celebratory
drink and given me a bottle of champagne, so we toasted
parenthood and a late Christmas in a very cosy fashion.

Two days later, back in St Albans, my colleagues gave
me a very warm reception and all the usual congratulations.
Kim and his wife invited me to dinner that night, where we
discussed the War, babies, and my renting a little house down
the street.

'You should be living with your f-f-family while you can,'
Kim advised. 'The chances are you may be posted abroad
at s-s-some point.'

Having thanked Aileen for the rather overcooked meal,
and Kim for the friendly advice, I walked home. As I listened
to the crunch of snow beneath my feet, I decided to move
Betty, her mother and our daughter to St Albans.

February 5th, 10.30 am: the dispatch rider arrived, skidded
a little in the snow, walked in, removed the icicles from his
moustache, delivered the Bag and left. Tim distributed the

contents and I looked through my batch for the telegrams. Finding one from Lisbon I quickly opened it.

'Lieutenant Demarest US naval attaché has informed me he has been approached by a Spanish national named Juan Pujol wanting to work for us in Britain. He has story about sending messages to Germans from Lisbon.' It was signed Benson, who was our shipping attaché in Lisbon.

Philby was in Curzon Street in London, conferring with MI5. Lisbon wanted a quick response. I read the message out to the others, rushed upstairs and knocked on Colonel Felix Cowgill's door.

The Colonel was sitting behind his large wooden desk, the photograph of his wife and green phone (scrambler) on one side, the red phone (his direct link to Menzies, the chief of MI6) and the black phone on the other. He was talking on the black phone. He put his hand over the mouthpiece and indicated for me to sit down. I noticed the maps he had recently pinned around his office, which showed our stations in Europe. A shy and secretive man, the Colonel always wore his uniform; the khaki green set off against the indelible tan gained from his exploits in northern India before the War, when he was a police officer tracking down Communist agitators. He hung up, and asked what I wanted.

'Felix, sorry to bother you. Since Philby is away I thought you should take a look at this telegram from Lisbon.'

When he had read the message he looked across his desk, and said in his quiet voice, 'Could be a double agent, we must be very careful. If we are too hasty we might give ISOS away, and the Nazis will know we have broken their codes.' His other reason for caution was to protect our secret from MI5; the rivalry between the two camps, perpetuated by Cowgill, was really quite amazing.

'Shouldn't we do something about it now?' I asked; this was much too exciting and important for us to sit about waiting, I thought.

'We wait for Philby to return.' He handed the message back, indicating it was time for me to leave.

I couldn't help feeling a little irritated by his apparent lack of interest and his willingness to fob off the responsibility of a decision on Kim. It also occurred to me that Kim obviously had not said very much to the Colonel about our suspect agent. In my mind there was no doubt that this was the man sending the phoney messages to the Germans in Madrid – the man we had Special Branch search Liverpool and northern Wales for; the man we had combed the Spanish Embassy and refugee arrivals for. This had to be Arabel.

4

Arabel Becomes Garbo

Kim arrived back from London at about 3.45 pm, walked into the office and stamped the snow off his shoes, and as he hung up his old leather jacket by the stove, I handed over the message from Lisbon, and said, 'I think we have something rather big here. I think it might be Arabel.'

He read the message, patted me on the shoulder and turned towards the door. He stopped, looked over at me with a smile of excitement and exclaimed, 'By God, Desmond, I think you're right.'

On that, he rushed up to the Colonel. Ten minutes later I heard him running down the stairs. He walked quickly across the office, picked up the green phone and, out of breath, rang Lieutenant Colonel Robertson of MI5, familiarly called Tar.

'T-t-tar, a Spaniard called Pujol has approached the Yanks in L-lisbon offering to work for us. He claims to have Abwehr connections in M-m-madrid and wants to come to England, where h-he feels he could be of use to us.'

Tar agreed with Kim that we must have Pujol interrogated in Portugal with the idea of bringing him over to England. When Kim raised the question of security once on English turf, Tar's voice boomed down the phone with a sarcastic tone.

'Oh, come on, Kim, I think we can handle this little Spanish sardine; once in England, where is he going to swim to?'

The following morning a telegram was sent to Ralph Jarvis, our head of station in Lisbon, instructing him to set up a discreet interview. Jarvis contacted his best local agent, Gene Risso Gill, and told him about Pujol. Between them they decided it was best for Gene to conduct the interviews as he was far less likely to be watched by the local Portuguese police, who were very pro-German at that time. Besides, he spoke the best Spanish.

Jarvis contacted Captain Benson and told him to arrange for Juan Pujol to go to a café in Estoril, just north of Lisbon. Gene, who recounted this story to me when I met him in 1944, told me, 'Never before or since have I been so nervous as I was at that first interview with Juan Pujol. Believe me, I thought every German agent was watching me and everybody around the area and in the café was a German agent.'

Gene arrived at the café; it was an unusually warm day for February and more people were out than usual, many of them sitting at the little cast-iron tables on the terrace. The café smelt of fresh coffee. The terrace was built like a horseshoe so that every seat was sheltered from the cold wind and benefited from the wonderful view of the Atlantic waves crashing on the white beaches, while the sardine fishermen wearing personally designed sweaters and colourful hats pulled in their catch, and their women sat on the sand repairing torn nets. Many day travellers up from Lisbon, and small groups of refugees, were wandering along the promenade to kill time before an evening's gambling at the famous Estoril casino. His task seemed totally incongruous with the setting, which apparently helped him relax. A man answering Pujol's description walked up to the bar and asked in Portuguese with a Spanish accent, 'Tea with lemon, no sugar, please.'

Gene sat down beside him. 'The view is much better at the table by the steps leading down to the beach.' Pujol gave the right response and got up; they moved across to the far table. After the initial five minutes of tension, with Gene constantly watching over his shoulder, they relaxed and started to talk. Gene was able to cross-question Pujol very easily as the latter was eager to prove his case. He handed over the invisible ink with copies of the messages he had sent to the Germans and gave Gene information to work on. They arranged to have more meetings in the same place but at different times of day. After these subsequent meetings the friendly little Catalonian seemed genuine enough to Gene.

Several messages came and went through our office in St Albans. Kim had taken to conferring with me during our evening visits to the pub, where he felt we had privacy from the others. When he and I became convinced this was almost certainly the German agent Arabel he sent a message off to Jarvis: 'Make arrangements for transport of our friend to Gibraltar as soon as possible.'

The tricky part was to make sure the Germans did not find out that Juan Pujol, their Arabel, supposed to be in England at this time, was in fact in contact with the British in Lisbon. Captain Benson made the arrangements and told Gene Risso Gill to escort Pujol through the harbour, up the gangway, past the Portuguese police, onto the British merchant ship due to leave for Gibraltar.

We received the message that 'Our Spaniard is safely on board and sailing to the Rock.'

Donald Darling of MI9, in charge of escaped prisoners of war and anybody else wanting to return to England, met Pujol, gave him money, showed him around Gibraltar and generally looked after him for two weeks. Donald quickly came to the same conclusion as Gene about Pujol, and with his sharp sense of humour named him Mr Bovril; this was to prevent that sinking feeling coming over any of us. The final message sent from us at St Albans confirming the go-ahead eventually put Mr Bovril in a seat on a Sunderland seaplane headed for Plymouth.

On the evening of April 25th the Sunderland landed in Plymouth harbour. Mr Bovril was met by Cyril Mills and Tomas (Tommy) Harris of MI5. The following morning Harris and Mills escorted Bovril on the train to the Royal Patriotic School for initial interrogation and filing of his arrival in England.

On April 28th I caught the morning train to London, the underground to Hendon and walked to 35 Crespigny Road, the house assigned to Bovril by MI5. Cyril Mills greeted me and introduced Pujol. My undercover name on this occasion was Captain Richards. Juan, a short man with slicked-back dark hair revealing a high forehead, and warm brown eyes with a slight mischievous glint, smiled as I shook his hand. The room was sparsely furnished, with just a table and four chairs set against a window overlooking the small back garden of the semi-detached house. I spent the next four hours translating the messages he had sent to the Abwehr into English. In the afternoon I started the preliminary debriefing. As the representative of MI6, it was my task for the next eight days to interrogate this enigmatic Catalan.

After our initial meeting, on the train back to St Albans, I reflected on how relaxed Pujol seemed, considering the ordeal he was going through. My train pulled into St Albans at 6.30 pm; I jumped onto my motocycle and sped to Glenalmond, wanting to tell the others about Juan Pujol.

When I stuck my head around the office door to find only Tim Milne and a new arrival to the Iberian section, Francis Watts, I knew where the others would be. Kim, Trevor, Frank and Jack were having their evening natter and pick-me-up in the snakepit. I asked Jack to pour me one of his specials.

Kim smiled at me through the smoke of his cigarette and asked, 'Well, Desmond, h-h-how is our friend?'

'Very well,' I replied, 'surprisingly relaxed, seems to enjoy answering any questions I put to him. He is delighted with the treatment he has received from everybody. He especially enjoys bacon and eggs for breakfast; apparently he hasn't seen bacon since 1936.'

'Being spoilt by our chaps in MI5 already, is he?' interjected Jack.

Trevor, never one to miss a dig, asked, 'Besides his culinary preferences, what else did you find out?'

'Well, without any doubt it is he who sent the notes to our opponents in Berlin. He is Arabel,' I replied.

'No doubt in your mind at all, Desmond?' asked Kim.

'No, none at all; he knows the dates and the contents of the messages, and I don't think he is a German agent; it seems as though he has invented himself out of some romantic notion about spying, or else just for the money. Apparently the Germans were paying him quite well.'

'Well, it's early days yet, but it sounds as though he is going to be useful. Have another drink, Desmond. Two more, when you are ready, Jack.'

Frank, who had spent time in Barcelona, asked whether Pujol's Catalan was any good.

'How would I know, my Spanish is Andaluz!' I thought it rather a silly question.

'Of course,' said Frank; then asked, 'How the hell did he understand anything you had to say?'

Jack, handing me my other drink and lighting my cigarette, laughed. 'Besides all that, do you like him, Desmond?'

'Well yes; he makes for better company than you chaps these days.'

Trevor asked in his gentle voice, 'Does his breath smell of garlic?'

'No! Skunk shit, just like your perfume, you ass. Joking aside, he seems to be a good chap with a phenomenal imagination, a good sense of humour and plenty of guts. I am sure 5 will be able to make good use of him.'

Trevor offered me another drink; I graciously refused, wanting to get home to my wife and daughter now living just down the road from Kim and Aileen. Kim and I left together; he had become a regular passenger on my motorcycle.

For the next few days I did not return to Glenalmond. After my daily sessions with Pujol I went straight home from the station to Sandy Lane.

The interrogation fell into a routine, and became more like conversations; about Pujol's life, the Civil War, his likes and dislikes. He was concerned about his wife and young son whom he had left behind in Portugal. A question I seemed to go over and over again with him was, how had he ended up working for the Germans? I'm still not sure of his reasons today.

On the fourth day, May 1st, I was greeted at 35 Crespigny Road by Tommy Harris, whom I had met a second time at

Kim's mother's Christmas party. I was relieved when he told me he had just been apppointed Pujol's case officer, as up to that morning Cyril Mills, who did not speak a word of Spanish and was far too pompous to make anything out of Pujol, had been working on the assumption that he was case officer. Instead Tommy and Pujol were going to be working together, to build up a phoney spy network which would feed false information to Pujol's German contacts.

We spent the morning going over Pujol's reports to the Abwehr, analysing his style: how he used punctuation; what letters of the alphabet he emphasised more than others; the way he crossed his t's and dotted his i's. Pujol had already developed a loose pattern of content, and it was essential the written dialogue remain in a similar vein to his previous letters to Frederico in Madrid. Coffee was brought in every so often by the watchman. Tommy seemed to have the size of Pujol very quickly and in between rolling and smoking his bloody Spanish black tobacco cigarettes, manipulated his new agent in any direction he cared to. This was going to be some duo, I thought.

In the afternoon I listened to Pujol's life story and his motives for wanting to be a spy all over again, watching how he responded to Tommy. His motives for working against the Germans were obvious; he told the story yet again about his brother witnessing atrocities committed by the Gestapo in France. He had all the right answers. (Interestingly, my wife became great friends with his wife after the war and apparently his brother had never set foot in France. This is why today I'm still not sure of Pujol's motives.)

By the end of the day I was saturated with Pujol's life story and in need of conversation other than spy talk. I offered Tomas a beer at the local. As I closed the front door, he rolled yet another cigarette, raised his eyebrows, shook his head, smiled and twinkled his eyes.

'Desmond, he is obviously Arabel, but I do find it hard to believe such an outwardly simple man still has the Germans fooled and had us worried for so long. He is such a dreamer and so willing, he is going to be a marvellous double agent to operate with as long as the Germans continue to swallow his communications. Well . . .' Tommy continued in the same breath, 'I'm not too keen on beer, how about a glass of vino at the Euston Hotel?'

The hotel interior was sumptuous compared to my normal drinking and chatting houses. Tommy was half Spanish, half English, an art dealer, artist, linguist and generally a very cultured, intense and humorous man. It was the beginning of a friendship that lasted until his tragic death in a strange car accident in Majorca in 1964.

By the end of the week Tomas and I had managed to convince the powers above us that Pujol was genuine. I could see that in the hands of Tommy Harris, Juan Pujol could be a marvellous line of false information, which would lead the Germans up all sorts of garden paths. Juan Pujol and Tommy Harris became 'Garbo'. Pujol was the person, Tomas the brains, mixed with both of their avid imaginations fuelled by the XX committee. Tomas and Juan started to create a large phoney spy network, using the fictitious KLM pilot Juan had invented in Lisbon as the spearhead. Within a few days the XX committee was supplying Garbo with information to send to the Abwehr. Garbo was IN.

My time with Tommy and Garbo sadly came to an end. I learnt a great deal during those ten days, giving me a background to the operations of double agents. I became especially aware of the huge ramifications required to maintain one side oblivious of the real intentions of the other.

I was invited to the XX committee meetings which took place on Wednesdays in MI5's headquarters. The full-time committee members chose the casual attenders, such as myself, very carefully. Our security and loyalty had to be one hundred per cent. It was indeed the most secret club of the Secret Service in Britain.

I remember very clearly waking up on the first Wednesday. I had spent the previous evening polishing my uniform buttons, belt buckles and shoes. This first meeting with all those important people gave me the butterflies. All I could eat for breakfast was half a piece of toast; the train journey to London was over far too quickly. I suppose I started to realise the heady responsibility and the fact that I was becoming a rather important cog in the Secret Service wheels; it had all been fun and rather easy up to this point – now, like Garbo, I was seriously IN.

As I turned into St James's Street I took a deep breath; 'Chin in, shoulders back, chest out,' I mumbled to myself. 'Come on, Derry, this is exciting, you are becoming important.' Another little voice told me it might have been easier had I been in the infantry. I was able to dismiss that thought very quickly by recalling the wounded soldiers I had seen at Oxford station. When I walked through the doorway of MI5's office the watchman seemed to know how I was feeling. It was the first time in a long time a watchman had stood to attention and saluted me. This simple gesture boosted my self-confidence. In reality he was saluting my uniform not me, but I had forgotten I was wearing one.

The room was square, bare and cold. So was the table in the middle with chairs around. Tar Robertson, a big haughty fellow with friendly eyes and an assertive way about him, came up and shook my hand.

'Hello, Desmond, glad you could make it, old boy. Don't worry, we're an informal lot here really, which is perhaps the best kept secret of all. Let me introduce you to the others; believe me, they know as much about you as you know about them.' Which of course was not true since they must have vetted my credentials closely before inviting me to attend. I'm sure you can imagine the type of people who were present: John Masterman, the head of the committee, MI5, Oxford University; John Marriot, the secretary, MI5, a London solicitor; T. A. Robertson, Lieutenant Colonel, MI5; Ewen Montague, Lieutenant Commander, naval intelligence; John Drew, Home Defence executive; Colonel Bevan, army; Flight Lieutenant Cholmondeley, air force, Cambridge, and myself for this meeting and the following four Wednesday meetings. We discussed the false information that Garbo should pass on to the Germans. My contribution was to advise on what information a Spaniard such as Pujol might initially put over to them and in what way he might text it. I liaised the information back to Tommy Harris. I suggested Tommy Harris became part of these meetings, and he was present at the last two I attended and from then on dealt directly with the committee. My workload at St Albans was growing since the Germans and Italians had started a spate of sabotage on our shipping in Gibraltar and around the southern coast of Spain.

5

Gibraltar

Early in May Felix invited me up to his office to discuss the growth of Section V and how well we were all doing. Several times during the conversation he brought up the subject of Gibraltar and sabotage and his feeling the need for someone to go to the Rock from our Section. I began to wonder where all this was leading. He stopped talking, rubbed his chin, stubbed out his cigarette, looked across his desk and said in his quiet voice, 'Desmond, you do realise that you are the man for Gibraltar. You like the Spaniards and obviously know that area better than most natives.'

Before he had time to say any more and officially ask me, coughing loudly and moving around in my seat, I asked, 'Felix, are you asking me to go to Gibraltar? If so I willingly accept.'

My car and boat trips to and from Gibraltar as a child and adolescent had given me a familiarity with the terrain, culture, and language (Andaluz) which would now be very useful. Besides, it was becoming increasingly frustrating for me dealing with messages about blown-up ships and German intelligence activities without being in a hands-on situation. By being in Gibraltar I would be in control of events and the flow of information to England.

I would need a secretary and after many interviews a

choice was made; his name was Dom O'Shagar. He had started his career as an Irish priest; at the age of twenty-seven he had given up the celibate life to open a shop in Vincent Square near Westminster Cathedral where he sold wooden and wax effigies, so popular in Catholic circles. How the department found him I have no idea, but his Spanish was good and having an ex-priest around made me feel spiritually safe if nothing else. He came up to St Albans several times to be briefed.

I made several trips to Medmenham, the headquarters of aerial photography, to study aerial photographs of southern Spain, Gibraltar and the bay of Algeciras. It was astounding to see the number of merchant ships only a few hundred yards from the Spanish shoreline of La Linea. I realised why sabotage was so easy for the Italians and Germans.

A farewell party was organised by Kim and Trevor in the snakepit. The evening was warm, many people from other departments joined in. Somebody had brought an old record player and the music of Gershwin and the new sounds of Duke Ellington floated across the back lawn of Glenalmond Manor. Luckily I had one day's leave in order to do my final packing and be at home with Betty and Rosanne which enabled me to recover from the hangover.

The next morning, June 4th, Betty accompanied me to Paddington where I boarded the train for Plymouth. We hugged and kissed, our tears and smiles came and went as we said goodbye. The pressure pushed the large piston, the wheels turned slowly, the steam from the boiler came hissing out and filled the platform, immersing Betty in a cloud. I sat back in my first-class seat trying to feel comfortable but feeling out of place and very excited at the same time. The beautiful English countryside, so green and sumptuous, flashed by the window. The clickety-clack of the wheels taking me closer to my new assignment brought the tune of 'Chatanooga Choo-Choo' to mind. For a brief moment, I wondered if I would see any of my St Albans pals again. This thought quickly disappeared as the thrill of heading almost home to Gibraltar, and flying in a Sunderland came over me.

At Plymouth I was met by an RAF driver who took me to a small RAF establishment near the harbour where they gave me tea and biscuits, to calm my nerves I assumed. O'Shagar was already drinking his tea when I arrived. At dusk we were taken to the harbour and put on a small boat which chugged through the mist, honking its foghorn. Then in front of us, looming up out of the mist, was a huge sleeping whale with wings on, or a Sunderland flying boat, my transport to Gibraltar. Safely on board, we started moving out of the harbour. It was exhilarating to feel the machine skid across the water and slowly rise out of the mist. At midnight a member of the three-man crew brought more tea and biscuits. The noise of the engines and the small bucket seats made sleep difficult. Early next morning we seemed to be miles from anywhere, no land visible; just the odd ship wallowing in the very rough seas of the Bay of Biscay below. By 09.00 hours southern Portugal was visible and the plane closed in towards land. By 10.00 hours, flying along the Straits, we could just make out the Rock of Gibraltar peering at us through the low cloud. I put out my cigarette, fastened my safety belt, my sweaty hands clamped tightly around the small armrests. The sea got closer and closer and the waves bigger and bigger. The flying whale landed in a big envelope of spray, crashing through the rough waters of the bay on the Atlantic side of the Rock. Section V now had a man in Gibraltar.

A small boat manned by field security crew drew alongside. A big man covered with oilskins and water came aboard to greet us. 'Captain David Thomson at your service.'

He handed a waterproof jacket to O'Shagar and myself, then turning around quickly to step back on the boat added, 'Better move it, this weather is getting worse and the plane must get back.'

Thomson, a very affable man, and a senior member of the Defence Security office, became a friend of mine and was very helpful in my task of setting up a Section V network.

I will use part of a letter I have received from Austin Baillon OBE, a friend who was in Special Operations Executive (SOE) on Gibraltar, to describe the Rock and a little of its history. Hopefully this will also help underline the importance of having a man from Section V there.

The 1895 edition of Chambers' Encyclopedia *describes the inhabitants of Gibraltar as 'a motley agglomeration of English, Genoese, Spanish, Jews and Moors'. 'Rock scorpions' was the unkind term applied by some when I was there, but I never had any reason to consider or call them so. Gibraltar has been in British hands since 1704 when a combination of Dutch and British forces took it from Spain. Several military attempts to recapture the Rock have failed and the Spanish have for the last hundred or so years tried diplomatic dialogue to recover the isolated mass of rock – 'jaw jaw, not war war', as Winston Churchill once said.*

In April 1941 myself and seventeen other Spanish-speaking officers arrived, not expecting to be in Gibraltar for very long as our mission was to enter Spain ahead of the expected German forces and to interrupt their communications behind them. Ours was Operation Relator, the Germans' was Operation Felix, neither of which took place.

Gibraltar was bracing itself for an impending attack. General Eastwood was replaced as Governor of the fortress by the more charismatic General the Viscount Gort VC, just as Crete was taken by German parachutists – the first use of such troops, and seen as a prelude to a similar attack on Gibraltar.

By then the Rock was a seething mass of activity night and day. It was the base for Force H, the Mediterranean fleet. The dockyard worked around the clock on repairs and refits. The original polo field and small airstrip were being extended into an important military airbase with the materials excavated from the bowels of the Rock by the Royal Canadian Engineer Company. Construction of an alternative city, with power plant, water storage, hospital and living accommodation for siege conditions was well under way.

Whatever else Gibraltar lacked at that time it was certainly not bars nor booze. At midday Main Street, Irish Town and Castle Street would be crammed with servicemen of all ranks, many in transit from passing convoys or naval ships. Desmond, one such passer-by composed an amusing verse unrepeatable in polite company, except for the opening lines:

Symbol of the British Empire
Haughtily Gibraltar stands
Never will this proud erection
Be reduced by Axis hands.

As you can see Gibraltar by the time I arrived was well established; it had become the victim of sabotage, and a potential den for Axis spies to send information about all sorts of Allied military movement in the Mediterranean.

A room had been reserved for me at the Rock Hotel where I stayed for two weeks.

The office was in a building just off Irish Town, near Mackintosh Square. The larger space was occupied by the four members of the Defence Security staff headed by Major John Medlam. A wide balcony, covered recently to create extra space, led to the MI6 office headed by Lieutenant Colonel Codrington. Donald Darling of MI9 had a small office next to that and in a corner sat Brian Morrison, one of the most intelligent and unused heads that I met during my time with the Secret Service. His is a sad story; he was treated very badly by MI6. The treatment extended to Donald Darling after the war by Her Majesty's Government was nothing short of cruelty either.

You will see in some of the following how dedicated and successful both of these men were in their work during the war, but when they were no longer required the Government discarded them in that thankless British manner, both financially and morally. Brian, who spoke German, Chinese, Russian, Spanish and French fluently, was at the beginning of the war stationed in Finland as an SIS officer. Towards the middle of 1940 when all others were recalled, Brian remained hiding in the woods operating wireless communications. He was the last SIS officer to leave Finland. After returning to England from Gibraltar at the end of 1943 he spent time training at HQ and St Albans in preparation for the invasion of Europe. Up to this point he had been a civilian and it was deemed necessary for him to become an officer in the Army. The selection committee known as the Warrant Officers Selection Board [WOSB] interviewed him. The first question asked by a rather typical small-minded pen-pushing individual was, 'What's a mouse when it spins?' Well, this was too much for Brian to tolerate. Brian made some rude comment – 'What the hell has that got to do with anything?' – got up and walked out. Brian was failed and spent the rest of the war as a Corporal in an SCI [Special Counter Intelligence] unit. After the war he was not offered a position with the Secret Services, despite the conflict with the Russians and Chinese, and discarded. He died tragically, an alcoholic, in Granada in 1983.

As for Donald Darling, after the war he spent time visiting and helping European members of the Allied Escape lines. In 1949 he was posted to San Paulo in Brazil to be locally engaged as the Press Officer, a rather lowly position for somebody of his calibre. On his return to England he was offered nothing and discarded. Donald died in 1980, alone in a small room of a public house near Trafalgar Square, having been befriended by the publican. Incidentally the answer to the (WOSB) riddle is: It's a weaving shuttle. Excuse this digression, but it does make me angry when I think how badly many worthy people have been treated by the powers that be, especially in the case of Britain.

The remaining staff consisted of the chief clerk, Sergeant McNeff, and Corporal Kevin Cavannah, an interesting Irishman, jokingly known as Red Cavannah because of his

Communist tendencies before the war. O'Shagar and myself had an obvious space problem which none of the above were going to help with since my appearance on their turf was upsetting for them. Codrington and Medlam made no effort to hide how much their noses were put out of joint.

I decided the best place for my office was on the covered balcony; this would put me in the middle of the two other departments, enabling me to eavesdrop and pick up information received by either one. O'Shagar used his Irish name to befriend Kevin Cavannah who, being the secretary of the others, knew exactly what was going on at any given moment. Kevin helped us gather a couple of old desks and chairs and had the telephone hooked up. On June 8th Section V opened their first official office on the Rock of Gibraltar.

John Codrington soon realised I was not the threat or bogey man he had anticipated, and showed me around Gib and gave me free access to information running through his office. On the other hand, Medlam was a pain in the rear end; but realising I was now working with him and from a department of the Secret Service he knew nothing about, he forced himself to be amicable and within a short space of time I was gathering information on local activities gleaned by his field security staff. Besides the information coming via these departments, I needed my own agents. David Thomson told me of Antonio Joseph, who did some work for the Defence Security department, and took me to the small office in Irish Town where Antonio ran his transport company. David formally introduced us, and went off to ferry in some new arrivals to the Rock.

Antonio tried to be suave and sophisticated; he always had his slightly receding dark hair brushed back, and wore the latest designer suits. He was a very light-hearted chap and we liked each other straight away. After half an hour of listening to the details of his company's business, and taking note of his affable attitude, I realised he was going to be very helpful.

'In these circumstances call me Desmond,' I said to him, 'but if we are anywhere else I'm known as Arturo. David tells me you have been more than helpful with certain lines of information and I am here to expand those lines.'

'Good,' he said. 'At last you English are realising how much information is flying around here. And there are some very willing Spanish friends of mine who don't like the Germans much.'

He told me of the network he used for his business, and over the next two weeks I had information coming in from Cadiz, Estepona, and very detailed accounts of German and Italian movements in the immediate area. He was my first and most helpful head agent and during my time in Gibraltar I liaised with him at least twice a week, usually in his apartment for safety reasons. The help he extended to me far exceeded what was expected. He gave me the use of his car, and acted as paymaster for the little money my agents ever received.

If indeed the Germans had taken Gibraltar, people like Antonio would doubtless have been executed. For this risk they were rewarded precisely nothing by HMG. Perhaps they did it for the excitement value, and their hatred of Nazi Germany.

Now settled into the routine of the office I needed to find alternative digs. Staying at the hotel any longer would draw too much attention to my presence on the Rock.

One evening while chatting over a glass of vino with Donald and Brian, they invited me to move into their apartment on the third floor of Plaza de la Verdura, a short walk up from Mackintosh Square. A more central location would have been hard to find, and more suitable room-mates impossible.

We each had our own small room set off from the central living room which had an old piano in one corner and four rather broken but comfortable chairs around a low oblong table. The two large windows had big sills covered with cushions where I often sat and watched the tops of people's heads as they walked in the square. When I sat against one wall of one of the windows I was able to see the docks of Algeciras and the battleships moving in and out of Gibralter. Every now and again Donald would put up an escapee for a few days, until their passage to England was organised.

The second Saturday after I had moved in, I got home late to the apartment. Jazz music filled the stairwell, growing louder as I climbed the steep steps. I was puzzled, as curfew was strict in Gibraltar, but not being too familiar with the exact laws was intrigued as to the source, and being a fan of jazz wanted to join in. When I reached the third floor, the door to my apartment was open; the piano and clarinet sounds were coming from the living room. Donald greeted me at the door and, not being too sure of my reaction, started to explain that every fourth Saturday he invited Cyril, a jazz pianist from the dockyard, to come over with any other musicians he was able to muster. He started a lengthy apology which I interrupted. 'Donald, I love jazz music; all I need now is a drink, you silly fool.'

Besides the odd escapee and the Donald Darling jazz festivals, our cosy apartment became a safe house in which we three Gib Musketeers discussed and plotted our activities. This apartment became the centre for MI9, MI6 and Section

V without the officials above Brian or Donald realising – I was my own master. The office was certainly not the place. John Codrington, Brian's boss, was not very interested in socialising, except occasionally in Spain with Jill Alvarez, whom he has been known to describe as his best agent! (She was an aristocrat who gave cocktail parties and tea parties, privy to almost useless information, and besides . . . she was his only agent.) Medlam just did not belong.

This is the moment to outline what we were all doing in Gibraltar. MI6 (John Codrington and Brian Morrison) watched Spanish army movements in the campo areas and any other relevant information or situation which had a bearing on what Spanish intentions were or might be, not only against Gibraltar, but regarding the Axis and Allies in general. The Defence Security office (headed by John Medlam) maintained the security of Gibraltar against espionage, sabotage and any other activities detrimental to our war efforts on the Rock. MI9 (Donald Darling) dealt with the escapees and refugees whom he screened before forwarding to London by boat or plane. Section V (I, Desmond Bristow) went to Gibraltar to build up records of German and Italian personnel and their agents operating in the area and establish a network of agents to help in this monitoring. Sixteen thousand Spanish people crossed into Gibraltar every day to work. These were all potential agents for the Germans or Italians and I started the area watch so we could possibly prevent some if not all sabotage and espionage as far afield as Malaga, Cadiz and Seville. The area being such an open book made work on counter-espionage almost pointless, so most of my work was to do with sabotage detection.

Jazz parties, living in an apartment often shared with

escapees and refugees, dangerous liaisons with my own agents, being my own boss: this was my 'Jolly Old Gibraltar'. Yes, Gibraltar was jolly in every sense; joyful, slightly drunk, festive – and I at last felt as though I was involved with a real war. It was good to be in or at least close to the battle arena.

Until October 1942 there was a strong possibility that the Germans, aided by the Spanish army, might invade – or so thought those who did not know the Spanish very well. As a result of this threat, during the course of my stay on this monkey-infested fortress we were instructed by London to organise a stay-behind network in the southern Spain area. (A stay-behind policy is the term used for the preparation of a network of agents to operate after the enemy has occupied territory.)

Early in July my agent in Cadiz sent a report: 'Spanish army on move heading towards Gibraltar. Transporting two 15-inch naval guns. Their progress, slow.' Ironically, the guns were made in Britain.

In the San Roque area, the hills surrounding the Gibraltar basin, gun emplacements sprang up like mushrooms. Large gasogene-driven trucks struggled up the slopes as far as they could, then their cement and brick cargo was taken further on by mules and donkeys.

Kevin gave me a copy of a London Sunday paper, saying, 'I think this will amuse you.' On the front page was a large cartoon showing the Rock with the monkeys looking down the barrels of guns of all shapes and sizes, dominated by the two fifteen-inch naval guns arriving from Cadiz.

A staff meeting was held at Government House. Brian and I had a hard time containing our laughter when they came up with the devastatingly bright idea of monitoring the movement of these two guns. Knowing the country well, I realised that the progress of the guns would be very slow. The roads had always been terrible, and had been damaged further during the Civil War. About five days after all the excitement I obtained passes for myself and Brian from the Spanish consulate to take the diplomatic bag to the British vice consul in Cadiz.

I posed as Brian's driver; he sat in the back being important. The security at La Linea was tougher than usual, and at the San Roque checkpoint I was a little worried. Having made it through, I was driving the 1936 Cadillac casually towards Tarifa up a bumpy road lined by oak trees. Suddenly four Civil Guards, rifles at the ready, jumped out in front of the car. Looking suspiciously at Brian they ordered me to turn around. Brian started to get annoyed with them, swearing in English; I translated, explaining how important Senor B. Morrison was, and showed the guards the passes. After some deliberation they reluctantly allowed us through.

On we went, hot and dusty, bouncing around in the large old Cadillac belonging to Antonio Joseph. The countryside was quite spectacular, the dramatic hills and mountains almost desert-like, with the odd patch of green olive trees. I started to laugh as we crossed a little old stone bridge spanning a small stream; turning to Brian, I said, 'I'm no engineer but I am sure of one thing, the bridges between here and Vejer will not take the weight of those guns.'

Brian sort of nodded. 'I'm ready for something to drink, and yes, you are most probably right.'

We stopped in a small village, which I don't suppose has changed much today. The little square with a small dry fountain in the middle had a couple of chairs and a table belonging to a little bar. We sat. A glass of vino and *tapa de jamon* arrived without a word being exchanged. Brian kicked up a conversation. The old boy with one tooth left in his mouth explained that many more Civil Guards had been around recently because of some gun or other.

He started laughing. 'What idiots they must be. None of the bridges would hold the weight of his donkey when fully loaded with his olives. Why do they think they will hold the weight of a big gun?'

On we went. As I turned a corner, from where one could see Tarifa on the other side of the valley, and headed down the hill, Brian noticed a large crowd of soldiers ahead. 'The bridge has gone – look, traffic is being diverted,' he exclaimed.

'Yes,' I replied, 'and there's the first naval gun, with its huge barrel sticking out of the mud down there.' We took the diversion, I slowed up and Brian took a photo of the barrel peering up through the muddy river.

It was pointless to continue to Cadiz since we had achieved our mission. After lunch in Vejer we returned to Gib passing through the same roadchecks as before, saying the consul had met us, to explain our quick return from Cadiz. We duly reported our findings.

The next three weeks brought in reports of Civil Guards and soldiers moving around Seville and Malaga. During that period of Spanish military activity we noticed how much building had started to happen. A house here, a storage shed there; La Linea was growing from the supplies of army cement and bricks. The gun emplacements didn't seem to be happening any more and had been washed away in the recent rain storms.

With regular reports arriving of Germans and Italians

visiting the area, confirmed by police files from San Roque, Algeciras and La Linea which showed these arrivals and departures, I came to the obvious conclusion that things were hotting up across the border.

The Italian ship *Oltera*, which had taken refuge in Algeciras at the beginning of the war on the pretext of needing repairs, had recently increased the numbers of its alleged maintenance crew. In reality, this crew, with large pieces of equipment which were being put on board, were making the deadly two-man submarines responsible for damaging a number of our merchant ships. Had the crews of these little subs been Germans, I am convinced the damage to our ships would have been much greater. Fortunately the Italians preferred to stay on board the *Oltera*, eating spaghetti and dreaming of their wives or mistresses. Nevertheless the threat of limpet mines from these subs being stuck to the bottom of ships made us work very hard at preventative measures. The navy laid many nets and regularly depth-charged the harbour in response to information I gathered about the Italian activity.

One morning in June, O'Shagar walked into the office having picked up the messages from London. Most were routine responses to information I had sent, but one instructed me to meet with an SOE officer, Austin Baillon, who told me a little of why he was there and that the SOE operation needed the help of my agents. I was mainly able to assist by spreading false rumours, to negate any information the Spanish police or army might have heard about this operation, so they would stay out of the way.

Since Austin Baillon has sent me a second letter explaining Operation Musson more clearly, I will use his own description of it:

All military operations must, I suppose, have code names – for record purposes if nothing else. Operation Musson was named after Peter Runciman Musson, born in Argentina, educated at Rugby, serving at one time with SOE's Special Section in Gibraltar during WW2. He was entrusted with the setting up of the clandestine activity of infiltrating SOE agents into Spain for onward passage to enemy-occupied territories. The exfiltration from Spain of SOE agents who had escaped, or had been withdrawn from occupied territories, was also part of this activity. The concept was the product of the agile mind of Leslie Humphreys of SOE's DF section, with the active co-operation of Victor Gerson – an English Jewish businessman who lived in France for many years. This was known as the 'Vic Line', and Operation Musson became the tail end of this very successful SOE escape route.

Peter Musson was one of the eighteen Spanish-speaking British officers trained at Arisaig in Scotland and sent to Gibraltar in April 1941 in anticipation of a German advance through Spain [Operation Felix], which as we know never occurred. I was one of the two who were privileged to serve under Peter Musson, the other being Arthur Fletcher, also born in Argentina with previous army service in the Blues. Operation Musson was created for the exclusive use of SOE agents and did not, as far as I was aware, deal with agents of any of the other intelligence organizations.

The quickest means of infiltrating an agent into occupied France was by parachute or landing from Lysander aircraft, or MTB (Motor Torpedo Boat). If the weather over the channel impeded this type of operation the fastest alternative, and perhaps the safest, was to fly the agent to Gibraltar whence he or she was en route through Spain to the Pyrenees, initially at least with the help of Spanish tobacco smugglers. There are in all nations stirring stories of smuggling, rich in romantic incident, and not least in Spain, where injudicious tariffs and the Royal Monopolies encouraged the practice to an enormous extent. The smuggler in Spain was regarded almost as a benefactor to the generally deprived population. Even so, in order to survive and prosper, it was imperative that the matutero *(smuggler) and his whole organization followed a rigid code of secrecy and security.*

Gibraltar, sitting on the southernmost tip of Europe, was always a unique platform for smugglers, especially of tobacco – picadura *as the chopped black leaf was called. But of course at the start of WW2 shipments of commodities were reduced to bare essentials, and* picadura *was not one of these. While scheming to open new and safer routes for the many agents trained to set Europe ablaze, Leslie Humphreys hit on the idea of using smugglers from Gibraltar. Musson was briefed and ordered to develop the operation.*

The Seruya brothers, who conducted a prosperous business from their premises in Main Street, Gib, could not have failed to be impressed with, and to realise the importance of, the suggestion that they be allowed to import quantities of picadura; *a commodity hardly likely to be required by the garrison in those days. Musson having obtained Seruya's promise of secrecy and acceptance of the proposal, asked him who he considered to be the best and most trustworthy smuggler in Gib. Seruya suggested Heredia Saavedra, a 50-year-old*

Andalusian who had been a resident of Gib since the end of the Spanish Civil War, with a long and succesful reputation as a smuggler. He had in fact been practising this occupation since the age of 10, and by 15 was the main support of his mother's large family. Having met, been amused and very impressed by José Heredia Saavedra, Musson asked him if he would be prepared, in return for the opportunity to smuggle, to carry a limited number of passengers on these occasions. He was told that suitable craft were made available for these exclusive smuggling trips and that passage through the British naval controls around the Rock would be arranged on each occasion, when they would be accompanied by at least one Spanish-speaking British officer. José, subsequently codenamed Jay, accepted the proposal and requested to be allowed to use the services of two of his most trusted men, also Spanish refugees resident in Gib. One was Manuel Pena, a marine engine mechanic, and the other an able-bodied illiterate sailor named Nicolas. Both were screened and found to be safe and more than suitable for the work at hand.

SOE Gibraltar had obtained three vessels suitable for the job. Our favourite and most used was a low-profile twin Perkins Marine engined launch named Calpe, *some 25 feet long with good storage space below decks and, more importantly, fast. We obtained moorings and the use of a small jetty near Blands wharf, close to the airstrip, where a Nissen hut was made available for us. We were each provided with a special identity document signed by the Defence Security officer, the senior staff officers from the navy, the army, and by the civilian Commissioner of Police: a document that even James Bond would have been glad to possess. Arrangements were made with the naval authorities in 'the Tower' for us to be informed of the recognition signals whenever required. The signals were for use when challenged by the naval patrol vessels constantly on guard against the approach of small craft like Italian subs and frogmen, and boats, coming from Algeciras. As an additional precaution against these mini-subs and intrepid frogmen, the navy lobbed anti-personnel depth charges at random into the sea off South Mole. On more than one occasion we were uncomfortably close to these detonations, bringing up shoals of dead or stunned fish and frightening poor Nicolas out of his skin.*

Two dummy runs, involving smuggling without the passengers, were made to familiarise ourselves with the drill and test the system. Having arranged with Jay a time and date for an operation the procedure was for us to meet in the night at Seruya's warehouse at the lower end of Irish Town where the bales of smelly tobacco, already bought by Jay, would be loaded onto one of our three-ton lorries. Each bale covered with sacking weighed about 70 kilos [155 lbs]. Two 6-inch ears of sacking at each end of the bale would facilitate handling. On the reverse side two strong straps of the same material provided loops through which the bearer of the bale could pass his arms once safely ashore and carry it like a large haversack. About 70 bales would be loaded onto the lorry, conveyed to the jetty and loaded into the hold of the Calpe, *where soon after the 'passengers' (in the case of infiltration) would be delivered. Jay by then would have arranged a time and date for a rendezvous; usually on the eastern coast of Spain near Estepona or Marbella: veritable hamlets of fisherfolk in those days. The* contrabandista *on the Spanish side would have made arrangements for the* carabineros *(police) to make themselves scarce. The launch would either tow, or carry abaft, a small flat-bottomed boat called a* patera. *We would approach to within half a mile or so from the coast; as familiar to our Spanish crew as the palms of their hands. We would strain our eyes for the expected* sena, *a pinpoint of light from a torch held by the expectant smuggler on shore. As soon as we saw the light the* patera *would be pushed into the sea and loaded with three or four bales, depending on how calm the waters were. Nicolas would then row ashore guided by the occasional pinpoints of red light. As Nicolas beached the* patera *on the sand a number of men would appear from the darkness, grab a bale and move as quickly as possible to the waiting lorry or often mule train. The passenger exfiltrating would jump into the* patera *for the return trip to the launch. On the second trip of the* patera *the infiltrating passenger would jump in between the bales and when on shore would quickly be met and conducted to one of the several safe houses along his or her route to the Pyrenees. One golden rule was that an incoming passenger should never meet an outgoing passenger. The procedure was always safe and sound except for the occasional close shave with a British depth charge. It never failed our end, and I have been told no casualties were ever suffered anywhere en route.*

Over the course of many months hundreds of agents went successfully en route until the Allied armies in France made Operation Musson obsolete, when we went our separate ways to fight the continuing war. I

*returned to my regiment, the First Airborne Division;
Musson returned to more active duties and won the
Military Cross. Arthur Fletcher after demobilization
joined, of all things, the Customs and Excise department
in England. As for the smugglers, until the end of the
war their activities were interrupted. No sooner was the
war over than Jay José was deported from Gibraltar as
an undesirable alien. Fortunately news of this came our
way and SOE were able to get the British government
to award Jay a medal in the Legation at Tangier and
organize his return to Gibraltar. After which I hope
José was able to resume the activity in which he was
such a master, and again become the benefactor to his
overtaxed and deprived countrymen.*

Back to my side of operations in Gibraltar.

One night in late July I drove across the border to the little
bar in Algeciras where I used to meet with one of my agents.
I parked near my destination and walked through the narrow
streets. It was a beautiful, clear summer's evening, the
Mediterranean was very calm and peaceful, there were even
little fishing boats out catching squid and prawns amongst the
battleships and cargo boats. Someone was playing a soulful
flamenco song which echoed through the streets. As I passed
a donkey loaded with sacks of white flour, Frederico, my
agent, caught hold of my sleeve indicating we must meet in
our prearranged second rendezvous. I turned and followed
behind the donkey, walked past three intersecting streets and
ducked into the hole-in-the-wall bar belonging to Frederico's
aunt. I waded through the usual crowd of bandits, smugglers,
tarts and off-duty secret police often there to buy black
tobacco. Pinching the bum of one of the tarts who shrieked

with delight I went into the smoke-filled kitchen rich with the smell of frying sardines and said 'ola' to auntie. From the kitchen I went into the men's loo where the hole in the floor politely known as the Turkish plate mellowed the smell of sardines. Asphyxiated, I opened the little side door relieved to be entering our tiny meeting room.

Frederico, excitedly spilling his sol y sombra down his jacket told me, 'Amigo, one of the Spanish guards of the *Oltera*, you know, the one who fancies my sister, has just told me that a submarine is due out at midnight tonight. He also told me he overheard reference to a British ship that arrived yesterday; I think it has oranges on board. Novo submarino was also mentioned.'

Thanking Frederico I scooted out of the back door onto the street near the police station. I looked at my watch; the drive back would take too long. There was enough time to catch the ferry, so I walked quickly down the cobbled street leading to the nearby docks, jumped onto the last ferry and twenty minutes later was debating with Captain Monday, the port security officer, a willing and able friend, the possibility of taking his launch, himself and two submachine guns to have a go at the Italians. He agreed, subject to my clearing it with his boss, Tito Medlam. I picked up the phone. Luckily Tito was still in his office, and readily agreed. Nevertheless, he had to clear it with the navy. Lieutenant Commander Pyke-Knott thought it a good idea in principle but felt forced to refuse clearance due to the dangers involved.

Disillusioned with our navy I went to the Embassy bar to recover from my disappointment; there I found Biaggio Damato, the Maltese owner, with tears in his eyes.

'Captain Britow! Oh, Captain Britow, Malta, Malta! All

the convoys to Malta are being sunk, what a tragedy!' He put his arms around me and comforted himself. He then took a deep breath, grabbed a glass, smiled and said, 'Have a John Collins!'

Not being able to tell him my own tale of woe, I asked if he had seen Brian. He shook his head, and told me he hadn't seen him for a day or two. There was nothing to do, so I sipped on the John Collins, ordered a sandwich and wondered what the outcome of the ship might be. Not feeling very hungry I left half the sandwich, said goodbye to Biaggio and wandered around the port area. Captain Monday had at least been able to advise the ship's master to move into shallow water and closer to La Linea. I watched the big boat slowly move across the bay and drop anchor.

Brian came up behind me and clapped his hands, almost making me jump into the sea. 'Biaggio told me I might find you down here; he said you seemed a little preoccupied.'

When I had finished telling Brian about the night's events, all he could do was laugh and swear at the same time.

'Bloody red tape and the silly bloody fools who always seem compelled to follow it. Come on, Desmond, let's go in here for a drink. I need one.'

Despite Brian's efforts to cheer me up I found it hard to respond. We left the bar and slowly walked around the port again. I kept on looking at the clear moonlit surface of the water in the hope of seeing the sub before it submerged to attack the ship. At 2.50 am there was a dull explosion as a limpet mine went off; a big spray of water erupted from the side of the ship. Brian and I waited for five minutes expecting a second explosion. Nothing happened. The following morning we heard there had only been one mine and the ship had received very minor damage.

About two days later the excitement continued. O'Shagar returned from the signals office with a coded message from London: 'Our impeccable source [meaning Ultra] has picked up reports of new sabotage operations being mounted against Allied shipping in Seville.' I should point out that the port of Seville, despite its distance inland on the ever silting up Guadalquivir River, could handle ships up to 10,000 tons. The ship most likely to be the target was identified and the Seville vice consul was asked to organise a strict watch. For two days I received messages from Ultra in London who were picking up German reports to Berlin saying that technical problems were making it very difficult to be effective against the British ships. At first the tide was too strong, then the technician became ill, most probably from the dirty water.

It was clear, however, that the sabotage war was becoming more sophisticated and that limpet mines were not being used. Extra vigilance was placed around the ship. The watchmen were vetted and given strict instructions to be very discreet so the Germans would not know that we knew what was going on. The problem for the Germans was they wanted Spain to stay neutral as much as we did, and therefore had to come up with a device that would not blow up in the river and cause a navigational hold-up which would upset the Spaniards.

Two days after the first ship sailed safely away with no devices on board, we received another Ultra report: 'Our impeccable source reports the sabotage operator [V Mann Rodriguez] has been successful, and with the help of a friend has fixed the device to the bilge keel. He assures Berlin the device will not blow up until the ship is well out to sea.'

I duly told the Admiralty in Gibraltar of Section V's findings; in order to cover up the possibility of this discovery coming from Ultra I was careful to imply that it was one of my agents in Seville who had discovered the German operation.

The ship's master, having been advised of his problem, set sail down the river as normal but when he reached open sea, instead of joining the convoy headed to Malta, he changed course and headed for Gibraltar where he dropped anchor in shallow water near no-man's-land. No-man's-land stretched between the Rock frontier port and the Spanish frontier at La Linea. Naval divers were waiting for the ship's arrival and soon established that the sabotage device was nothing less than a torpedo, five feet in length, with three propellers, one at the front, one in the middle and one at the back.

For those of us on shore it was nerve-racking watching the procedures. Eventually three frogmen appeared on the surface with the device which they tied to the back of a rubber dinghy. All three climbed carefully into the little boat and gingerly started to row towards the small crowd of us standing in no-man's-land. Every stroke they took made us wince in anticipation of a loud bang. Their journey with the deadly catch took about fifteen minutes: for me it seemed to take hours; I can't imagine what it must have been like for them. Once on land two of the frogmen were relieved by an engineer whose name I do not recall, and George Berry, an ex-Scotland Yard detective now with Defence Security staff. The third frogman was Lieutenant Commander Bailey, the bomb disposal expert. They placed the torpedo in an old trench left over from the Civil War, and started to dismantle it. Hot tea was served to those of us watching. The second time around, the tea-serving sailor asked me what I was doing there. When I explained, his response was, 'With all due respect sir, since you don't have to be here you must be bloody mad.'

Two hours later, when Commander Bailey announced that all was safe, I started to shake and needed to sit down.

The torpedo was a distance time bomb. Very fine wires connected to a shaft driven by the propellers would trigger the large explosives when the ship had travelled a certain distance; luckily for us, that point was not reached while they were rowing the thing ashore.

Sir Samuel Hoare, the British Ambassador in Madrid, issued a protest to the Spanish government based on the information we provided to the Foreign Office about the German operation in Seville, and V Mann Rodriguez's activities soon stopped.

6

Pencils and Rubbers

During July and August, Brian Morrison spent considerable time organising the limited stay-behind set-up, which he formed from Gibraltar. He would recruit my assistance as often as he could. London kept insisting that we recruit avidly anti-Franco people, a policy with which both Brian and I strongly disagreed, since in those days such people tended to be rather unreliable and basically anarchists. Besides, a combined military attack by the Spaniards and Germans on Gibraltar would have meant Spain falling into the hands of Germany, and even the pro-German Spanish would not have allowed themselves to be taken over to that extent. We sat up into the early hours and watched many a sunrise while debating various courses of action. After consulting with John Codrington we decided to hide only one wireless set and distribute 300–400 lots of instructions on how to frustrate the enemy.

Through Antonio Joseph I established contact with a retired Spanish merchant ship's captain called Wenceslas Garrido who lived in Cadiz, and who was neither pro- nor anti-Franco but more than willing to co-operate against the Germans. For some reason which I never discovered, he also strongly disliked the Italians. Wenceslas was able to recruit one of his old shipping wireless operators, and also agreed to distribute a few dozen instruction leaflets amongst his friends and associates.

We created many sets of instructions, all containing particular information for agents in certain areas and allowing for their own special circumstances. I am not going to bore you or myself repeating any of the instructions; besides I don't remember half of them. We typed these instructions onto foolscap edible rice paper, just in case anyone had to eat them at some point. How to hide and distribute these pieces of paper became our next problem. For two or three days we tossed around ideas, none of which were very practical.

Brian and I felt we deserved a break, so we took up a Spanish friend's invitation to a downtown bar in Algeciras where the alcohol company Negrita was giving out gallons of free drinks as a promotion for their new rum. All along the bar sweaty people clamoured for more than their share of the very tasty rum. Juan came back from the bar with three full glasses and four or five pencils. The pencils had the company name down the side and a rubber holder at the top; you know the type. It was the first time advertising material had been used in Spain since the Civil War. Brian's pencil had a loose top and the rubber came straight out. We smiled at each other and said in unison, 'Now doesn't that make a nice hiding place for small pieces of paper?' We pushed to the bar and filled our pockets with pencils.

The next evening I came back to the apartment to find Brian nursing a badly cut finger.

'What the hell happened to you?' I asked, looking at the drips of blood on the floor.

'The f—ing knife slipped.'

He had been taking the rubbers out of the tops of the pencils and cutting them in half. Brian had very large fingers, which made holding a small rubber rather difficult, and he had almost cut his finger in half.

Our hiding place was in the top of the pencil under the rubber. To make space for the paper we had to remove the rubber, cut it in half, then slip the rolled-up piece of paper into the top and push half of the rubber back in. We did this in shifts. For three days in our spare time we cut rubbers and our fingers and put rolled-up pieces of paper into four hundred pencils which then had to be distributed amongst our agents and their friends.

We set off to Cadiz in the old Cadillac with the pencils and the radio set. About an hour outside Cadiz we took a diversion, carefully noting landmarks. For fifteen minutes precisely we made our way up a tiny dirt road, then stopped. I spotted an old twisted olive tree on its own next to a clump of rocks. We buried the wireless set at the foot of the tree, and for extra security I cut a small V into the bark just below the first protruding branch. We set off to Cadiz and found old Captain Wenceslas. We explained where he would find the wireless and gave him a number of pencils to distribute amongst his anti-German friends. Our next stop was Estepona where we visited a fisherman friend of mine, Paco Churro, my agent in that area, and told him about our activities. We gave single pencils to various others, and told the owner of the Miraflores bar to issue pencils to his gang of potential agents in the event of a German takeover.

During all this time reports were coming in about Italian and German movements in the area from Antonio's agents. By August I felt it imperative to extend my line of agents.

On a hot sweltery evening not long after handing out the last pencil, I strolled into the Embassy bar. Biaggio, who was cleaning glasses, looked at me in surprise when I ordered a Coca Cola with ice and lemon, a refreshing rare beverage in those days. 'What's wrong with you tonight, Captain Britow?' he asked.

'Biaggio, do you have somewhere we could talk in private?' I asked.

'Yes! I have a little office at the back, but can it wait for five minutes? My brother Angelo is finishing the accounts with Bianchi.'

'Yes, of course.' I went outside to the large terrace with its spectacular view of Algeciras and the bay. It felt strange to have this moment's peace. The sea was red under the setting sun, and the bay sparkled with the reflections of the dockyard lights where they were repairing ships and building the lovely little Spanish fishing boats. It was hard to imagine the death and destruction that was taking place in many other parts of Europe. Two days before a refugee who had been staying in our apartment under Donald's care had told us about the Gestapo, the firing squads, and something about concentration camps, a concept I did not really understand at that time. The sounds of flamenco guitar and castanets came from the mainland, interrupted by a married couple arguing tooth and nail about her mother coming to stay. Mule hooves clipped along the cobblestone streets taking their owners home. The palm trees on the terrace rustled in the warm summer evening's breeze.

'Well, Captain Britow, enjoying this beautiful evening are you?' Biaggio continued talking as he walked to the far side of the terrace. 'Come this way, Angelo has finished the accounts and can look after the bar for me.' He led me through a gate into a well-furnished, well-organised little office shared by him and his brother. He already had a John Collins and another Coke waiting, and offered me a seat.

'Biaggio, I'm not sure how to ask this delicately, but I need your word that you will repeat nothing of what I'm about to say outside this room. If you do it will be the end of our friendship. Um, what I am about to say could be dangerous to you, but I would like your help.'

He shifted in his seat, sipped his drink, glanced out of the window which looked to mainland Spain. 'Captain Britow, I don't read or write very well, but I own this bar and the hotel in La Linea, I like to take risks and if it will help you win the war, I am at your service, Captain Britow, sir.'

Biaggio had become a good friend and his serious comments always ended in a joking manner, which made me laugh.

'Well, actually I want you to become my agent and find out what you can about the Italians and Germans. Listen in the bars, or more importantly your hotel lobby on the mainland.'

I had imagined it was going to be a lot harder to recruit Biaggio, but he was always full of surprises. He looked at me and nodded. 'I thought you were more than a Captain, Captain Britow. Yes, of course I will. I suppose you have already worked out the possibility of me recruiting others as I go across the border every day to and from my hotel.'

Due to Biaggio's added line of information I was able to confirm the existence of a German monitoring set-up which enabled the enemy to watch all the shipping coming in and out of the Mediterranean. It was thanks to this monitoring station that the Germans were so successfully sinking convoy after convoy. Biaggio, epecially excited about this discovery, gave a small party for Donald, Brian and myself. He thought we would be able to get supply ships through to his beloved Malta more easily. A similar monitoring station had already been dealt with in Tangiers, and London suspected the Germans had some other method of monitoring the ships now confirmed by us, just no information on where and how.

Two days after the party Biaggio came up with the location – a beautiful house twelve kilometres west of Algeciras, high on the cliffs overlooking the Straits of Gibraltar with a good view of Morocco. Our confirmation and finding of this monitoring station created a lot of excitement and anxiety amongst naval intelligence and the navy. Obviously they needed to blow up the site, but since it was on Spanish territory the Foreign Office were forced to negate this possibility. It was out of the question also, perhaps more importantly, because our findings had coincided with the last preparation period of Operation Torch (the Allied invasion of North Africa). Someone more qualified than myself and in a position of power decided it better to leave the monitoring station alone and concentrate on the invasion. Mind you, it would have taken only a small shell or small amount of explosives placed near the house by friendly Spaniards to destroy the equipment. So unfortunately for Biaggio and his beloved Malta, convoys still sank at the hands of the German and Italian U-boats.

'I have a friend who last night told me about a pending visit by a very important German intelligence officer to our area. It could possibly be the head man himself,' was Biaggio's next piece of spy news, obviously received from one of his Spanish police friends. I suspect it was Commandante Molina, head of the Spanish security police in the campo area. I asked Biaggio if he could find out the intelligence officer's name. The next evening he indicated for me to follow him into his office, where he gave me a crumpled piece of paper which bore the name CANARIO.

'This man will be staying at the Hotel Reina Christina from this coming Friday to Monday,' Biaggio stated, looking pleased with himself. He had every right to be.

I promptly telegraphed London asking for instructions and suggesting that if indeed it was Admiral Canaris (head of the Abwehr) we have a go at capturing him. London's response confirmed it was Canaris, but said that on no account should he be threatened in any way whatsoever.

On thinking about it I realised the foolishness of my suggestion, because had we captured him the Germans would have changed all their message codes, rendering Ultra useless – and after all Ultra was telling us everything the Germans were up to.

Brian and I decided it would be rather amusing to have tea at the Hotel Reina Christina that Sunday. I managed to persuade Donald who, unable to resist the temptation of cucumber and tomato sandwiches, dared himself to cross the La Linea frontier for the first time.

Sitting in the back seat of the Cadillac poor Donald, a rather nervous character, just managed to contain his panic as we negotiated the police passes at La Linea, into Spain and through the second security patrol at San Roque. He enjoyed seeing how the 'Green Line' worked, and the San Roque train station. The Green Line was the route and method used for his refugees and escapees from the station in San Roque to Gibraltar.

In the grand hotel we wandered through the tatty but luxurious lobby to the terrace, which was unoccupied despite the sunny Sunday afternoon. We sat at a corner table from which we were able to see everything. We looked across the bay of Gibraltar over to Morocco. The odd ship, including Allied merchants, sailed by on the horizon.

Brian ordered tea and sandwiches. Donald started to tease us both. 'Well, I can see why you two don't do any work. How often did you say you came here?' It was not often the three of us sat and relaxed; Donald especially. He now allowed his wonderful sense of humour to have Brian and I in stitches, about what I don't remember. The tea, with an assortment of sandwiches and shortbread biscuits, arrived. While Brian was playing host and pouring the tea, I noticed the waiter laying a table for three, just two seating places from us.

Casually Admiral Canaris walked onto the terrace with one henchman in front and one behind him. In that polite German manner he acknowledged us as fellow tea-drinkers, obviously unaware of our nationality – or maybe he knew exactly who we were. I kicked Brian under the table almost making him spill the milk. Brian, who had his back to their table, turned around to look at the Admiral and nodded. Canaris was a smallish man with distinguished facial features. He almost looked too kind and nice to be the head of Germany's secret service.

Donald, quite oblivious of who was about to drink tea on the same terrace as us, was almost euphorically enjoying the cucumber sandwiches, the view and the Chinese tea. With rather a full mouth he said, 'Desmond, I can't thank you enough for persuading me to join your Sunday tea party; these sandwiches are absolute perfection and the view makes Gibraltar seem like a different world altogether. I wonder why we are doing what we are doing?' he asked rather despondently.

'It beats being in the infantry,' I answered. I leant forward and whispered, 'By the way, do you realise who is sitting at the table over there?'

'No. And why should I?' he asked rather indignantly. 'Does it really matter so long as they behave themselves and don't disturb us?' Not able to hold back a smile, knowing he would be very disturbed by what I was about to tell him, I whispered again, 'The one in the middle is none other than Admiral Canaris.'

Donald, unable to contain himself, stood up and spitting bits of sandwich everywhere exclaimed, 'Don't be such a bloody fool, Desmond.' Not wanting too much of a scene I admitted it was a joke. Sitting down Donald said crossly, 'Your jokes are often in very bad taste. You have spoilt the flavour of the cucumbers.' He turned to the three gentlemen and apologised for his outburst, explaining it had been my fault.

We finished our tea and paid the bill. Brian and I nodded to the Admiral as we slowly walked past his table. He looked up and smiled. He certainly knew we were British, as he could not have helped overhearing some of our conversation; I still have the feeling he knew we were British agents.

Pale and somewhat shaken, Donald got into the back of the Cadillac. 'Tell me, Brian,' he asked, 'was that really Admiral Canaris?' Brian said it was. 'You are both bloody liars,' said Donald, 'and you have ruined the best afternoon I've had in ages.'

Anxious to restore Donald's feeling of well-being, Brian and I agreed to treat him to a sol y sombra at the Miraflores bar between San Roque and Algeciras. He calmed down, and was able to appreciate the comfortable bar where many of the escapees stopped on their way to Gibraltar, sometimes staying the night. José, the owner, came over and I introduced Donald.

José was a jolly character who took endless risks for the

British escapees; if he had ever been caught by the Spanish secret police there is a chance he might have been shot. I am glad to say Donald's humour returned and safely back in the apartment eating baked beans on toast, he reminded us to keep Saturday night free as he had a special jazz player coming over.

7

BMWs and German Sunglasses

I received news from all of my Spanish agents, Biaggio, Fruity, José, etc., that the Iberian government had decided to change the policemen around. The present police force around Gibraltar had apparently become too tolerant of, and even friendly with, the British, at least that is what the rumour was. Donald, Brian, David Thomson and myself analysed that the change of location of police personnel was due to corruption, and the friendly attitudes the police had towards the smugglers and local councillors.

For the first few days of that very hot August we watched as the local police with their friendly Andaluz faces were replaced by hard faces from northern Spain, mostly Irun, wearing German sunglasses. I must admit that when we saw the arrival of these obviously hardened police with their German vehicles a feeling of anxiety crept through the Rock. Our security and army patrols were all increased as the threat of a Spanish-German invasion of the Rock seemed imminent. Still finding it hard to believe, I decided to go across the border and do some spy work myself.

Slowly I drove up to the frontier at La Linea. There was an air of efficiency about these unfamiliar faces and clean uniforms, but I did not get the feeling they were about to attack. Next the check at San Roque, always

more daunting than La Linea. I noticed the brand new
BMW motorbikes lined up outside the frontier cabin, and
a new German transport wagon parked at the back. Three
policemen with new Germanic-style uniforms and Zeiss dark
glasses sauntered over to me. In a northern Spanish accent I
was ordered to get out of the car; when I hesitated the door
was opened for me by one officer while the other two stood
either side of the car. A distinct feeling of submission came
over me and I followed their orders. As soon as I stood
up two of them grabbed me, put me up against the side
of the car and frisked me, while the third searched the car.
When they had finished showing off and demonstrating their
control of the situation, they duly handed me my papers and
ordered me to proceed. The car decided that this was a good
time not to start. For a few minutes I tried, but the engine
was not going to fire. The policemen helped push the car to
the side of the road. I opened the bonnet and one of them,
intrigued by the big American engine, immediately stuck his
head in and started to fiddle about.

'You seem to know a lot about engines,' I commented (all
this was in Spanish, of course), 'very good of you to help.'
He made some remark about the expertise of American
engineering. I could not help noticing that his accent was
Andaluz, not northern Spanish at all. Pausing for a moment,
not wanting to seem too inquisitive, I asked, 'Where do you
come from?'

'Oh, I was born in Valverde del Camino,' he replied. 'It's
in Huelva; you won't know where that is.'

'You don't think so?' I laughed and told him, 'I come
from the mine of Sotiel Coronada, ten kilometres from
Valverde.'

His father had worked on the mine for my father, and he

himself attended school on the mine and could remember when I was given the donkey on my birthday. A remarkable coincidence, and a lucky one, as I found a new ally amongst the Germanophile police. These new police had been trained and had served for two years on the northern and the Portuguese frontiers. He and many of his fellow officers were glad to be in the warm climate and to be eating good healthy food. From him I was able to discover there was no threat of an invasion; Franco was more concerned about Spanish bandits in the surrounding mountains, the smugglers and about basically tightening up on his own people. When he told me the German motorbikes had been brought down from the north to facilitate high-speed chases, I could not help laughing. The idea of a high-speed chase after the jet-propelled donkeys used by the aforementioned criminals along the bumpy tracks amused even him. Despite his amusement, he made it clear that the smuggling would soon be stopped as these new police arrivals, including himself, were going to be very tough.

The engine started up and he closed the bonnet. As a token of my gratitude I gave him half a pack of Craven A cigarettes. We shook engine-oil-covered hands and agreed to go out for a drink sometime. As I drove away I leant out of the window, waved and said, 'Adios, amigo.'

Within two weeks, these tough northern policemen started to enjoy sugar, white flour, tobacco, and other more refined essentials which they had not seen since before the Civil War. Smugglers again crossed the border to Spain quite freely. The threatening atmosphere transformed overnight into one of smiles, salutations, 'ola amigos', chats over the odd cigarette. Our would-be foes allowed the 'Green Line' to continue and any number of Brits crossed the border whenever we wanted.

All those hours, and Brian's damaged finger, so gladly contributed to the stay-behind plans, had been a waste of time, apart from generating a few amusing anecdotes. Now we were confronted with the task of collecting all the messages up again. I asked Fruity to take the bus to Cadiz, call on Captain Wenceslas and help him collect all the pencils and instructions in order to destroy them.

Two days later I met Fruity in our usual meeting place; a bar at the end of a little square full of palm trees in La Linea. Looking around furtively, he pushed his hat to the back of his head, took a sip of wine and began to laugh.

'What's the joke?' I asked.

'Well,' he replied, 'I caught the 7 o'clock bus, arrived at Cadiz at 10.30 having slept most of the way. I walked to Wenceslas's house. Francisca, his wife, very excitedly told me that only a few minutes before I arrived, Wenceslas was shaving in his pyjama trousers. Suddenly he let out a cry; she thought he had cut himself. He looked at the door, then her, and with soap all over his face rushed out of the house.' Fruity took a sip of wine. 'So I waited about thirty minutes, I helped Francisca stay calm and wondered what the hell could have happened to the Captain, normally such a quiet chap.'

Fruity looked at his empty glass. I took the hint and ordered again. 'The Captain arrived back still only wearing his pyjama pants and with shaving soap all over his face. He sat down, obviously relieved about something and exhausted from running. Panting like a dog he was. "Oh, Santa Maria, last night I took my suit to the cleaners," said the Captain. While he was shaving he had suddenly remembered he had left some pencils in his suit.'

Fruity took another sip, and chuckled. '"Here they

are," said the Captain and handed them to me. I couldn't help it; I laughed so hard I fell down and broke his favourite chair, which upset him even more. Can you imagine Wenceslas running past his neighbours dressed like that, to the cleaners, to save the pencils and messages I was there to tell him to destroy!'

The following week started with another amusing day. David Thomson invited me to Four Corners, the frontier post.

'I want you to witness something, Desmond. I have just discovered the new method they are using to smuggle tobacco.'

At midday, the daily caravan of donkeys and carts taking the garbage to La Linea approached. David walked up to the first donkey, lifted up its tail and grabbed a fine piece of rope. The donkey kept walking, David stopped and held the rope tightly. Slowly out of the donkey's rear end emerged a string of eight black sausages. Condoms filled with black tobacco, to be more precise. David then ordered the donkey caravan to stop. He and I found four more donkeys similarly stuffed. He had to stick his arm in the last one and fish around a bit; it rather reminded me of little Jack Horner, sticking in his thumb and pulling out the plum. I looked up as David pulled out his string of plums, to see the congenial customs officers all laughing.

David washed his hands and we had lunch. I told him that on my recommendation to HQ he was going to be taken on by Section V. Kim Philby and Felix Cowgill had decided to make him our man in Tangier. I had spent social time with David and was going to miss him. During lunch I told him how much I enjoyed being a member of Section V. I recounted the amusing times at St Albans with Kim and the gang; the pub sessions, the snakepit, and the cold winter freezing my bum off in the St Albans office. He was due to leave for Morocco a few days later so we wished each other luck over a couple of brandies.

Feeling warmed up I went back to the apartment, having promised Donald I would be there at 6.30 pm. He had some special guests arriving to stay with us. Brian and I waited for a short while, then Donald arrived with two chaps dressed in RAF uniform who did not speak a word of English. They were Russian escapees whom Brian could translate for, being fluent in many languages including Russian. They told him how they had escaped during their exercise period in Hanover POW camp by pole-vaulting over the fences, and running like crazy, somehow escaping the dogs and search parties. They managed to get to Belgium where they were picked up by one of the escape organisations and given passes and clothes, following which, on bicycles and by train, they made their way down to southern France, where they were put on a boat (*Tarana*, captained by Nobby Clark) and brought down to Gibraltar. Now they were depending on Donald to get them to England, so they could fight against the Germans. Donald, through Brian, explained that they must stay with him and he would show them the Rock.

The following evening, after their tour of Gibraltar, we cooked for them. I was quite good at preparing spaghetti and had picked up some red wine in Spain and some mince from Biaggio. Whilst I was chopping the onion and garlic I wanted to listen to some of Donald's jazz records; at one point I felt like leaving the apartment because they would not stop yabbering. Brian, sensing my frustration, explained what all the excitement was about; they could not get over the Key ceremony.

In the morning the Governor (then Major General Mason Macfarlane) hands the keys of the fortress over to the civilian authorities. During the parade the General, dressed in shorts, was given a message and as soon as he had handed the keys over he ran off the parade ground. For them to see a general in shorts was very shocking; to see a general run even more shocking; and to see a general in shorts run off a parade ground, unimaginable.

Two days later they left, and when I returned to London I found out that they had been handed over to the Russian authorities, and on their return to Russia it was apparent they had been shot by the Stalin regime.

Which is a cue for me to indulge you by giving you some of my private thoughts. During war, somehow we are able to minimise the depressing side of life. For all of us it is necessary, from time to time, to find moments of solitude in a private place, where one can forget everyday occurrences and reflect on friends, family and life in general. For me, in Gibraltar, this place was near the ramparts below the Hotel Bristol. I had found a large rock shaped like a chair that looked over the bay. Some evenings I would walk along the beach and sit in the rock chair and reflect while watching the boats create their wake across the bay. I would stare up at the wonderful Mediterranean sky and think of Betty and my daughter, and wonder how they were dealing with the bombing raids. I would think about the terrible destruction going on all over Europe, and the fact that I could not go and see Spanish friends, such as José Muñoz, who lived in Antequera, just north of Malaga, because I was a spy. I might have put him at risk.

I was privy to information which I could not tell anyone about, which in a certain way makes one feel very important. After all I was the only person in Gibraltar who knew anything about Ultra and at that time (September 1942) was most probably the only person who knew why Spitfire planes were arriving in Gibraltar to be assembled. Everyone believed it was to help Malta, but I knew it was for the Allied invasion of North Africa, due to happen very soon. I realised working as a spy was a lot of fun basically; nevertheless, internally, it often made me feel separate from others, especially friends and family. The sound of the sea washing over the sand always reassured me that the world was still spinning around and I was not all that important.

In mid-September our department was put under investigation for bad practices. Thyl Vischer, a naval lieutenant attached to John Codrington's staff, quite often acted as courier for the Special Intelligence Service (SIS) to and from Tangier. Sometimes he would carry the diplomatic bag. On one occasion he decided it would be a treat for the staff to enjoy a meal of suckling pig. So the silly bugger bought four little pigs in Tangier, put them in a large canvas bag similar to a diplomatic bag and brought them over to Gibraltar as part of the diplomatic package. As he walked through customs, the pigs decided to squeal. The customs police confiscated our meal and reported the incident to the Governor. Importing live animals was a very serious offence. Thyl received a severe reprimand and the office was investigated in case we might be up to other smuggling antics. Fortunately the Governor was blissfully unaware that sixty per cent of our operations were so successful due to the help of smugglers, pickpockets and assorted criminals.

Shortly after the investigation I received a message from London advising me that three new Section V officers, fluent in French, would be arriving. They were to remain in

Gibraltar where Brian and I were to teach them coding and decoding, and generally help them to visualise their future. I decided to tell Brian why we were coaching these people about field operations as spies.

We were on the terrace of the Embassy bar. Biaggio served us with the normal John Collins, I made sure we were alone, and leant over the table. 'Brian, I've got something to tell you which can go no further than your ears. I'm telling you since I think it ridiculous for you not to know. The Allies are going to invade North Africa in early November, that's why we are teaching these bods about coding, etc. They are to be SLU (Special Liaison Unit) officers.' (In other words they were going over after the landings to infiltrate and gather information about the feelings of the natives.)

Donald in the meantime was increasingly occupied by the successes of the feluccas (small coastal fishing boats such as the aforementioned *Tarana*, used for transporting escapees).

Brian and I walked into the apartment feeling jovial but a little cheesed off with our students. We found Donald sitting hunched up over the table, almost in tears, chewing on his fingernails. Brian got out the bottle of whisky reserved for these occasions.

'Oh Christ! I think something has gone dreadfully wrong with one of the boats,' said Donald. 'I was supposed to receive a communication yesterday, and I have heard nothing. The boat is apparently on its way back here . . . empty. I can only assume the people are dead, or possibly stuck and waiting for the boat somewhere in the South of France.'

'Calm down and have a drink,' said Brian.

'Unfortunately there isn't much you can do about it, is there?' I suggested.

'No, but I can bloody well panic, can't I?' he retorted.

'Yes, of course, but you won't help them, and you won't do yourself much good either,' Brian pointed out.

We sat in silence. Donald took another large swig. 'Of course you're right, I must think of what to do . . . calmly.'

Donald decided to go to the signals office and, encouraging him that this was a very good idea, I went with him. A message had arrived for him saying the rendezvous had failed. He immediately telegraphed London saying he would radio *Tarana* to return to southern France and London must get the message back to the people in France to organise a new rendezvous.

After forty-eight hours of more nail-biting, nerve-stretching, and radioing for Donald, the boat turned around and successfully picked up the escapees. They all arrived safely a few days later.

Two of them stayed with us, French Canadians who had been taken prisoner by the Germans during the terrible Dieppe raid. Lucien Dumais and Ray Labrosse camped on our floor for three days. Lucien was a marvellous cook, so in the evenings we would sit around, eat and drink and hear stories of the war in Europe and how tough the Germans were. It was fun practising our French with these two disciplined fighting men who, through Donald, joined MI9 and volunteered to go back to France and help with the escape routes.

Brian and I had to go to Madrid and talk directly with our fellow workers stationed there, simply to familiarise ourselves with other members of our business. So on October 18th we packed up Antonio's Cadillac with twenty two-gallon tins of petrol and the diplomatic bag. Laden down and stinking like a refinery (we agreed it was not a good idea to smoke on this trip), we drove along the coast road to Malaga, passing through the little fishing villages of Estepona, Marbella and Torremolinos. Palm trees were being planted, and streets and roads damaged in the Civil War were being paved. The port area of Malaga was being rebuilt and modernised. We called in on the consul to pick up his diplomatic bag and left Malaga at 19.00 hours, having spent more time with the consul than intended.

The mountainous countryside between Malaga and Granada was wild and wonderful, and many areas were being planted up with pine trees. The twisty and very bumpy road was terrible and was being repaired in places. With all the petrol sloshing around, this section of the journey was very gruelling, but despite the hazards by 21.30 we were sitting in the wonderful coffee house in the main square of Granada facing the Hotel Victoria. People were wandering around in the warm evening atmosphere, lovers arm-in-arm closely followed by their chaperones, gipsies selling their handwoven lace, flamenco guitarists entertaining us on the streets; this part of Spain was slowly returning to its colourful self.

Refreshed by the strong coffee we set off towards Jaen only to be stopped by a Civil Guard patrol. They checked our papers, and looked suspiciously at the tins of petrol. One of them smiled and told us about the bandits in the mountains just before Jaen, warning us that it could be fatal to continue during the night. We thanked them for their advice but with a certain bravado decided to drive on.

'We must be bloody mad. One stray bullet and we will light up half of Andalusia!' exclaimed Brian.

'They are not going to shoot us,' I said confidently.

For the first half hour every corner we went around we quite expected to find a roadblock with rifle-bearing bandits at the ready; Brian kept on asking what I thought it would be like to be shot by a firing squad, or even worse, to be burnt alive due to a stray bullet setting fire to the petrol. As midnight approached our concern about bandits lessened, and staying awake was more of a worry; mind you, Brian managed that quite well by discussing the outcome of the car going over the edge and possibly dropping three or four hundred feet. As I edged around a corner he would come out with some stupid comment about how beautiful the stream in the ravine on his side of the car looked and how if I went any closer to the edge we could both benefit from a cold bath – if we did not catch fire on the way down.

Tired and hungry, at 3.20 am we arrived at the Albergue Hotel in Bailen. I remember this so well because I was surprised to find a security guard, and even more surprised to be offered fried eggs and toast for supper. Tired out, I fell asleep with my clothes on and the diplomatic bags tied to my wrist.

Washed and refreshed, we were on the road to Madrid by a quarter past ten, and to top our surprises of the previous night we found a telephone that worked, at a coffee bar which served roast barley coffee. Brian made a call to the Embassy in Madrid and gave our estimated time of arrival at about six that evening. We had lunch at the Albergue outside Manzanares and were thankful to be driving across the flat and arid countryside of La Mancha. Don Quixote and Sancho Panza might well have been attacking the windmills on the surrounding horizon.

Feeling as though the worst of the journey was over, Brian opened up the Cadillac only to hit a very large pothole. Rather shaken, he slowed down to a crawl as he manoeuvred in between the patchwork of hundreds of large holes in the road. The Messerschmitts and Stukas now fighting in northern Europe had used this area as a practice ground and left torn-up tarmac and shot-up vehicles as an indication of their expertise; another hangover from the Civil War. Despite our caution suddenly a loud crack came from the rear right-hand wheel, which immediately locked up. I crawled underneath the car and looked; realising there was nothing for it I told Brian to pass me the pliers and screwdriver. The rear spring had broken and the axle was jamming the brake cable. After two hours, with the brake cable tied around the axle to stop it from moving around, we were back on the slow move.

Our arrival at the Palace Hotel looking like tired-out grease monkeys was not welcome, and they refused to give us our rooms. Swearing at the manager and anyone else in earshot, I turned to Brian and loudly said, 'Let's break the Embassy rules and go to the National where I will be welcome.'

Juan, the receptionist, remembered me from when I stayed on my way to England in 1939. He put us in the best suite where we bathed and changed, then headed down to the restaurant.

Walking across a dining room full of Japanese and Italian faces felt somewhat strange, considering we were at war with both. It appealed to both Brian's and my rather wicked sense of humour; consequently we spoke in English as loudly and obnoxiously as possible; Juan and the waiters made the most out of it as well, and as we were leaving said how nice it had been to see English faces for a change.

The following morning, Alan Hilgarth, the Embassy security officer and naval attaché, sat us down in his plush office and gave us a severe reprimand, telling us never to stay in out-of-bounds hotels again. Brian and I split up after our hand-smacking by officialdom.

Kenneth Benton (head of Section V in Madrid) and I shook hands, rejoicing in being able to meet each other after all the messages we had exchanged about Garbo. After discussing the practices and character of each other's agent's, what Gibraltar was like, what Madrid was like, Kenneth took me to the Meson. A short drive out of Madrid and I found myself in a restaurant full of Brits and Secret Service folk. Basic wooden tables and chairs, a friendly atmosphere and, despite the shortage of food in the area, an excellent lunch. Here in this homely establishment, as Kenneth introduced me to many others working in the espionage game, I started to feel as though I belonged to some kind of special club.

On the way back to Madrid, Kenneth told me how they had been watching Frederico (Garbo's Abwehr connection) for the last year. The German secret service were rather useless in Spain, certainly in Madrid, by then.

To be English in Madrid in October 1942 made one feel rather special. Everywhere I went, with or without Brian, the Spanish always made extra efforts for one's comfort and well-being. Sitting in a famous German restaurant, I overheard the group of Spaniards at the table behind us wondering what and who we were. They thought we were Americans, or some other English-speaking people. One of them turned around and said, 'Well, they are foreigners anyway.' The fellow next to him smiled and patted him on the shoulder. 'They are not foreigners, they are English.'

The next morning must have been a Sunday, as I remember the people all dressed up waiting outside the church for mass. Unlike in London there were no sandbags, no temporary air-raid shelters, no one walked around with gas-mask bags; on the other hand there were very few cars, and food and clothing were in short supply.

Very early on Monday morning, the car full of petrol cans, Brian driving, the sound of the engine exaggerated by the empty streets, we headed south to Seville. Until we reached Valdepeñas the road and country seemed to be totally deserted apart from the occasional gasogene-powered truck. Valdepeñas, famous for its wine, was like a different country: trucks coming and going, donkeys, mules, people – it was as though Franco had decided Spain needed to drink wine, and it was all being produced here. We found a very busy bar-cum-restaurant full of truck drivers and muleteers and had lunch. Then back in the car, and on and on and on, our slow progress making the trip, although spectacular, very long and tedious. We were both grateful to be in the large, newly-sprung Cadillac, a wonderfully comfortable car which allowed whoever was not driving to sleep.

At last Seville and the lovely Hotel Inglaterra. We drove around, taking a trip through the world trade fair area of 1926, the port area where English and German merchant ships were moored next to each other, and went to a few good bars and consumed some very tasty tapas. We picked up the vice consul who took us to a restaurant for a marvellous paella. We made the most of our short stay in that beautiful city before going on to Cadiz, where we picked up a very ill marine engineer suffering from gangrene. He lay in the back as we drove as fast as we could to Gibraltar's military hospital. Fortunately the car had consumed about ninety per cent of the petrol and we only had a couple of cans left in the boot, because when we were about three hours away from Gibraltar the car caught fire. With the help of a Guardia Civil we managed to put the fire out without it causing any real damage to us or the car.

When the Guardia saw the man in the back, who at this stage was very ill indeed, he promised to telephone the frontier police and ask them to stay open until we had crossed into Gibraltar. As Brian drove up to the frontier, to our relief the two guards immediately opened the barriers and waved us through; by this time our companion was in a coma. At the hospital we ran into the lobby and, taking no notice of the protests from the night duty nurse, grabbed a stretcher. As soon as she realised the condition of the man she ran off to fetch the doctor. If the Guardia had not helped, firstly by putting the fire out and secondly by calling up the frontier guards, I am sure our patient would have died.

Back at the apartment, Brian and I collapsed on our beds and slept for a good twelve hours. We were woken by the loud noise of assembled Spitfires and Hurricanes being test-flown in preparation for the invasion of North Africa.

Three days after the first Spitfires had had a practice run, Brian and I crossed the border to spread rumours with our agents telling them that we were preparing for an up-and-coming relief of Malta. We hoped this would stop any conjecture as to our real destination.

We returned late in the evening to find La Linea Control in a state of mayhem. A policeman, Juan Llegado, told me 'The Americans have arrived and made a mistake. Look at those lovely planes buried in the trenches.'

'No one hurt,' I heard one official say.

A squadron of American Lightnings had started landing

on the Gibraltar airstrip in the early hours of the evening; some had missed the runway and landed in no-man's-land between the runway and the Spanish frontier.

I asked Juan Llegado, 'What will Madrid say?'

'Nothing for a few days, but get them out quickly please.'

Brian and I went home, to find Donald rather amused by the whole situation. Early next morning I went to the office and reported by phone to the Governor's office what I had been told. He told me the American representative on the Rock was worried because one of the planes had something called George on board. George was a new autopilot device developed by the Americans to help flying at night. 'It didn't help them much yesterday evening,' I said.

I missed all the action. Some SOE chaps and a couple of the American pilots, with the help of a few diversions created by some of my agents and a lot of other people, recovered George safe and sound from no-man's-land. Biaggio's Embassy bar was full of blue uniforms most of the day; it was the regular hangout for British and American pilots. He was a happy man, and I found it hard not to tell him that the planes were going to North Africa not Malta; he was going to be so disappointed.

The dockyard was working day and night. The workers consistently ignored the demands of the union leaders to go on strike. Due to all the extra activity I demanded double vigilance from my agents and their networks, as the chance of sabotage attempts was greatly increased. They kept me extremely well informed of any suspicious goings-on on the mainland and Gibraltar. I must admit my work seemed relatively easy, and certainly a lot of fun, due to the men I had working for me.

The streets were crowded with navy, air force and army

personnel wandering around. The white hats of the American military police bobbed up and down, so obvious amongst the other uniforms. Pieces of Hurricane planes were trolleyed down the road towards the north front where they were assembled.

One evening, around November 5th, I can remember going to Europe Point, a viewing area overlooking the Straits. Planes taking off and landing, ships sailing in all directions, boats coming in and out of the bay, soldiers drilling in the barracks, and all the people standing around watching; it was incredible to see. Suddenly – bang, bang, bang, bang, in rapid succession. Perhaps for Guy Fawkes night, they had decided to fire the rocket guns: twenty-five rounds a minute for four minutes, what a display. The sky lit up, reminding me of the firework displays at Crystal Palace I had illicitly watched when I was a boy at Dulwich.

Early in the morning on November 8th all the planes started taking off and the ships sailed away with supplies and troops; the drone of the Spitfires, the Hurricanes and Lightnings continued for hours, and the honks and whistles of ships and boats went on longer still.

The Allied forces landed in Casablanca and on the beaches just west of Algiers. Some of our intelligence officers were in at the very beginning doing their bit; Major Trevor Wilson volunteered and rode a motorcycle into Algiers to find out if the natives were going to be friendly or not. But for the most part the Brits were not involved directly with the initial landings. Algiers was taken by the Yanks quite peacefully, with big celebrations held in the streets.

On November 17th a trusty DC3 flew me to Algiers airport where Trevor met me and filled me in on all the latest news. Trevor had already settled into the offices on the second floor of number 8 Rue Charras. I could not help noticing some Algerian artifacts he had hung on the wall behind his desk; mostly pictures of rather busty belly dancers and a big poster advertising Molyneux perfume. The building was shared with Field Security who were rather a dry, humourless lot. Trevor informed me of the connection he had made with the French intelligence personnel who, according to him, were willing to help as much as they could. I'm sure they could not have been other than charmed by this fluent French-speaking, English skunk shit collector. Of course he had managed to acquire a beautiful Chrysler from the American consulate in Algiers; on the strength of his daring motorcycle trip, I expect.

I returned to Gibraltar – to do what? I'm not quite sure. The only useful action I was involved in was with Pilot Officer Butch Gerrard (the Fixer). He asked if I could help him out as he wanted Christmas turkey for his lads in the Fleet Air Arm. I made the necessary arrangements and he came across the border with me to the Miraflores and helped me load fourteen plucked turkeys into the back of the Cadillac. A very merry Christmas was had by one and all, at least on jolly old Gibraltar.

O'Shagar, my trusty Irish secretary, was to keep the lines of communication going with the network of agents I had built up. The next port of call for me was Algiers. My task there was never clearly defined, other than being to liaise with the French and start deception work; what kind of deception, I was to find out. On January 20th I made my last trip in wartime across the border to La Linea and Algeciras to say adios to my friends and cohorts.

Biaggio, who had drunk a few John Collinses to help him recover from his disappointment at Malta not being freed, provided food, drinks and location, Donald had his jazz friends play the night away, and I had a goodbye party to remember my friends and Gibraltar by. The following morning Brian took me to the airport, we shook hands. He started to walk away then turned, coughed slightly as he often did when about to say something slightly emotional, and said, 'It has been fun, hasn't it?'

With that he turned and walked off.

8

Algiers

As I turned away from Brian the hot morning sun hit my face making me squint, which was quite painful due to the hangover I was suffering. The American DC3 was waiting, its engines ticking over. On that bright January day in 1943 I joined eleven other passengers also heading for Algiers. The Americans had accumulated so many transport planes in North Africa that they were now responsible for carrying personnel and most of the freight to and from Europe.

I made myself as comfortable as was possible on the hard steel bench on the port side of the plane. Flying always made me nervous, and still does. But on this one occasion, I was so filled with a mixture of sadness at leaving Gibraltar and the excitement of a new adventure in Africa that the flying part did not worry me, at least for the take-off.

The engines revved up and the plane slowly taxied along the runway. We waited in line while two other DC3s took off in front of us. I checked my seatbelt and smiled at a couple of passengers, when suddenly one of the engines stalled. The high-pitched whine of the starter motor kept on and on. I began to feel nervous and was about to go and ask one of the crew what the problem was when the engine fired up. The navigator stuck his head round the door and told the marine sitting up front to pass a message around that all was OK. The plane jockeyed into position for take-off, the engines revved up with a deafening roar, the plane accelerated, then slowly started to climb, thankfully only to a low altitude. We were on our way to Algiers.

Spain slowly disappeared into the heat haze; the Mediterranean was full of ships rushing around; some heading to Gibraltar, some to Algiers, some, perhaps, back to England; I hoped, for Biaggio's sake, that one or two were on their way to Malta. The sea was so calm I could see schools of dolphins in the ships' wake. It looked like an aerial painting, where the artist had pencilled in the lines from the bows of the boats and added the delightful creatures as strange contrast to the large warships.

Although the sea was so calm, the air turbulence was terrible and a couple of times when the plane dropped rapidly, reviving my nagging fear that the engine might stall at any moment, I wished I had taken up the navy's offer of a ride on a destroyer on that nice calm sea. The bumps and dips broke into my reminiscences of how good life and work had been during my seven and a half months on the Rock. What was in store for me? The plane suddenly made a very severe lurch, and I stopped wondering. Thank goodness the reason for the last big-dipper effect was our descent to Blida.

The airfield at Blida was no more than a flat piece of land with a wooden hut at the southern end. The airstrip was muddy and rutted after the rains, so the engineers had laid down strips of steel mesh all over the surface in the hope that these would stop the planes from sinking into the soft mud. The steel strips worked quite well, but there had been so much air traffic that the surface was incredibly bumpy. Two planes that had obviously tried to take off before the mesh had been put down were sitting just off the runway, mud completely covering their wheels.

The airport was mayhem; it felt rather like being at a rugby or soccer game for the army and air force – or perhaps I should say an American football game. The Yanks were everywhere. Trevor Wilson met me, threw my bag into his requisitioned Chrysler and drove me towards Algiers, filling me in on who was who and what was what. At that moment I was not sure what was expected of me, except to be his number two in the rank-and-file of Section V, and to start up a deception network with the co-operation of the French.

I watched the scenery of adobe houses, and camels being ridden by their Arab masters; obviously neither beasts nor men were used to there being so many military vehicles running around. Trevor just managed to avoid two camels which suddenly ran straight in front of the car, due to two American jeeps racing towards an airplane that was preparing to take off.

Trevor looked at me over his glasses and said, 'Good to see you, Desmond. It has been a little confusing around here recently. The Americans like to do things on such a grand scale and always in such a hurry.'

'Yes,' I replied, 'it looks as though the natives are slightly bewildered and in a state of shock.'

'I think they are,' Trevor said. 'I know I am in a state of shock from dealing with the Americans, they are so sort of loud and big and there are so many of them. Your arrival has given me the excuse to start liaising with the French, which has been refreshing and somewhat relaxing. By and large they are very pleasant, and definitely will help you a lot.'

The French navy, despite their bitter memories of the British raid on Oran (then an important French naval port) in 1941, had decided to join the Allies. Members of the Deuxième Bureau and the Bureau de Renseignements, both well established in North Africa, presented themselves as more than willing allies. Trevor had struck up a particularly good relationship with Capitaine Paul Paillole, the head of the Bureau de Renseignement du Territoire (this bureau monitored the flow of information in and out of the area). His department had about thirty German and Spanish agents under their control. Before the Allied landing it had been relatively easy to give these agents enough low-grade information to keep their German masters happy. The invasion of American forces in Morocco, and Anglo-American forces in Algeria, was a shock to their masters and after a short period of inactivity these agents' Spanish and German masters began to ask different questions, and designated new targets for espionage.

Trevor continued, 'You will have to deal with the double agent problem. I have set up a meeting for you with Paillole tomorrow; after that you will have to sort out the situation with his staff. You must get Captain Paillole to introduce you to Captain Germain, who seems to be involved with the DAs (double agents). The question of free information is up to you to deal with.'

Trevor stopped talking to avoid an Arab boy who had just run into the middle of the road and stopped; he turned, looked at us, and raising both fists started to yell at the top of his voice. Trevor continued in his calm fashion as though nothing had happened.

'Lieutenant Colonel Hill-Dillon, a very likeable chap, will give you all the support you need. He is the British G2 at AFHQ, and a very supportive friend of our activities – our man in AFHQ as it were.'

Trevor was right, I did like Hill-Dillon, and he was very helpful. It made our life very much easier having a friend in Allied Forces Headquarters, as the regular army chaps did not like us cloak-and-dagger boys very much.

Trevor had organised an apartment for me in the centre of town. Having disposed of my bag and taken a shower I walked down the narrow staircase to the street.

The contrast to Gibraltar was one of noise, to start with. In Gibraltar vehicles were not allowed to honk their horns; and the language heard in the streets of Gib was a kind of Spanglish, interspersed with Hebrew and Pakistani; in the centre of Algiers it was predominantly French. American, French and British soldiers milled about like ants. The roads were full of honking military vehicles, ambulances, troop carriers and of course jeeps. (These tough four-wheel-drive vehicles were the envy of the English, as the Austin pick-ups we used were always breaking down or getting stuck in the sand – in fact they must almost have lost the war for us. I often wondered how much manpower was wasted repairing these hazardous vehicles.) All this hustle and bustle gave off a tremendous chaotic energy.

Just around the corner and down the hill from my apartment I found a little French bar next to a grocer's shop. A glass of Algerian wine and some goat cheese with stale French bread made up my first meal in Algiers.

The farmers from the very fertile surrounding area travelled by camel, by donkey or by foot to the market in the centre of Algiers to sell their herbs, spices, rice, goats, etc., as they had done for hundreds of years. The antiquity of the streets and the faces juxtaposed to the tanks and army vehicles made their normal life seem very tranquil. Algiers was a beautiful Arab town, with the blue Mediterranean to the north and the snow-covered Atlas mountains to the south.

On the morning after my arrival Trevor gave me a guided tour. The large port area was very simple and not mechanically equipped to deal with the destroyers and merchant ships toing and froing. The port's busiest time until 1943 had been in the eighteenth century, when it was the haunt of the famous Barbary pirates. The French Foreign Legion conquered Algeria in the 1830s, and Algiers had been an important Arab-European trading point since, but only for carpets and spices, and of course fishing. Now lorries, sailors, mechanics, cranes, large crates, small crates, armoured cars, tanks, jeeps, tents, and packages of canned food in abundance seemed to be disappearing in all directions; and not all to the Allies. The Arab workers had extremely dexterous fingers. The passing of information was an old-established trade which was also becoming much busier and free-flowing in Algiers.

The Arabs' distinctive adobe houses made up the outskirts of the town. Many of these Arabs worked and sold their goods in the souk, the small labyrinth of shops and mint-tea houses one could very easily get lost in, which regrettably had to be more or less out of bounds to the Allies. I am sure that every conceivable crime in the world happened in those tiny streets. The women, hidden behind their yashmak face masks, walked around in groups, constantly haggling. Many of the men wore French clothes, and seemed very European in an Arab way.

Trevor drove through the Arab section at the southern end of town, and we slowly climbed into the upper outskirts, where beautiful palatial houses with tree-lined drives and

grassy rose gardens revealed the rich colonial element of
Algiers. He turned into the gateway of one of these grand
houses.

'MI6 HQ is here.' He looked at me over his pince-nez
specs and added, in answer to my unasked question, 'Yes,
we are going up in the world.'

Another contrast to Gibraltar became apparent; here everybody wore uniform most of the time. We needed to be
recognised in Algiers and our presence needed to be felt.
The British army was on the move and counter-espionage
was playing a very important role in the decision-making of
the generals. Due to our success in transmitting confusing and
wrong information to the Germans, which they believed (e.g.
we were going to save Malta), the Torch landings in North
Africa had been very successful and not very expensive in
the loss of material or life. This success had convinced many
of the generals of the importance of good deception work.
Now, with counter-offences being planned, every false piece of
information which the Germans believed would help us win the
battles quickly, cheaply and with as few deaths as possible.

The gardens at MI6 HQ were beautifully laid out. Small
pools with fountains in the middle fed small canals, which
flowed through the shaded gardens that extended around the
house; pepper trees, pine trees, mimosa trees and a couple
of olive trees.

We walked into the tiled lobby, where marbled stairs led to
the upstairs section, and through a brass-handled door down
into the basement. Trevor's introductions were interspersed
with the usual idle chat, and swigs of Algerian vino.

'Captain Cuthbert Bowlby, Desmond Bristow. Cuthbert
used to be head of station in Cairo; took over here a couple
of weeks ago.'

Cuthbert was a very good chap, ex-naval officer and all that jazz. He had joined SIS just before the war. His quiet, discreet manner made him popular with the French; his easy way went down well with the Americans; all in all he created a co-operative and congenial atmosphere. His staff consisted of three assistants, several secretaries and a signals unit, handling MI6 signals.

'Desmond, I believe you already know Lieutenant Morgan, head of signals. He's waiting for you to find some good agents to operate the radios for us so he can retire and spend the next few years on the beach.'

Lieutenant Morgan smiled as he shook my hand. 'Good to see you, Desmond. I hope this is good reading.' He handed me my first message which had arrived that morning under my new codename of Tapwater. This made us all laugh. I remember wondering who in London had decided I should be Tapwater for my duration in Algiers.

After lunch, Trevor dropped me off in the Rue Charras. 'I'll see you at seven in the orifice,' he yelled as he drove into the thick traffic. The memory of all those people and vehicles running around in Algiers will always daunt me. It never stopped. It was rather how I imagine New York to be. Back in the office, which was shared with Field Security, there were five messages on my desk, all unimportant, from various chaps inviting me to meet them. A brief note from Brian and Donald wishing me well made me feel better.

I sat at my desk thinking around the fact that Trevor was going to introduce me to the French secret servicemen, and practising my French. (Où est la plume de ma tante?)

It was thanks to Trevor building up a very positive relationship with the French that the Allies were able to utilise their network of agents so quickly. It became clear that I was in Algiers to take over and enhance Section V's liaison with the French specifically for the purposes of deception operations; at certain moments I was indirectly operating thirty double agents through and with French officers. Despite the English/French rivalry that has become so fashionable, I can honestly say they were wonderful people to work with and certainly knew what they were doing.

French HQ was very near MI6 HQ, and the houses had obviously been built by the same architect. Captain Paillole, Captain Germain (an unfortunate name, I thought), Colonel Rivet and several other officers were at this first meeting. Captain Paillole was one of the most striking characters I met during the war. He was one of those people who could walk into a crowded room and everyone would notice him; tall, quiet, very good-looking, cool, calm and collected, he was in charge of the French double agent operations. Captain Germain was a shortish, balding, fairhaired man, who prior to the war had been a professor at Metz University. Colonel Rivet was an affable man in charge of the overall Secret Service proceedings. He appeared to be very overshadowed by Captain Paillole.

The following day I was introduced to the Frenchman with whom I was to work most closely: Captain Doudot. Captain Germain took me to Doudot's little office in a sidestreet off the main Algiers Boulevard, introduced us to each other and left.

My newly found cohort and I gave each other a brief life history, and then started a conversation which did not finish for nearly eighteen months. There were a few full stops and paragraph changes, but from this moment on he and I saw each other almost every day to talk about agents, troop movements, messages to and from Cairo, London, Gib, army camps, bars, street corners etc., etc.

Captain Doudot was in his early forties; he had gingerish hair, a freckly face and stout build, and wore very strong glasses. He was from Alsace, which gave him an under-standing of the German mentality, and his stamina gave both of us the strength to deal with our forthcoming task. Luckily he had a very lively sense of humour, very much like my own, so we were able to laugh at the frequent times when the intensity of the double agent game might otherwise have broken us.

Realising that, besides having to work with each other, we genuinely liked each other, Doudot offered to take me to lunch at a little restaurant out of town, which he thought I might enjoy. Indeed I did! It was owned by a Spaniard whose speciality was fish with mimosa eggs.

It is strange how the fortunes of war could take one down a road which might have death at the end of it – or might turn into an exciting journey in the best of company; company I am enjoying writing about, nearly fifty years later.

The Spanish restaurateur, José, could not believe I was from Huelva; he immediately embraced me, and made a great fuss. Of course it became a favourite eating place for Doudot and me. It was worth the drive, to sit amongst the lush palm trees, planted in large pots with Arab designs. Punka-type fans rotated in the ceiling, creating a cool breeze. At the exclusive end, high-backed wicker chairs formed four-seat private tables.

On this first visit, Doudot and I took a table in the back corner near the kitchen, affording us a good view and privacy. The chances of us being overheard were less than in the office. It would take too long to give a detailed account of the conversation, which was all in French; besides, I remember only the context, being rather confused at the time. (Trying to remember all the agents Doudot told me about is giving me as much of a headache now as it did then.)

He told me about a French air force officer who had volunteered to become an agent for the Germans, and had managed to get himself sent to Tunisia by Lufthansa. He parachuted in, landing somewhere near Tunis with a radio and receiver. 'The Germans trust him implicitly,' Doudot said.

I wondered how this man had dared and managed to do this; but the hows were not important, the fact that he had, and that I could use him to feed the Germans with what we called chicken feed, was very important. 'What type of information can we send, and how often, without jeopardising his position?' I asked.

'It is essential that he works his cover and keeps fairly quiet until it becomes clear that he is entirely trusted by the Germans, and we in turn can continue to trust him. We have given him a notional post in the French liaison department in AFHQ. What do you think of that?' Doudot asked.

Shifting in my chair I realised that with the right handling this man could become the best agent for our purposes. Most of the agents then working for us as doubles had direct contact with their German or Spanish employers, which was a very dangerous situation especially for deception work.

Doudot continued, 'I would like to add, Desmond, that as far as I am concerned there is no question of this man being disloyal and the Germans obviously see no reason to believe he is double-crossing them, since they chose to drop him in Tunis.'

'We must build him up very slowly and carefully for the next few months,' I said. 'Since he is in AFHQ the information we give him must be very selective.' I quickly added, 'We must not be too ambitious yet.'

This daring air force officer became known as the highly important and successful agent Gilbert.

For the next three hours or so we discussed the strengths and weaknesses of many other agents, and how best to use them. It became clear to me that the French had been working against the Germans and Italians in North Africa in depth and in a masterly fashion for some time, without any defections. I felt elated and surprised at the end of this meeting that the French should be handing over this intricate network for us to use.

Doudot and I, smiling and happy, arranged to meet the next day. I found Trevor in our office looking through telegrams, and described my meeting.

'Right,' said Trevor. 'Tomorrow we see Hill-Dillon.'

9

Deception

In those relatively early days, when ideas were abundant and untested, and no definite plans could be made, my first task was to analyse each agent the French presented to me. It was imperative to reduce the possibility of detection by the Germans to a bare minimum while maximising the potential of each informer.

I had dinner with the two French refugees who owned the local grocer's shop where I bought my food when tired of bully beef. They told me that in 1920 they had been professors at the Sorbonne University, teaching foreigners French; I had spent six weeks brushing up my French at the Sorbonne in 1937. Though I usually take up any excuse for conversation, that occasion, despite the delicious meal and good wine, was very quiet. I was in no mood for talking, and my hosts very politely must have sensed my need to be undisturbed.

I went back to my apartment and studied the names and characters of our AFHQ staff. It was part of my job to obtain permission from AFHQ for the information we needed to pass on. At this early stage, it seemed that the military could be persuaded to give us information on troops, their badges, movements and general activity. On the other hand the naval element, under Admiral Sir

Andrew Cunningham, was very reluctant to bless any kind of information, even non-consequential chicken feed. The following story illustrates how stupid this was.

We knew an enemy plane had been doing reconnaissance over Algiers and Bône, and had without any doubt spotted the destroyer and merchant ships in the port. Cunningham would not allow us to confirm through our potential agents what the Germans were looking at photographs of, and if the agents were not informing their masters about ships in the port, when an airplane could take photographs, what good were they? This had to change for us to be able to build up the Germans' trust in the agents we were using as doubles. I realised our department was going to have to put pressure on these elements of resistance to deception, and persuade them how important it could be. After all, we were trying to make life easier for the likes of Cunningham.

I made up my mind to suggest to Doudot we take a tremendous risk and give some chicken feed to Gilbert to radio over to his German masters.

Lieutenant Colonel Hill-Dillon had big bushy eyebrows which set off his aquiline noise and the permanent twinkle in his eyes. He walked as though he had been in the saddle of a horse from birth. As Trevor had predicted, I liked him and he was very supportive of us. He listened to our makeshift plans with great enthusiasm; we told him very little about our work, but he understood our need for information about army activity and that it was for deception and it would be going to the Germans.

'Well,' he said, 'you do realise there are a lot of chaps who neither trust nor like what you are doing, but I shall see what I can do. You know, if it wasn't for you chaps I'd get awfully bored around here; you give my brain something to do. Besides that, it tickles me how stupid some of the people around here can be, and you make me feel as though I'm not one of them.' He smiled. 'By the way, I reckon if you are seen with us army chappies often enough the old naval boys will get jealous and want a bit of the attention as well.'

He showed Trevor and me around the enormous complex of AFHQ. Trevor had of course already seen it many times. It was a very large building on the eastern end of town. Again constant comings and goings of personnel and vehicles, naval, air force and army. I took note of some apparent new arrivals. Hill-Dillon confirmed they were new, and that they were not important and could be used as chicken feed. I'm sure, had they known, they would not have liked the idea of being chicken feed.

I then called on Doudot in his tiny room. Papers and books were everywhere. He was sipping coffee out of an enormous cup, and poured me some, strong and black.

'Doudot, last night I came up with a plan,' I said, pacing the two metres of floor space. 'I think we should send some chicken feed to Gilbert as a trial run. You see, in our camp there are some people who are not convinced deception works, and really don't like us very much. Part of my job is to convince those bods that deception with your network of agents is very worthwhile. I thought if we could send a little something to the Germans via Gilbert it might help.'

I knew that any message Gilbert sent to the Germans would be picked up by Ultra in England, who would then be the first to realise the potential of at least one of the French agents. I told Doudot of the new arrivals at AFHQ and he agreed to contact Gilbert. He understood it was essential to start some activity to help me convince the likes of Admiral Cunningham how vital our operations were to the war effort.

Doudot and I worked on the wording of the message for hours in his little office; we ate sandwiches, talked, drank copious quantities of coffee, and smoked cigarette after cigarette. It was vital this first message gave enough to the Germans to make them trust Gilbert, and even more vital we did not over-indulge our German friends, and thus get into trouble with AFHQ. It was a trial run for everybody involved, and very hard work on the brain, made fun, however, by the interaction between Doudot and me.

Doudot got the message to Gilbert, who sent it to his German masters. Four days later I walked into my office and sitting on my desk was a triple Z envelope from St Albans. I opened it very quickly, thinking that it must be confirming the success of Gilbert. It stated: ACCORDING TO US AND OUR FRIENDS HERE [Ultra], WE FEEL YOUR MAN IS SUSPECTED OF MAKING BREAD IN THE WRONG BAKERY. I.e., the Abwehr suspected Gilbert of being under our control. I could not believe it. I must have re-read that telegram twenty times. My heart sank through the floor. After an hour or so of deliberation I called up Doudot, who came over straight away.

As he walked in he exclaimed, 'Mon Dieu, Desmond, what's happening? You look as white as a sheet. Some brandy perhaps?' He offered me a silver hip flask.

'No, thanks. Here, take a look at this.' I gave him the telegram and translated for him. My previous deliberation had been over the dilemma of whether to show Doudot the telegram. By giving him evidence of England's ability to intercept German communications I was informing him

On my horse Rozinante accompanied by Feliciano (the groom) on a donkey with panniers full of picnic supplies, outside the front garden at Sotiel Coronada.

The Roman bridge and Roman mill, still operating at the time, on the River Odiel near the mines. I watched sunbeams and collected flour there.

Diving with friends into the dam on the mines at Sotiel Coronada, near Robinson Crusoe Island.

Rowing for Magdelene College, Cambridge.

Betty Weaver carrying potatoes in the Land Army in 1940, the year before we were married.

Getting married in Oxford.

Facing page: In Gibraltar, 1941. In the back row, from left to right, the first man is Austin Baillon (SOE), the third man is Brian Morrison (MI6), and the fourth man is Lt-Col. Tito Medlam (MI5).

This page: Madrid, 1949. I am in the centre, Betty is on the left, Marjorie Presley is second left, and Joe Presley of the FBI is on the right.

Donald Darling of MI9 in his office in Gibraltar.

Joe Presley in Madrid.

Waiting for wild boar on a shoot outside Madrid in 1949.

With Betty and Father Ransome on
holiday at the summer house owned by
the Catholic Church.

Relaxing during a wild boar shoot at
Yebenes outside Toledo.

about Ultra, one of our great secrets of the war. I had decided that if we were going to work together efficiently and freely we could afford no secrets from one another.

'Desmond, how come they even know Gilbert sent a message? I assume from this that England can intercept everything. Do you realise what a risk you have taken in showing me this telegram?'

'Yes, I do realise, and I thought about it before I called you, but if you and I are to work together like this and we cannot trust each other we may as well stop here and now.'

'I agree with you, but your countrymen will not. I am honoured by your trust and obvious understanding of our situation.'

I explained some of the details of Ultra and other aspects of British Secret Service capabilities. He reciprocated my trust, and divulged secrets which I'm sure the French authorities would not have been too pleased to have me know. This mutual trust enabled us to discuss, to plan and to operate much more freely and comfortably. We were able to achieve many of our goals much more quickly. From that moment on our work relationship was never questioned by either of us.

Doudot left the office and returned an hour later. 'Desmond, I want you to telegraph London and request they thoroughly check their findings of discrepancies which make them think the Germans know we are controlling Gilbert.'

He knew the Germans called their wireless transmitter operators 'piano players'. Maybe some confusion had occurred over this code the Germans used. He felt sure a mistake had been made; he had checked all the details of his agent's message, and the call signs, and had found nothing odd at all; and believe me he had been reading and sending messages for a long time.

That sleepless night went on for ever. I tossed and turned, got up, made coffee, smoked, paced the room, listened to the traffic, and I worried a lot. I had run a risk by having the message sent by Gilbert, but nothing compared to what might happen if HMG found out I had let Doudot in on Ultra.

Early next morning I received a phone call in my office from HQ to say a triple Z telegram had arrived for me from London. I borrowed Trevor's car and rushed up there. I ran into the radio room and grabbed the telegram, which read something like this: FOR TAPWATER, REGRET ERROR MADE ON OUR BEHALF, V MANN REFERRED TO AS PIANO PLAYER CONFUSING, ALL A OK.

Laugh? I almost cried out with jubilation. I rushed over to find Doudot in his office, who apparently had also had a sleepless night. I gave him the good news.

Gilbert went on to become our best agent and extremely important in our game of deception. He has been compared by some historians to Garbo in their examination of post-war Abwehr records. By early February continued messages were being sent by Doudot and myself through Gilbert and other agents; my knowledge and comprehension of his network grew every day. We spent hours sifting through snippets of information, formulating a message to be sent by one agent, usually Gilbert, and supporting messages to be sent by others; that is, the important message would be sent by one agent, then we would put together subsequent information supporting the contents of the first. With a time-set plan we would have other agents transmit the supportive information a day or two, sometimes a week later. As we became visibly successful in confusing the Germans, our department was able to put ever-increasing pressure on AFHQ and Cunningham. We were also able to persuade Brigadier Dudley-Clark, who visited us regularly from Cairo, to apply some highbrow pressure in the right places.

Official clearance was obtained, and the reporting of anything which Field Security sections overheard in the camps, town, or wherever, proceeded. We studied carefully all indiscretions which came our way, and worded them in such a fashion as not to tell the Germans anything of real consequence (rather like legal documents of today). We now had a steady flow of information being sent by our various agents. Sometimes we had to send something meaty but we always managed to phrase it so that the Germans either reacted too late or, when the wording was really vague, ignored it until after the event. Then they most probably sat down and told each other they should have listened to the agent.

I was now attending regular meetings with the French: Captain Germain, Captain Paillole, and others. I was also attending many meetings with Hill-Dillon and field security officers. All this information became too much for me to cope with. I was to all intents and purposes a lone committee for a short period. Thank goodness Major (later Lieutenant Colonel) Michael Crighton arrived from Cairo with his A Force experience. He became chairman of the committee and brought in Colonel Golbranson of the US general staff. He in turn brought in Lieutenant Arne Eckstrom, a member of the Office of Strategic Studies (OSS). Michael Crighton had Captain Thomas as his aide. I was the MI6 representative at these meetings, during which we decided what information I should sift through with Doudot and send via the appropriate agent. I insisted that either Doudot or Germain be present at some of these meetings and I would translate for them.

Doudot and I were essentially the joint controllers of about thirty double agents at this point – around the middle of March, 1943.

The Americans on the committee were not familiar with the idea of deception, and this presented a rather similar problem to the one we had just got over with the navy: how to persuade them to co-operate as much as we needed. Arne Eckstrom fully understood our predicament, since he well knew how stubborn many of the American generals could be, especially General Marshall. Arne kept chipping away at the US delegates, and eventually we had the authority to start sending American chicken feed through our network.

These various hurdles having been dealt with, it was time for me to visit our man in Oran, Captain Bobby Lloyd.

I acquired a car, and went to the grocery store for basic supplies. When Albert, the ex-professor turned grocer, heard where I was going, he asked if I could do the shop a favour. I owed them a few meals and other favours, so of course I said yes. He asked me to get eggs.

'Where do I go?' I asked.

'Three kilometres after Tenes, the road leaves the lie of the coast. About two kilometres on, you will see four huge straw stacks on the left. Just stop there, press the hooter three times and wait.'

This I did, and after about two minutes out from one of the stacks crawled two young boys, who approached the car timidly. 'What do you want?' they asked in Algerian French.

'I am looking for some eggs.'

They looked at each other. 'Are you American?' the taller one asked.

'No, I am English,' I replied, trying not to laugh at their interrogative methods.

The short one said, 'We know you are not French by your uniform.'

'Good, now what about the eggs?' I asked, getting a little impatient. 'I don't want them today. I will be back in two days at 12.30 pm.'

'How many eggs do you want?' the tall one asked.

I thought for a bit, and as a joke I asked for five hundred, thinking they would laugh at such a quantity.

'Very well,' came their reply, 'we shall have five hundred eggs ready for you.' The little one added, 'In boxes.'

'Very good, and thank you,' I replied.

As I was leaving the boys ran back to the stacks and seemed to dive under the straw; immediately about twenty heads of men, women, and children appeared from the inside of the stacks to take a look at the Austin pick-up and me. Where on earth were all the chickens, I wondered.

I arrived in Oran late in the evening. It was not such a busy place as Algiers, and luckily I found Bobby's apartment near the centre without any problem. The European influence was not as strong here in a cosmopolitan way, but there were a few French Foreign Legionaries wandering around.

Captain Bobby Lloyd, a short, good-looking, aristocratic Englishman who had a sort of gurgly laugh, and as far as I remember never lost his temper, was the MI6 man in Oran and had established a very close liaison with the resident French Bureau de Renseignement officer Eduard Douare. There was a covey of French-controlled agents in the pay of the Spanish and Germans, ostensibly working for the Spanish in neighbouring Spanish Morocco, or for the German vice consul in Oujda. Most were doing no more than satisfying inquisitiveness, rather than giving information on intelligence targets. Ship movements in and out of Oran had a certain degree of intelligence interest, especially the types of vessels, but were of very little consequence to the Allies.

Bobby's apartment was very close to Douare's house and after I had cleaned up after my dusty trip across the desert Bobby took me around to meet Eduard and his delightful wife, who had a slight squint. Eduard took us out to a small bistro around the corner. Gigot was the *spécialité de la maison*, stuffed with garlic, surrounded by peppers and aubergine. It was quite excellent – it must have been, for me to remember it so clearly nearly fifty years later.

The next morning we reviewed Douare's agents and their possibilities, selecting the few who could be useful in a future deception campaign. I spent some extra time with Bobby working out which agents would be in the best positions to put out messages or stories to back up details coming from Algiers. A lot of this work was hypothetical, but it was necessary in case the Germans started to do better in the desert war. Also, if at any time there should be a particular tricky piece of information going to the Germans it was comforting to know that an agent in Oran could put out a story to substantiate it.

In the late afternoon Bobby took me for a guided tour of Oran and its environs, and of course to Sidi Bel Abbes, just to have a look at the headquarters of the French Foreign Legion. There seemed to be 'Spais' and 'Goumiers' – French Moroccon regiments – everywhere. Moroccan troops under

French command marched across the quad and back again; these later proved themselves in the Italian campaign; especially with the women, I gather!

Early next morning I got back into the Austin pick-up, praying it would not break down, and headed back to Algiers. I was egg bound, and after a long and uneventful journey through the northern desert I stopped the car to become involved in a minor black market operation. To my surprise, when I honked the horn three times, the lower part of two of the straw stacks came alive. Fifteen or twenty boys ferried the forty-two dozen eggs into the back of the pick-up. When the last box had been loaded, the tall boy came up to me to be paid.

'Just one thing before I leave,' I said.

'Yes, monsieur?' He sounded rather impatient.

'Where are the hens?'

He looked at me as though sizing me up, then pointed in the direction of the straw.

'You see the two stacks at the back?' he asked. The chickens live under those and my family and some friends live under the front four.' He turned away on the ball of his bare foot, then turned back to say, 'Goodbye, monsieur, and thank you.' He held up his hand, with the few extra Algerian francs I had given him.

I drove with great care over the bumpy road, and when I made my delivery I was invited to a supper of scrambled eggs, which I gratefully accepted.

10

My Feluccing Friend

Doudot and I started to relay messages to our agents which would confuse the Germans about the Allied plans concerning an invasion of Europe from Africa. We agreed it would be a good idea for me to visit Gibraltar and substantiate some of these messages.

Brian had been recalled to London. O'Shagar, now on his own, was gathering more information on German personnel in the campo area, and keeping tabs on the Italian frogmen. Donald was still hard at escape work. The flow of people escaping had almost doubled, partly because the Germans were having to use prison guards to fight on their front lines, and partly because the escape organisations were much more efficient.

I arranged with Donald that I should spend the night in my old bed, and left the office, noticing how comparatively quiet Gib was these days, except for the shipyards that were full of vessels waiting for repairs and being repaired.

Quietly opening the door I crept up to the bar and coughed very loudly. Biaggio jumped up from behind the counter.

'Captain Britow!' he exclaimed. 'Have a John Collins,' as though it was only yesterday when we had last seen each other.

'Don't mind if I do. How are you, Biaggio?'

'Very well, Captain. Malta is able to eat reasonably good food again and my family are healthy. Thanks to the English.' He started to mix my drink.

'Nice little party you are having with the Americans in North Africa.' He placed the John Collins on a tray and led me to the office. I apologised for having had to lie to him about Malta, and he seemed to understand.

'I assume you are here to ask me something, or have me pass some information around,' he said with a smile.

He had guessed correctly. Having thought about all the agents who had worked for me in Gib, I had decided Biaggio was the best person to ask to spread stories around Gib and La Linea which would substantiate some of the messages our agents had been sending to the Germans.

I wish I could remember exactly what the stories were, but time and training are working against me. It is of the utmost importance when one is travelling around as a spy to forget the reasons why as soon as possible.

I do remember that Biaggio was arrested by the British for passing on the information to his agents in his hotel. Whether or not he tried to get hold of me I don't know, but I did not learn about his arrest until after the war. I was infuriated since the officials responsible knew very well he worked for me. This is just another small incident of British justice towards a man who had risked his business and life for no reason other than love of the English. Amazingly, he was not very upset as the authorities released him when they realised their mistake. The irony of it all is that just before I arrived in Gib to give Biaggio the information which was used to put him in jail, he had donated £2,000 to the Spitfire fund.

A week after my return from Gib, Bobby Lloyd was

moved from Oran to join me. He moved into the spare room of my spacious apartment, and the two of us moved the office from Rue Charras to the consulate general, which initially was shared with Kenneth Younger, a typical English gentleman.

It was a great relief for me to have Bobby as my co-worker; I liked him, and the workload was growing to enormous proportions as more generals and admirals started to wake up to the benefits of deception work preceding a major strategic offensive.

When I returned from a top secret A Force meeting, where the tension and excitement had been exhausting and exhilarating at the same time, Bobby asked me, 'How did that go, Desmond? Have they fired you yet?'

'I wish they had. Close the door, will you, Bobby.'

He did so, and came and sat very close to me so that our speech was a mere whisper.

'We are going to invade Sicily, and you and I have to do some storytelling which will put the Germans to bed in the wrong place at the right time. The fun is about to begin. The Americans are still not convinced that deception will work, silly buggers.' I got up and opened the door. 'I'm off to see Doudot and tell him about the party . . . Why don't you come with me?'

We again analysed in depth the potential of Doudot's agents. It was agreed by the committee that our job was to convince the Germans of a big build-up of Allied forces in Algeria.

'What's going on with the French troops that we can keep the Germans interested in for a while?' I asked Doudot.

'Well, we are enlisting more locals and Moroccans into the

French forces. We can show this activity by the movement around Fez, Mostaganem, Rabat and Sidi Bel Abbes.'

Bobby chipped in, 'I think we should report more military insignia being seen all over our area.'

The conversation covered all the details about the French network, and possibilities in Spanish Morocco of using Douare's network. We continued discussing all the alternative amounts of information we could pass to the Germans, on into the night.

The next day I arrived at the committee meeting with a breakdown of our discussion, and our ideas of how to implement our phoney programme.

Arne Eckstrom looked around the table and said in his gentle American accent, 'This is definitely making the most of the only means at hand. The French, from what Desmond tells me, are incredibly well organised, so my feeling is to get on with it.' The rest of the committee were in agreement.

That evening Bobby, Arne and I met Doudot to tell him of the committee's approval. The task of designing misinformation for our double agents began.

I should explain how deception works. Since Gilbert was a plant by the French to begin with, he does not follow the normal pattern of agents, so I am not referring to him.

To start with one needs to find a person who is in a position of free movement around the public places, such as bars, restaurants, repair shops, newspaper vendors. The Germans tended to choose barmen, waiters, mechanics, etc.; the Spanish were keen on journalists on local newspapers. Doudot had spent long hours following and watching such people, looking for one who was obviously making extra money somehow, and assessing whether this money came from being an agent for the Germans or Spanish.

When sure of his man, or woman, he would allow some time to go by and, choosing the moment very carefully, perhaps when the person needed even more extra cash, approach the person and suggest they give information to their paymasters, which he would feed to them. These agents often did not even realise what they were involved with so long as they received money. For them it meant receiving two paychecks, tax free.

I must add that some of these agents volunteered their services, but this added an extra worry since they may have been triple agents, as they had the freedom of meeting their German or Spanish masters in private. It did however mean they could reply to the German or Spanish questions with the answers we wanted them to receive. The fact that the French had thoroughly researched into these people's loyalties reduced the risk considerably. Added to this we could also put in the reply a small piece of information which would lead them to believe things we wanted them to believe, over and above whatever they were curious about. Yes, it is nothing more than lying. But very creative lying.

For example: Jean the waiter is asked by the Germans to find out about the shipping movement going east from Algiers port. We would tell Jean as much or as little as we wanted known about the shipping, which he would then send to the Germans. This information would always be close to the truth. Then we would add some information about new tanks heading south. The Germans would then start a line of questioning about the tanks, and they would obviously assume there was a build-up of forces in the south. With luck, they would send troops south, and our troops could then attack from the north and meet less resistance.

During this time in Algiers, information put out to the

Germans by the agents had to be co-ordinated with A Force in Cairo and the XX committee in London. Since AFHQ was a joint US-British organisation. A Force Algiers incorporated joint American and British deception planners for the first time in the war. As I have mentioned, the French also became part of this committee.

Arne Eckstrom, Bobby Lloyd, Doudot and myself had our first meeting in Doudot's cramped office. Bobby sat on the corner of the old French desk, Arne on a wooden packing case and I on a tiny chair; Doudot went on smoking, filling the room with the aromatic smell of black tobacco.

I explained. 'Doudot, we are somehow trying to convince the Germans that our next expected attack will be in the eastern Mediterranean. We must put over the idea of Crete, and try to get Turkey on our side. We must give the impression of military interest in the Peloponnese area in general. Nobody seems to know exactly where we are going to attack next. Theoretically we could attempt to cut off the German forces in Italy, by attacking the north east and the north west in the Ligurian sea, and around Venice. We will have more positive instructions in the next week or two. For the moment we should allow agents to be quite negative about our future intentions and the significance of the military movement going on around Algiers, and eastward towards Tunis. All this movement is not going to be engaged in the final liberation of Tunis, it is for something bigger; where that something bigger is going to happen we do not know, as far as our agents are concerned.'

'Yes, that coincides with how we Americans feel,' said Arne, who spoke perfect French – for an American.

'We ought to involve Douare from Oran in our next meeting,' suggested Bobby.

Subsequent meetings were concerned with the deception leading up to the Sicily landings. Douare attended several of these, and Captain Germain began to add his intellectual abilities, attending a couple of times a week. I am glad to say not many of these meetings were held in Doudot's office. I don't mind the smell of black tobacco but when one started to feel as though one were sitting in the Black Hole of Algiers, the smoke did not help.

A Force meetings were now receiving regular visits by Brigadier Dudley-Clark and Lieutenant Colonel Noel Wild, as the build-up for the Sicily landings needed more deception. The date of the landings was a constant subject of conversation; it kept changing. This was partially due to how the desert battles went, but it was particularly influenced by what we in deception were able to get the Germans to do with their forces. For a short time the committee wondered if we had too much true information slipping through to the wrong places, and I was concerned by the Spanish consulate general, for no specific reason other than not being able to recruit or control them. I had failed to recruit one of the Spanish consulate secretaries who was going out with a British officer. As we left a meeting together Brigadier Dudley-Clark said, 'Desmond, do you think you could find out what our Spanish friends are up to, if anything? This business of the girl going out with the lieutenant may be harmless; nevertheless, I for one would like to know, not about her especially, but what the Spanish are up to in general.'

'I'll see what can be done by the time you return,' I replied.

Walking through the crowded streets I formulated a plan. Doudot had recently taken a professional safebreaker into his employ. This man had been one of the top safe mechanics in Madrid before the war, and had made good use of his abilities since being in Algiers. Doudot had heard about him from a rich French lady who, having lost the key to her Louis XIV bureau, employed Carlos to open it. He did so without leaving a scratch on it. Doudot employed Carlos for information, and safe cracking if needed. As it now was. My plan was to break into the safe in the Spanish consulate and take copies of all their cypher codes.

So on a moonless night, with watchers all around, Carlos slid through a window, and one and a half hours later slid back out again.

'Where are the codes?' asked Bobby, wanting to photograph them very quickly and have Carlos return them.

Carlos handed over the cypher books and we photographed them. Meanwhile he pulled out another package from his large pocket. Twenty-five pairs of silk stockings and six Omega watches appeared.

'I found these in the other safe, which I must say was very easy to open.' His eyes twinkled as he held up the ill-gotten gains.

We distributed the booty amongst ourselves. I received a watch. The cypher books were returned to the safe, and no more was said or heard about the break-in, not even from the consul. I expect he thought it was an inside job, or perhaps the stockings and watches were stolen goods anyway.

After that, the Spanish consulate general appeared to stop making intelligence reports. This indicated that they were probably using their diplomatic bag, so we kept a flow of deception material going their way.

Not long after this episode I was in the bar around the corner from my apartment chatting with the local carpet trader, who was also selling camels for his brother. He smelt more of camels than carpets. We had talked on many occasions; he thought I was with the regular British army. This time he told me his brother had been to a monastery near Boufarik and had heard strange noises like a wireless set or something. He thought the Italians might be involved. The next day Francisco, my newly acquired driver, with my newly acquired Chenard Walker (automatic, you know), took me to the monastery.

The Abbot received me very politely and showed me around. He did get a little upset when I asked him directly about the radio set, which of course he denied all knowledge of. I remember my footsteps echoing on the stone floor and how cool the air was in the passageway when we passed a door which he ignored and did not open.

'Monsieur, this door needs to be opened as well,' I said with as much authority as I could muster. He nodded and tutted a lot. I continued, 'If you refuse me I shall return with some army chaps who like nothing better than knocking down doors in monasteries.'

After a few moments' deliberation he unlocked the door to what appeared to be an office. Amongst the papers I discovered hundreds of Bordeaux wine labels. Further on, in a small yard full of wine bottles, were two monks pasting labels and another carrying the labelled bottles into a room. It was a bottling plant, turning Algerian wine into French. No radio set was discovered, but I did return home with a case of very good Algerian Bordeaux, a bottle of which I took to the next meeting with Doudot and company.

A few days later I was invited by a friend of Doudot's to take a trip into the desert near Hassi Messaoud beyond Ghardaia, and visit a sheik friend of his at his palace. I was able to borrow a jeep from the friendly American mechanics who had just repaired the Chenard Walker. They were often very helpful, in return for a few cans of bully beef, the occasional meal at the British mess at AFHQ, and bottles of Johnny Walker which I acquired every now and again.

We set off early in the morning, driving further and further into the desert, getting hotter and hotter and dustier and dustier. The only interruptions on the first leg of the trip were the crossings of camel trains. We rolled into Ghardaia with virtually no petrol in the tank and looking like dust-covered zombies. We stayed at a flea-ridden rooming house where we ate couscous and slept in very uncomfortable beds. The shower, however, was greatly appreciated. The next morning we filled up with petrol and drove for three hours to Hassi Messaoud, where we stopped for petrol and coffee. About half an hour out of this little desert town we came across an American personnel carrier heading in the opposite direction. We both stopped, creating a large cloud of dust.

'Hi, limeys!' roared a large sandy Texan sitting in the back seat smoking a cigar. 'Do you know the neighbourhood well?' he asked. 'We need somewhere to stay tonight not having seen or felt a bed for two days.' He lifted his arm and sniffed his armpit. 'We could do with a shower as well.' With glee I described the rooming house in Ghardaia as having marvellous French beds – 'It's the best hotel between here and Algiers,' said I, scratching my bed-bug bites.

After a quick exchange of Anglo-American ruderies, I said, 'This is a restricted area. What are you doing here?'

'We're sort of lost. We've been driving along this sandy road for the last few days, from Morocco,' the Texan drawled. 'We are catmen.' Looking them up and down,

I said, 'Oh, of course; but you won't find many cats around here.'

Laughing, the Texan explained, 'We have been sent out here to look for oil and are returning with soil samples. That's what catmen do, look for oil, and I used to think it beat the hell out of fighting for a living, but after a few days in this desert I'm not so sure.' He leant forward and tapped the driver on the shoulder. 'Well, nice meeting you limeys. Maybe we'll see you at the end of the war somewhere. *Au revoir*,' he yelled through the dust as his driver accelerated.

We arrived at the sheik's palace, where we were shown to our rooms. Water and a large fruit bowl were brought to my room. It was strongly suggested that we take a bath in the large pool.

It was marvellous to relax in such surroundings; Persian rugs everywhere, a cool breeze in every room, and a stable of fine Arab horses. When it came to meal time I enjoyed the couscous and lamb, but the eyeballs floating in garlic sauce were a bit hard to chew on.

On my return to Algiers I attended a series of important meetings held by A Force. We went through the plans being made for the Sicily landings. I was informed of the deception activity that had been consistently flowing in northern parts of Europe and was successfully keeping many German forces in that area. We were instructed to indicate to the Germans that southern France was to be the Allied forces' target, which hopefully would divide their forces in France and keep them out of Italy. We were to play down the possibility of an invasion in Italy as much as we could without it appearing suspicious. In our deception messages we emphasised the Italian forces' unwillingness to continue with the war, and how quickly and easily they surrendered in the desert battles. Many of our messages gave accounts of conversations between the prisoners, who were expressing great relief at having been captured and how very fed up they were with Hitler and the Germans walking around their country expecting them to fight or die for the fatherland.

Messages of this type were starting to work very well as many of the Germans who were reading or hearing them were probably also fed up with the war.

The fall of Tunis put many more prisoners at our disposal for questioning, and made it possible to keep feeding this form of information to the Germans. Of course the other fact which helped was that under no circumstances did Hitler want to lose many troops in an Allied invasion on Italian soil.

We judged that the Germans would be quite inclined to believe an invasion would take place elsewhere; with the Italians about to surrender, why would the Allies invade Italy? While all this misinformation was being received by the Germans the Allied troops were of course preparing for the invasion of Sicily.

In early May the well-known Operation Mincemeat took place. This involved placing a dead body dressed as an officer of the Marines off the coast of southern Spain. It was discovered by fishermen, who handed it over to the Spanish authorities, who in turn handed the documents in the briefcase over to the Abwehr. Amongst the documents was a fictitious letter from Sir Archibald Nye to General Alexander (Commander in the Middle East), detailing London's wishes for a planned attack in the eastern Mediterranean, with a hint that southern France was a possibility.

On July 10th the Sicily landing was successfully executed with token resistance from the badly shaken 15th Panzer Division, the Hermann Goring Division, and the Italian 6th Army. Unfortunately, after the landing our troops dug in at the beach-head instead of pursuing the retreating German forces, which enabled the latter to regroup and put up a very tough fight which was to last for a long time.

For the next few weeks it was our job to supply agents with irrelevant and mundane information. The A Force committee had decided that for the time being we were to give no indication of future Allied force plans, false or otherwise.

One evening I was invited to see operational agent training in the basement of our HQ. The lieutenant in charge went to great lengths to explain the details. I was visiting while volunteers were being trained to land in northern Italy and report back their findings. The lieutenant showed me a photograph of an agent; a dark-haired man, who looked convincingly Italian. I suddenly noticed his shirt; the collar had buttons at the tips.

'Who is this?' I asked casually.

'Oh, him, he is half-Italian and half-English; scheduled to leave for northern Italy tomorrow, as a matter of fact,' replied the lieutenant jovially.

'Not wearing that shirt I hope, nor with a copy of this picture as his ID,' I said, a little perturbed.

'Why not?'

'That shirt style is only made in Cambridge or America. They don't exist in Italy, so if he is caught with this photo in his papers or he is wearing that shirt, he will be for the high jump.' I was rather angry at this obvious lack of thought concerning dress. 'No doubt whoever decided what this man should wear has no fashion sense at all, which under normal circumstances is all well and good, but when dressing a man to go into enemy territory I would have hoped a little more interest and initiative would be applied.'

'Oh God! I'll have to find an Italian shirt and take his photograph again. I shall be up all night.'

'I should bloody well hope so.'

I then asked to see the instructions and questionnaire being given to this poor unsuspecting agent. All the questions were about German troops and their movements. I pointed out that since this man was running a very high risk of being caught questions should be added about the beaches in the area. Such questions might make the German interrogators think we could be planning to invade northern Italy, which hopefully would make them divide their troops in central and southern Italy. Appropriate questions were added to the papers of all agents going to northern Italy.

After this distressing episode I went to the bar at HQ, and who should walk in but Trevor, whom I had not seen for a while. We chatted, and he told me he was perpetually involved with liaison and sorting out communications problems. He invited me to to go somewhere; I don't remember where, but I do remember what happened on the trip.

We left HQ late in the evening and drove slowly along the desert road, because the headlights were restricted by slit-eye covers. The Chrysler soaked up the bumps and felt very comfortable compared to Austin pick-up trucks. We must have been travelling for about half an hour on the road leading south out of Algiers, when an Arab, screaming at the top of his voice, sprang from the darkness on our right-hand side and ran straight into the side of the front wing. Trevor immediately slammed on the brakes, causing the Arab to somersault on the bonnet and land on his feet on our left-hand side. He turned around very quickly to look at the car, then carried on running and screaming into the dark distance of the desert.

Trevor looked at me rather bewildered. 'Desmond,' he said, 'I was not aware that the Arabs had opened a circus around here, were you?'

I laughed like hell. Only Trevor could have come up with a comment like that. It was the best antidote to the fiasco with the lieutenant.

The episodes of the wrong shirt and the screaming Arab were by no means the only incidents, serious or comic, which I vividly recall from wartime.

As I have explained, the office in Rue Charras was opposite a US army vehicle repair unit, which occupied the ground floor and basement of an old warehouse. The efficiency of this set-up always fascinated me. They possessed racks of supplies of spare parts for every single Allied vehicle involved in the war: engine parts, suspension, drive shafts, fan belts, radiators, everything. Being Americans, they were quite willing to repair our motorcycles and cars in exchange for something they wanted or needed. A bottle of whisky, as I have said, or two cans of bully beef (they hated the constant American cookhouse supply of lima beans and tinned liver), would purchase a full repair job on a motorcycle, or a transmission rebuild on my Chenard Walker. The number of vehicles the twelve or so mechanics would get through in a day was astounding. I remember watching one chap take the motorcycle engine to pieces, replacing every old moving part with a new one. On the back wall were crates marked 1st grade, 2nd grade and 3rd grade where each old part would be deposited, depending on its condition. The bike arrived at 8 am and was ready by midday, looking brand new. The American arms supply to the front was as efficient, but thinking about that reminds me of a rather sad joke that went around the British mess.

A very green American battalion received their battle baptism at the Heights of Kasserine. They had been fighting for a few days, and every time their machine guns became too hot to continue firing the guns were replaced. This was of course unheard of in any British action. The young, inexperienced American soldiers, despite the abundant supply of weapons, suffered large losses of men, used a large quantity of ammunition, and had very little effect on the German battalion facing them. On the sixth day the losses incurred by the Yanks forced them to withdraw, being replaced by the very experienced and effective fighting unit of the Scots Guards who, within twenty-four hours, had forced the Germans to surrender. As you can imagine, this story was widely used for teasing purposes.

A story of medical interest also occurred in Algiers. The 1st Army hospital was in Algiers for a time, where I used to visit Robert, a friend from Cambridge, who had been wounded in the leg. The flow of ambulances to and fro was horrifying and some of the poor chaps I saw arriving – well, it was bad. The first time I went to see Robert he was lying in bed, the wound on his leg pegged open and a seething mass of maggots wriggling around inside the bloody gash. He woke up from his anaesthetic just as I arrived and was rather taken aback by the sensation and sight of his leg. He asked if I knew what was going on and if this remedy was necessary. I explained that a Spanish medic, Dr Trueta, had discovered during the Civil War that the best way to prevent gangrene setting in was to allow maggots to eat the bacteria. A medic confirmed my story and we convinced Robert to accept it as, in the heat, many men had lost their limbs due to gangrene. Sickening as the remedy may sound, two weeks later Robert, his leg stitched up, was limping around the hospital with a very insignificant scar. I must tell you the smell of putrifying flesh in the ward was sickening.

Here is a story of circles, which is a reflection on how efficiently records were kept during the war. After the Sicily landings, my American friends had some jeeps to spare, and kindly asked if I wanted one. I duly signed the papers and used the jeep for a short while; then it was taken to Italy and used by an SCI (Special Counter Intelligence) unit which later took it to Trieste. This vehicle had been in the thick of some heavy fighting, and had travelled extensively through southern Europe. Despite the number of flat tyres, boiled radiators and other hazards it must have suffered, ten years later, in 1954, I received a letter from the War Office enquiring how I had obtained a jeep in Algiers; when I told them, they informed me that it was being auctioned in Oxford and asked if I wanted to put a holding price on it. I didn't; I should have; but it is amazing that they tracked me down.

Now an ironical story, which started when I employed a Spanish driver for nostalgic reasons. He was a refugee from the Vichy concentration camp in northern Algeria. His name was Francisco and he reminded me of the chauffeur on the mines who had taught me to drive the old Model T Ford when I was a child. Not long after he had proved himself a competent driver but a lousy mechanic, he told me he was a Communist and that the Russians had approached him in a mint tea house and asked him to work for the NKVD. Two days later I walked into the office in the British consulate, where Kenneth Younger, a political warfare rep (I think), introduced me to two Russian officers who were supposedly aiding Russians lost in the desert who had been released from the Vichy concentration camp.

After Sicily there was a lull in our activity and many of the small-time agents were paid off by the French. Changes in staff took place, essentially people leaving. Malcolm Muggeridge came for a spell, taking up a glorified liaison position, which he graced with his inimitable amusing and cynical manner.

For those of us remaining in Algiers the war had moved on. The port was almost back to its picturesque and primitive self. No more jeeps, trucks, tanks, ambulances, large cases, small cases, soldiers or sailors running around. The French language was all I heard in the streets, at the bars and in the restaurants.

Doudot took me and a new friend of mine, Reggie Braybrooke, for a stroll around the souk. Flies; I remember a lot of flies, and women breastfeeding their babies while selling the tomatoes and maize they had brought into town in the morning. The rich smells of cinnamon, vanilla, pepper, and aniseed filled the air; with all the dark alleys and tiny doorways it was no place to get lost. Luckily Doudot was known by many of the more wealthy traders, some of whom invited us to sip mint tea with them. We sat on moorish carpets with our legs crossed and talked about the war, and the differences it had made to us, European and Arab. One trader told us he had made the same money in that year as he would normally have made in three years. 'The Americans buy everting,' he said in his broken English. But against that he had lost a lot of camels, either shot or stolen by the army, and to replace them it would cost him the same amount of money as he had made in his shop.

It was amazing how quickly the military forces moved out of the town, leaving very few signs of their occupation. The road from Algiers to Tunis, once seething with army vehicles, was now deserted, apart from the occasional truck or staff car, or camel or donkey rider who would wait to be honked at before moving out of the way. The closer one got to Tunis the more conscious one became of the recent battles. Vehicles, mostly German, some American and English, were strewn along the roadside having been either deserted or blown up. There were tanks, armoured cars, trucks, troop carriers, guns, helmets and other war-torn metal objects all starting to rust and be covered with sand, as though time and the wind were trying to hide the destruction.

As things were so quiet, I decided this was a good time to take some leave. I visited my good friend Mr Stephanos Souliotes, the Greek consul in Casablanca, and stayed in an apartment near the beach. I swam in the turquoise Atlantic, ran along the beautiful white sandy beaches, and ate freshly-caught tuna and sardines at the beach-side restaurants. Stephanos offered to drive me to Fez via Rabat. The hundred-kilometre road from Casablanca to Rabat was empty and very straight. The two-hundred-kilometre journey from Rabat to Fez was also empty but not so straight or flat. Some of the potholes could have hidden a camel train without much difficulty. The two of us stayed in the famous Hotel Palais Jamais, and languished around the superb gardens swimming, drinking, eating and talking idly about nothing, and about the war of course. It was very hard not to, although one often wanted to talk about something completely different.

Refreshed by the week of pleasurable nothingness, I was able to get back into the routine of constructing messages for the Germans with a new verve; telling them southern France was again a very strong possible invasion point. This was reinforced by the Allied occupation of Corsica, where a large contingent of French troops was garrisoned. The coastline round the Ligurian Sea became very important for deceptive purposes. Many of our agents landing in northern Italy to spy on German troop and supply movements would have leading questionnaires about gun placements, building construction, minefields, and points of interest which might concern our armies if they were to invade the area from the coast. Many agents were taken to their drop-off points in Italy by MI6 naval personnel in boats called feluccas. A felucca looked like a fishing boat typical to the area it was operating in, usually the Mediterranean, fitted with very large inboard engines and bren guns instead of fishing nets. These boats would drop off or pick up agents in enemy territory, often carrying explosives and supplies, and taking tremendous risks. The amazing fact about these non-fishing fishing boats is that, for all the risk involved and the 150 or so operations undertaken, not one was ever caught.

One evening, someone walked into the office whom initially I took no notice of. I was aware of this person standing by my desk but, wanting to finish my paperwork, I continued writing without looking up.

Suddenly a loud voice said, 'Ola, cono!' I jumped up, recognising the voice of my childhood friend Frederick Elder.

'Good God! Frederick! What the hell are you doing here?' I asked, unable to control my smiles and laughter of delight.

'Well, I've been meaning to try some couscous and this chap told me that someone stationed in Algiers called Desmond Bristow is an expert, so I stole a fishing boat from the Liverpool docks and here I am.' Then he stood on one leg, put his head in the air as though trying to touch the ceiling with his nose, and made the cry of the male stork when wanting food; an old ceremony we practised when we were thirteen years old. He stopped, and stamped his foot. 'Now where's the couscous?' he demanded, as we embraced.

I took Frederick to my favourite couscous house, arriving early so we could talk without the bells and drums that accompanied the belly dancers. Pierre the French-Arab waiter presented us with the usual hot, scented towel and warm water to rinse our hands and faces with, then brought over the best bottle of Algerian wine and took our orders.

Frederick explained how he had been recruited from the navy by MI6, to become second-in-command of a felucca. He recounted some of his crazy adventures; of course, all were near fatal. Frederick tended to be overly dramatic.

'Here, Desmond, read this little ode written by my skipper, Lieutenant Commander Letts; that explains who and what we are,' he said very seriously as he handed over a crumpled piece of paper, looking around as though making sure no one was watching us. Instead of a list of instructions or missions, the following is what I read:

Special Service

We are not just common seamen,
We're above that sort of rot,
We are hand-selected he-men,
A tough and desperate lot;
If we have a thing in common
It's that little daily tot,
We are Special Service Sailors; Special Service – What!
(Dei gratia in Slocomotion)

Our lives are fraught with danger
And our deeds are frightfully hush,
We are awfully Lone Star Ranger
And all that sort of gush.
We seldom see a harbour,
For us no gilt and plush.
We are Special Service Shoeflies; Special Service Slush.
(Sic transit Schickelgruber)

We explore the Riviera
In our quaint old-fashioned craft,
And cry 'Bueno sera' from a twin-screw rubber raft
To make them think we're friendly or simply rather daft.
We are Special Service Sleuthhounds in Special Service craft.
(Pro bono Benito)

Our engine rooms are smashing;
We can speed at nearly nine
While the chiefs and chaps are dashing
Valves and pistons into line,
And the whole thing's tied together
With lengths of binder twine.
We are Special Service Speedsters; Special Service Swine.
(Floreat Meccano et Gibb)

When this bloody battle's over,
Will they send us silly suckers
To the old white cliffs of Dover?
No: they'll very quickly chuck us,
Crying 'Eastward ho, my hearties,'
In junks or Jap feluccas.
Pukka Service Sahibs; Special Service Fuckers.
(Per ardua ad Norman)

We can spin a spiffing story,
And spin it frightfully well
Of how we rolled to glory
On a rough and ruddy swell.
But there are precious few among us
Who won't roll down to hell –
We are Special Service Sinners; Special Service? . . .
  Well.
(Requiescat in barque)

After the meal Frederick and I went to the notorious Hotel Alletti for a nightcap. The Alletti, a large modern hotel close to the port, was the meeting place for many officers engaged in non-orthodox warfare. The large, comfortable lounge bar, decorated with French can-can posters, witnessed some very shady conversations and dealings, as well as ridiculous party behaviour. This night was potentially one of those nights.

I don't like to lead the reader on, but for me to write any more about this night would mean recounting events I don't really remember; it's best for you to use your imagination as to what we did. We drank a bit, I remember that.

11

Russian Agents in Lisbon

As the Allied armies advanced slowly northward through Italy, they captured the Adriatic port of Bari, where an SCI unit was set up and required staff.

I was in my office packing up files and writing to my wife and parents when the telephone rang.

'Major Bristow, please.' I recognised the voice of Captain Monday, the port security officer.

'Speaking. How can I help you, Monday?'

'I was wondering if you knew anything about two signals corporals who have just reported to me, having just arrived with the convoy from Gib?' Despite his gentle way of speaking Monday sounded rather concerned.

'My guess is they should be on their way to Bari, it is the only place in the area needing signals operators. Put them back on the convoy headed for Bari,' I said. 'Don't worry, I'll take responsibility.'

'Desmond,' he replied, 'the convoy set sail about five minutes ago.'

'Blimey!' I exclaimed. 'Get in your boat quick and get them on board somehow.'

He managed to catch up with the convoy, and put them on board one of the destroyers.

That same afternoon I received a ZZ telegram: TAP-

WATER, PLEASE MEET SIGNALS CORPORALS
ARRIVING BY CONVOY NO 37 AND FORWARD
TO BARI. I could not resist sending back the following reply:
LONDON, CORPORALS ALREADY ON THEIR WAY,
PRESUME YOU SENT TELEGRAM BY SLOW BOAT
AND THE CORPORALS BY WIRELESS. TAPWATER.'
I was reprimanded for using government communications
inappropriately during wartime. There was a new man han-
dling administration of Section V in London, Major Roland
Adams, a lawyer by trade, with no sense of humour.

The end of 1943 and beginning of 1944 was a dull time
from a work point of view. AFHQ was disbanded, Trevor
left in early '44. The French friends went back to their normal
routine, and I kept a spattering of liaison going, sending
messages every now and again. I would spend evenings
with Paillole, Doudot and Germain. We would take trips
to various parts of Algeria and generally have fun.

In February 1944 I received a ZZ telegram instructing
me to pack a bag with civilian clothes and to board the
next DC3 bound for Lisbon, where I would receive further
instructions from Charles DeSalis, the head of Section V,
Lisbon.

Lisbon remained blissfully unaffected by the war compared to other European cities. I stayed in a little Victorian
hotel called the Europa.

Before my arrival I had established that I was to pretend
to be a tourist, and that the work was of a very clandestine
nature. This was the closest I ever came to being James
Bond. Although – or maybe because – it was just an act, I
enjoyed being a tourist for a few hours. I asked the concierge
about the gambling at the casino in Estoril, fishing trips, the
museums and other local tourist attractions, making sure the

policeman sitting in the corner reading the newspaper heard my loud enquiries.

The only evidence in Lisbon of stressed circumstances was the shamefully obvious policing by the over-zealous Germanophile Portuguese secret police, the Policia International do Defensa do Estado [PIDE]. There seemed to be a member in most hotel lobbies, and certainly a large number had been hanging around at the airport.

That first evening I toured several hotel bars to try and pick up on the current topic of conversation in Lisbon. As far as I could tell it consisted of the news reports of the Allied advance through Italy, and how well the Germans were fighting back. There was a definite Germanic slant to the reports received by the Portuguese people. After leaning on four or five bars and chatting with several bartenders I went back to the hotel to dinner and bed.

The following day I made some loud enquiries about the location of the British passport control office, saying I had to renew my visa. The concierge very kindly drew me a map which I followed, occasionally stopping to ask someone to confirm my directions, for the benefit of the secret police who were following me. To have tried to lose them would have been pointless, and would have created too much suspicion.

I reported to Charles DeSalis at the passport control office in Rua da Emenda. Charles told me of several agents who were in touch with the Abwehr, and how I could get in touch with their controllers. One occasionally visited the office under the disguise of being involved with shipping. Another, Rita Windsor, was an experienced operator in the Firm working at the Embassy as a personal assistant.

'As you know, Desmond – ' said DeSalis.

'But I don't know,' I replied.

DeSalis continued, 'Well, there is a much more pressing engagement for you here in Lisbon. MI5 have lent us and asked us to look after a long-standing agent of theirs who is due to arrive in a few days. This chap is a German expert, who I understand fought for the Germans during the First World War and has worked for 5 for some time. He is on his way to make contact with some old pal of his, a member of the anti-Nazi group, so it seems. His name, not the German's but the agent's, is Ustinov and you are to make sure his back is covered and everything runs smoothly. It's very hush-hush, so watch out for the PIDE; they are devils.' Charles went on to explain that I had a secretary at my disposal. My God, what luxury, thought I. Mrs Jenkins was an American volunteer, the minister's wife no less, who obviously enjoyed being part of the cloak-and-dagger department and was extremely efficient. 'She will inform you of Ustinov's arrival,' said Charles.

On leaving the office I watched for followers and footed my way around Lisbon to familiarise myself with streets, bars, hotels and restaurants further away from my hotel. It was indeed great fun playing the tourist and playing spy, looking in shop windows, admiring the architecture, taking bus rides, train trips and one short boat trip up the river.

On the third morning, the hotel receptionist gave me my train reservation to Estoril, and a note from Mrs Jenkins: 'Your friend arrrives at Hotel Avenida Palace at 6.30 this evening. Table for two reserved at his hotel restaurant . . . in your name.' After breakfast I set off to the gambling casino of wartime Europe.

The casino at Estoril was grand, with red velvet curtains and sparkling chandeliers everywhere. One of the English croupiers was very helpful in showing me around. After getting his name and address and chatting about clients and the problem of the English nannies left behind by their employers at the outbreak of the war, he showed me the short cut to the bar, where Garbo had met Gene Risso Gill. I ate a seafood lunch, chatted up a couple of abandoned English nannies and continued to behave like a tourist for a few hours before the train took me back to Lisbon, where I put on my best clothes, caught the tram down the hill to the centre of Lisbon and walked into the Palace Hotel restaurant to meet this Russian-German MI5 agent whom I was to help rendezvous with a German.

A gentleman of forty-five or so, with greying hair, a smiling face and an interesting air about him, was already sitting at our table. 'Iona von Ustinov,' he said, as I approached.

We made polite conversation about his trip to Lisbon and drank a glass or two of vinho verde. Ustinov had already ordered lobster for both of us. I was glad MI5 were paying, and that Iona von Ustinov's visit warranted first-class treatment.

'Klop,' he said.

'Beg your pardon?'

'My friends call me Klop; because I like horses, most probably.'

'My friends call me Derry, short for Desmond.'

We laughed and talked and I really enjoyed our first meeting. He told me about his time in the German calvalry during the First World War, and how in the early thirties, working as the German press attaché, he became an English spy, and then defected. He was a fascinating and amusing man with adventure and culture running through his veins. We arranged to meet the next day, by the river.

After a good night's sleep and hearty breakfast, I caught the tram to our morning rendezvous. With the noise of the boats and traffic, Klop and I could talk freely.

'I was an active member of an anti-Nazi group before I became English, and I'm here to meet an old friend who is involved with some German officials who want to get rid of the Nazis and Hitler,' he told me. 'Apparently there are one or two groups but none dare talk to the other for fear of being betrayed to those lovely Gestapo.' Klop stopped walking and looked straight up into my face. 'For obvious reasons I shall not tell you his name.' We continued walking.

'Thank you, I'd rather not know more than I have to.' This time I stopped and looked around. Sure enough there was a PIDE standing by the tram stop, where the ferry terminal was.

'I don't know how often you have been to Lisbon' – I leant on the back of a wrought-iron bench – 'but the police are everywhere. I have heard they are quite pro-German. My feeling is they are cautious, and don't want trouble. Even so we must be careful.'

'Yes, I was briefed about the police here before I left. It is half the reason why 5 chose Lisbon, because if they have any information about me or about the man I am supposed to be meeting with, they hopefully will assume it is to do with my working for the Germans.' Klop laughed.

We continued talking, walking and watching the boats and the horse buggies; we lunched at a table on the pavement, underneath a beautiful old elm tree, then set off walking again, this time up the hill to the Europa.

The famous Lisbon trams were rattling along the very wide main boulevard, O'Rossio, with its lovely wrought-iron baroque street lamps on pedestrian islands. We were in no hurry, and continued exchanging stories about ourselves and our families; we loitered on one of the islands, tram wheels hammering over the tram tracks on either side. Klop, who was wearing a long Russian astrakhan coat and a wide-brimmed black hat, offered me one of his gold-tipped Sobranie Black Russian cigarettes. Accepting one, I brought out my lighter and put the flame to his cigarette then my own. The wind blew the flame out a couple of times, and we started laughing, when suddenly two hands grabbed us by the shoulders.

'Senhor, please show me the licence for your lighter,' demanded a very serious-looking PIDE officer, in Portuguese. I shrugged my shoulders, Klop kept quiet.

The other secret policeman looked hard at Klop's coat and hat, and at our cigarettes. 'Here in Portugal, gentlemen, you have to have a licence for a cigarette lighter,' said he. 'Passports please, senhores; you are obviously foreign.'

Klop and I looked at each other, not quite able to comprehend the situation. After examining our passports, the older policeman took me aside. 'Desmond Bristoff, you are obviously English, but of Russian descent, are you not?' Meanwhile the other officer cross-questioned Klop, who indeed was of Russian descent. Greatly influenced by the fact that Lisbon was busy with spies, they came to their conclusion: 'You are Soviet agents, are you not?'

This was not a good situation to be in. To avoid going to jail we would have to prove our identity, and therefore our connection with the British Embassy. I started to protest very loudly as they guided us towards the police station. Eventually one of them asked which hotel I was staying at. When I told them, they escorted us very politely to the Europa where the receptionist confirmed that I was British, and that in fact the Embassy had reserved my room. Not totally convinced, the younger, more zealous, policeman said, 'We shall take you to the Embassy and see what they have to say.'

Finally satisfied of our legitimacy the two officers went on their way, but from that moment on we were never left alone; PIDE eyes followed us everywhere, in a very obvious fashion.

That night Klop and I decided it would be safer and easier to deal with this problem if we moved to Estoril, trains being an easy form of transport to lose a tail on. DeSalis agreed that Estoril was a good idea and gave us the use of his Embassy car, so that we could split up if necessary. The car was a black Citroen, identical to the cars used by the secret police.

Luckily the croupier I had met at the casino rented out a spare apartment; it was ideal, with two bedrooms overlooking the pine forest on the cliffs above the beach. From the lounge window we could see the access road and the casino, making it easy to spot the PIDEs.

For two days the police watched and followed us in a very conspicuous manner. Klop and I made a joke of it, and resigned ourselves to playing hide-and-seek. This suited us for the time being, since the presence of the PIDE would keep the Germans away from us. Klop tended to stay around Estoril (secretly gambling, I think), while I made daily trips to Lisbon and around the general area, and tested out the resilience of our shadows. On the third day it appeared that they had become fed up with watching Klop win or lose, and following me doing my tourist impression. In the evening we decided to go to the town centre and hang around the cafés. No one appeared to be following us, but just to be sure we never stayed in one place for too long. Sometimes

I would walk on ahead while Klop sat hidden behind a café window and watch for a follower to appear, or I would stand in shadow under a tree while Klop crossed the road; we did not see any secret policemen or other followers of any kind. Thinking about it now, we had a lot of fun, and I certainly learnt a lot from Iona von Ustinov in the techniques needed to lose a tail and then have them refind you at your own convenience.

This absence of followers bothered Klop. As he said, 'Better we see them seeing us, because then we can all see together, but when not seeing them seeing us we might not see them seeing us doing what we are doing.'

'Yes, absolutely, I couldn't agree more,' I replied. 'Shouldn't we return to Estoril and see if they are waiting for us up there?' On the drive back Klop told me his rendezvous would be taking place in four days time.

As I parked, I noticed the red of a reflector light shining from a car up in the pine trees. 'Klop, the pine trees seem to have company.' At that moment their headlights flashed, obviously signalling another watcher. 'Into the apartment quick,' I yelled, and rushed up the stairs and into the lounge to watch the black Citroen roll down the road without its lights on. We went out to inspect the parking space they had used. 'Klop,' I said, 'we have to repeat this for the next three nights; same time everything. Hopefully we can bore them by keeping to a strict routine.'

The following three nights we repeated the scenario. I parked the car, they flashed their headlights, we rushed into the apartment, they had a lightless cruise down the hill, we went for a walk. What fun they were having, and what hilarity we found in the situation. The last night before Klop's rendezvous was nerve-racking. We sat up and made our plans, repeating the details to each other. It was our hope and the hope of MI5 that this rendezvous might bring the war to an earlier end than could possibly happen without inside help from this German anti-Nazi group.

We spent the morning in the semi-circular arena of seats overlooking the Atlantic just below Estoril station. After two hours of chatting and reading, two gentlemen seated themselves to the left and down from us. About five minutes later, two more similar looking gentlemen arrived and sat to the right and down from us. The last two arrivals Klop and I had seen hanging around outside the station early in the morning. As I stood up to leave, one from each pair got up to follow me. I went to the Tamaris restaurant just next to the station and surveyed the men's-room window and the back entrance, hoping my followers thought I was just peeing. After twenty minutes, as agreed, Klop and I met in the front entrance of the restaurant, went in and sat down at a window table overlooking the ocean and ordered our meal. Five minutes later a young nervous chap, about nineteen years of age, obviously sent in by the four police, who must have realised we knew who they were, sat at a table near the door and ordered lunch. I then went out, as if to the toilet – in fact I paid for the meal in advance, to allow for a rapid exit! On my return to the table Klop pointed out the four policemen sitting in the shade of a tree across the road.

'Klop, when you go down to the loo, there is a small door next to the broom cupboard that leads to the back garden. At the end of the path is a wrought-iron gate which opens onto the side alley of the station by platform 3, which is where you go for the 1.15 to Lisbon.' Pretending to have said something funny, I laughed at my own joke; Klop followed my lead. He had an exceptionally good false laugh. I continued, 'I think you'd better go now, it's 1.10. Good luck and hopefully see you tonight.'

'Thanks, old boy. Yes, see you tonight,' he whispered. Then he loudly asked the waiter the way to the loo.

I sat quietly, sipping my coffee and looking around as if expecting Klop to return. At last I heard the Lisbon train-whistle blow as it puffed out of the station. Klop was on it, otherwise he would have been back by now. As I sauntered out, the young man hurriedly called the waiter. About a minute later he rushed out of the restaurant to find me sitting in the shade of a tamarind tree reading a newspaper and wearing Klop's hat, which he had left at the table. The young man looked at me, I smiled at him and nodded. Poor chap, he looked very annoyed and went rushing off, presumably to find the four others.

I slowly wandered up the hill to our apartment. There was another follower! Soon the black Citroen appeared, picked up the follower and drove off as I opened the front door.

Late that afternoon I sat in the arena to watch the sunset and the fishing boats coming in with their day's catch, hoping Klop's catch was to be as good as theirs appeared. Klop did not return until early the next morning, and nothing was said about his endeavour other than that it was a good meeting.

The black Citroen and our followers lost interest after this, enabling Klop to have two more meetings without the same harassment or excitement, and my watchdog work mostly consisted of sitting around waiting.

At the end of March Klop and I said farewell, promising to get in touch when I was next in London, which we did.

*   *   *

It was impossible to implement positive deception from Lisbon via our double agents, but it was possible to feed information through them that would complement other deception stories. I fed stories that confirmed the rumours I had been sending from Algiers; for instance, that the South of France would be a landing place for combined French and US forces coming in part from Corsica and in part from North Africa. The other supportive deception story the Germans received from our agents in Lisbon was that since the Normandy beaches were too well protected, the main Allied attack would possibly be near Calais, or the beaches thereabouts.

It is important to note that the two agents in Lisbon were reporting directly to their German controllers, which meant that Allied intentions became a subject of normal conversation between the controller and agent. It was important to keep the stories vague since there was no reason for anyone in Lisbon to have particularly good information. It had to be a balancing trick. Obviously the balance worked, since the Germans had no idea they had been deceived by our two agents even after the D Day landings.

Besides working out deception stories and wandering around Estoril, I would meet with Gene Risso Gill, unfortunately not very often as it was too dangerous for me to be seen with this well-known British agent. It was at this time that he told me about his meetings with Garbo. I left a few stories with him and Charles DeSalis to pass to the double agents at various dates. At the end of April 1944 I returned to Algiers.

By early May I was back in the almost routine work of

sending off deception messages to keep the confusion going amongst the Germans. Italy was proving to be a tough battle with the well dug-in German troops fighting very hard. For a short period Algiers was again busy with troop and shipping movement as supplies and reinforcements had to be sent to the slowly advancing Allies. Amongst the reinforcements preparing to leave for Italy were American and French troops being gathered for the real landing in southern France, to take place in August. Now that this area was the real target for a landing our deceptive messages contained information to mislead the Germans into believing that Genoa would be our next troop landing area. Fortunately the Germans fell for it, and moved troops towards the Genoa area. I remember sending one message about Genoa via Gilbert on June 2nd or 3rd, mentioning the possibility of a major offensive near Calais on June 6th which was in fact D Day. This message was sent to add to the total confusion the Germans were in, and also to make it seem as though Gilbert was receiving information of a very important nature from time to time.

For obvious reasons we in Algiers were not told very much about the specifics of the D Day landings. Doudot and I often discussed possible dates and places; we actually thought the offensive would take place sooner than it did.

During some of our earlier discussions we were joined by Ricardo Sicre who was being trained by OSS to drop behind the German lines in France with his radio operator, Betty Lucier. He also thought the landings would be earlier, as his departure for France was set for May 12th. I had last seen Ricardo when he had walked into my office in the late spring of 1943, filthy dirty. He had hitch-hiked from Marrakesh to Algiers, and the official in the OSS office would not believe who he was; unable to have Tangiers confirm his identity, Ricardo found me. I knew him from a brief trip I had made to Morocco not long after I had arrived in North Africa. Betty Lucier, who became his wife after their stint in France, had been flying wrecked Wellington bombers and other planes to repair-yards in Britain. It was a nice surprise to see them again, and between May 5th and 12th we spent a lot of time together. We truly thought we would never see each other again.

June 6th; D Day. It happened, and successfully. Of course we all know that now, but at the time we did not know how successful it had been. As the Allies slowly struggled through France and Italy, we were kept busy throwing as much confusion at the Germans as possible. When the South of France was successfully invaded in August, deception work became rather pointless so I cleared my office and said goodbye to my French comrades. Bobby and Trevor had already left for London; now it was my turn to go home.

There were four of us in the steel seats of the DC 3, smoking, looking at each other, not able to talk above the noise of the revving engines. We all looked very nervous as the captain had warned us that turbulence over the Atlas mountains would be bad due to a storm. I was especially nervous, as my right hand clutched a bag containing special intelligence military consignment documents.

The plane heaved itself off North African soil. No sooner were we in the air when we hit some very bad turbulence. We passengers were jolted around and must have turned several shades of green. The storm was worse than the captain had anticipated. The route to Oran took us over the eastern end of the mountains, a bumpy ride under normal circumstances; on this occasion the air currents were so bad the plane lurched and dropped like a stone, sometimes for a hundred feet or more. Normally I would have started vomiting all over the place, but the fairground switchback sensation left me totally numb with fear. Suddenly one engine failed. I started to pray and realised I would not have enjoyed being a parachutist. For half an hour or more I quite expected to die. Thanks to the cool head and skill of the young American pilot the plane stayed in the air until he landed us safely at our first destination of Oran.

As I was leaving the plane, a US sergeant suggested it might be safer to leave the bag under my seat as the airport canteen was very busy and it might be a while until the engine was fixed. 'The plane will be locked,' he assured me. There were after all other documents staying on board, and there was a guard.

I telephoned John Fisher, who was meeting me at Marrakesh. The Americans had already informed him of the engine trouble and that my arrival could be delayed by up to three hours. About an hour later, the plane was ready. I stepped on board and headed to my seat.

'This is not the same plane,' I exclaimed, panic creeping into my blood.

'What do you mean, sir?' asked the sergeant, as I kept looking around, not wanting to believe what my eyes were telling me.

'The bag, where is my bloody bag?' I demanded.

The pilot casually informed me that the bag had been put onto an RAF plane flying direct to London. My heart sank. To lose any bag was bad – but this bag! I would rather have lost my life.

On the flight to Marrakesh my fingernails disappeared. I smoked feverishly, prayed, feared and walked up and down the very empty and now stable airplane. What was to be done? If only I had stayed on the plane; if only I had taken the bag with me – my mind kept nagging away.

John Fisher was waiting at the airport; he consoled me as much as possible, but agreed that to trace a missing bag was difficult; even so, knowing I needed comfort and that I was leaving that evening, he undertook the task. He informed London of my dilemma, and the probable destination of the bag, since the only RAF plane to have left Oran that day was arriving at Debden air base in Essex.

I left Marrakesh at dusk. The flight to England was smooth, long and in no way helped appease my worry.

On arrival at Prestwick airport at 9 am I telephoned the office and spoke with Kim, who suggested I go home and report back two days later. He made me feel less worried and did not seem overly concerned about the lost bag. It was good to talk to him, and to be back on British soil, despite everything.

I caught the train and headed home; at last I would see Betty again at the cottage in the country. The English countryside looked so peaceful as I walked down the twisty lane from the station. Birds sang in the trees, the green lush grass swayed in the gentle breeze, smelling marvellously fresh after a light shower of rain. No more palm trees and camels. Seeing Betty again was quite simply wonderful. Her hazel eyes shone and her wavy brown hair glistened in the sun as she called Rosanne, who was now two and a half years old. Betty had shown Rosanne photographs of me in uniform, and when she came waddling around the garden wall she put out her arms and yelled 'Dadda!'. Gosh, how quickly children grow when one does not see them for a long time. I think it must have taken me a while to realise I was home, and that the two previous years had not been some kind of a dream. The contrast from rushing around the desert sands of North Africa and the copious amounts of food in the restaurants and at AFHQ, to being back in a domestic surrounding and in a country suffering from food rations was a bit of a shock.

Betty had become very strong having continued her work with the Land Army, and was now a well-established member of that very efficient agricultural unit. She had two Italian prisoners of war working under her who lived in the cottage at the end of the road; they seemed very happy and willing, if not too good at English. For two days I wandered around getting in the way, making lots of suggestions as to how they could improve the farming system, which of course was already working perfectly, and generally enjoying myself and being a nuisance. I was able to forget about lost bags, double agents, secret policemen and all.

Those two days went by very quickly. I walked up to the phone box on Kerswell Green, and rang the office.

'Philby, please.' I waited for what seemed ages while the receptionist put me through.

'K-k-kim Philby here,' he said, with that familiar stutter. 'Oh! Desmond, you will be g-g-glad to hear that the bag turned up yesterday.' I breathed a sigh of relief. 'I'm s-s-sure you need two more days off; report here on Friday morning. See you.' I was about to hang up when I heard him yelling, 'Desmond! Don't forget that the office is now in Ryder Street just behind the renowned J-j-jermyn Street and no longer at S-s-st Albans. Bye.'

The bombing must have stopped, I thought.

Tommy and Hilda Harris in Madrid.

Tommy Harris experimenting with
photography at Camp de Mar, Majorca.

1950: In the British Embassy line-up (wearing glasses) waiting to shake hands with General Franco, who was accepting the credentials of the British Ambassador.

Betty, Rosanne, John and Annette on a visit to our pre-war summer resort at Punta Umbria.

Right:
Frederick Elder in Madrid, 1951.

Left: Waiting for Peter Wright at the St Anne's Castle, Gt. Leighs, which is said to be the oldest pub in Essex.

Below: With Juan Pujol (Garbo) at a D-Day reunion at Gold Beach memorial, 1984.

Left: Looking over Glenalmond, which was MI6's Section V headquarters, at St Albans in 1985.

Below: The 'Snake Pit' at Glenalmond.

Outside the Peahen Inn in St Albans, which was the up-market pub for the Iberian Section V and where Kim Philby would often pick up the tab.

The King Harry pub was very popular with the Iberian Section V. I had many private chats with Philby there.

I rushed out of the call box and jumped for joy, and ran all the way back to the cottage to tell Betty the good news. Two more days to relax and enjoy being with my family. Oh, what marvellous medicine it was!

12

London: I Spy Beer

The Ryder Street office was totally different from St Albans. For a start, the atmosphere was quite obviously much more relaxed. The early days of developing filing systems, creating deception and undermining the strength of the German infiltration in neutral countries was over. Espionage work had become a matter of monitoring movement and helping agents behind the ever-decreasing German lines.

I shared an office with Martin Lloyd who was MI6's representative on the XX committee. Robin Campbell, a commando who had been badly wounded during the daring raid on Rommel's HQ in 1942, also shared the office; what he was doing I'm not quite sure. I found out from him that an old schoolfriend of mine had been killed and another, D.G. Gardner, had won the Victoria Cross.

My job was to read over ISOS reports with information about France and the French people as the Germans retreated. Intermittently I attended XX committee meetings and LCS (London Control Section) meetings, now controlled very effectively by Lieutenant Colonel Noel Wild whom I knew from Algiers. He seemed to appreciate the tightrope Bobby, Trevor and myself had walked in the early days of the Algerian campaign, when we had formed our relationship with the French. The committee sessions felt more like business meetings and were very informative and open, discussing the details of how various operations had worked. We even discussed whether or not to continue deception. The success of Operation Overlord's deception had not apparently gone to anyone's head; perhaps we were blasé, or perhaps we all felt as though the hardest part of our work was over. Despite all the questions, deception work was to continue as a result of the V1 bombs dropping on London.

During the week I shared a flat with Donald Darling again, this time in Ebury Street. We of course had fun, talking about the good old days in Gibraltar and listening to jazz and wondering what had happened to Brian. Ebury Street was also quite dangerous and perhaps the closest I had been to being blown up during the whole of the war. Three nights after I had moved into the spare room I was sitting up in bed reading, when Donald appeared in the doorway to say goodnight. At that very second a V1 bomb landed about a hundred yards away. The flash created a halo of light all around Donald's plump form. 'Good God, Death appeareth,' I said. At that moment Donald was pushed against the wall, my bed shook and moved around the floor, the loud blast temporarily deafened us; it broke windows, cracked the walls and made powdered plaster fall from the ceiling. Donald shook the dust off his terrified head, and turned into the hallway, stumbling over fallen plaster. He stopped and said quietly, 'I'm having a drink. Can I get you one?' I could not help bursting out laughing, he looked so white and dusty.

I was able to introduce him to many of my friends such as Kim Philby, Tommy Harris and Trevor Wilson. In late August the German V1 launching pads at Arras were taken over by the Allies, so I looked for a flat or house around

London. A friend's mother owned a house in Kew, just in front of the gates to the gardens; Betty, Rosanne, Betty's mother and I moved in.

That September was a beautiful month; the autumn colours seemed especially spectacular. There were no bombs, I was around the family and old friends, I started rowing on the river again; it was good to be back in England.

Having said that, at about 2 am early in October one of the first V2 bombs landed alongside the Great Western Road, damaging the Firestone Rubber Company's spectacular factory. This was worrying from my family's point of view. For a few days we debated whether they should return to the country, but my confidence in our department's deceptive abilities convinced me all would be well.

I was attending meetings dealing with the flying bomb problem. The XX committee had several consultations with scientists and proposed they report the place of landing to the Germans – except that, of course, these reports would not give the true landing places. The newspapers and radio news would put out false reports to the British public. We sent reports to the Germans via our double agents which indicated that the bombs were going too far west, or north, and gradually the bombs started landing in harmless places like Romney Marsh.

This was not quite as straightforward as it sounds, due to the risk of bombs going astray, and arguments with borough councils. Meetings with politicians wanting to protect their own constituents occurred every week. Plans also had to be submitted to the Ministry of Production, essentially in charge of arms and work areas, and the Home Secretary, Herbert Morrison, who was very concerned about possible unnecessary loss of life. Despite objections full authority was given to the XX committee to go ahead. Political objections continued, but there was a directive that the north west of London be protected as much as possible.

Early reports given by Garbo convinced the very accurate German launchers to shorten their range; this persuaded the sceptics, unaware of the amount of deception we had used during the war, that deception would work. Funnily enough, Garbo's deceptive bomb-message reporting and his notional arrest – a ruse planned by Tommy Harris to make the Germans think that he had seen assessed for spying on the V bomb areas and that therefore all the information passed was genuine – coincided with him receiving the Iron Cross from his German masters.

In October 1944 I was posted to Paris. This posting coincided with Dick White's appointment as head of a joint intelligence set-up housed in Baron de Rothschild's mansion in the Versailles area. My particular role was to control the dissemination of ISOS to the various SCI units and to decide how much information any given agent should have. The nearer to the front line the less they received. By the same token, German stay-behind agents, left by the Getsapo mostly, had to be rounded up, turned and used, or simply arrested. The SCI unit commanders had to be given their names and identities where possible, and this information was then shown by ISOS so that field security could find them.

There was some resistance to my passing ISOS to Ricardo Sicre who, after his brave and successful undercover job in southern France, had become a US SCI man. Despite the resistance I decided it was essential for him to have the benefit of any ISOS reflections pertinent to his area, and sent it to him.

It was the coldest winter I have ever had to sustain, and with only one log fire in an enormous mansion it was no fun.

Luckily I was recalled to head office in London in February 1945. I say luckily, but as I drew up to the dock at Dieppe and saw the motor torpedo boat and the condition of the weather I did not feel so lucky. The rough sea and gale-force winds, the rain, and a boat that started to flood from the moment we were in the open sea, made me so terribly seasick that the possibility of drowning was not such an unpleasant thought.

The end of the war was clearly approaching. The office sensed this and an air of relaxation wafted through the narrow corridors of Ryder Street and we started to look for distracting pastimes. Beer being in short supply, some of us deployed our espionage expertise in a serious endeavour. Within half an hour of briefing, Tom and Bertie had learnt how to find out which pub had been supplied with beer in the morning: the secret was to spy on Watney's drays (the horse-drawn carts which carried the kegs around London); they appeared more frequently than Whitbread's. Tom, I may say, became the best beer-wagon tailer in London town. I developed counter-espionage and deception channels to inform falsely those we wanted to direct to the pubs that had not received a delivery.

I had leave due, and spent most of it rowing at London Rowing Club and walking around Kew Gardens with Betty and my daughter, which made the war seem as though it had never really happened. We bought our first house; a pretty, leaded-windowed house in a cul de sac on Strawberry Hill, in Twickenham. We made several trips from Kew to Twickenham in Betty's Ford 8, carrying our bits and pieces of furniture. Betty had to be somewhat careful since she was expecting our second child in June.

In April 1945 Section V became Section IX, and many of us hoped Felix Cowgill would continue to overlord the post-war counter-espionage department within SIS. None of us, except perhaps Tim Milne, appreciated how Kim Philby was manipulating Colonel Vivian, the deputy head of MI6. When Felix was posted to military government in Germany, we all believed it was a temporary position and he would return to take up his rightful post shortly. This was not to be the case and his masterly wartime role, especially in the protection of ISOS, went almost unrecognised by the authorities. Philby took over as head of Section IX.

The end of the war, in May, brought about a different requirement for the secret services and lessened the need to have so many people within its invisible walls. Some of us were invited to stay on. I willingly accepted the invitation, and soon found myself assisting the Iberian G officer, Hamilton Stokes, whose last post had been as the head of station in Madrid. The officer dealing with Iberian affairs was in charge of receiving and distributing reports from stations abroad and administering their needs. Reading Marxism, and many books and papers on the subject of Communism and the increasing threat from Russia, took up a lot of time. A real war had just ended and something which became known as a cold war was beginning. Many changes of personnel took place, many associates left, and those of us who stayed on became the butt of Malcolm

Muggeridge, who described us in somewhat scathing terms in his humorous and highly cynical book *Tread Softly, for You Tread upon My Jokes*.

Most of us thought it not only a very worthwhile job but very interesting and of national importance at the time. The in-tray was still being filled with aspects of cleaning up Europe after the war. But the coming challenge was Soviet Russia, as its spying branches became the post-war enemy.

Physical sabotage was not part of the USSR's programme. Realising how backward it was industrially, and therefore incapable of competing with the West, Russia resorted to a campaign of upsetting the working capacity of the West. It spread feelings of discontent amongst Western workforces, provoking strikes even if it meant funding certain elements in the trades unions, such as shop stewards, who were potentially susceptible to the preachings of the Communist way.

Without a clearly defined programme either politically or industrially it was very hard to grasp the situation and deal with the problem. Britain, a declining world power, entered a long period of apathy, when fear was able to get hold. I might add, Britain is still reeling from the effects of that time, economically.

Shortly after I joined Hamilton Stokes, the department received a letter from Madrid suggesting we visit Señor Valverde Gill, who was staying at the Piccadilly Hotel. Hamilton Stokes told me Gill had been our vice consul, or honorary consul in Zaragoza.

'Why is he here then?' I asked.

'Well,' replied Stokes, removing his thick glasses. 'Señor Gill was our vice consul in Zaragoza and by that, Desmond, I mean he worked for our department on and off; right in the thick of a lot of German activity. At the end of 1941 a priest from one of the local churches reported that the Germans were about to dispatch a mass of propaganda wrapped up in Catholic tracts on the vessel SS *Cabo de Hornos*, bound for Latin America. Señor Gill took a risk and broke the normal lines of communication to get the information to us directly. As a result, Section V had the ship intercepted in Bermuda, the documents were found and confiscated. This broke a small German ring in Spain and embarrassed the Spanish Church. Subsequent enquiries made by the Spanish police – rather pro-German in that area, I might add, Desmond – exposed Señor Gill; and owing to, I assume, pressure from the High Church, the Spanish Government labelled him persona non grata and gave him five days to leave Spain or be arrested. We brought him over to London, where he has been ever since, and he is now at the Piccadilly Hotel.'

I immediately rang the hotel. Valverde Gill sounded very pleasant, and agreed to have lunch with me. We met at Martinez, the best, perhaps the only Spanish restaurant in London at the time. We ate paella and chatted about his dilemma. Valverde Gill explained that he was waiting to be allowed back to Spain but had not heard anything for a few days. I promised to do everything I possibly could to help and suggested we meet for lunch next day.

When I enquired, the FO confirmed that Valverde Gill was being taken good care of, and his return to Spain was imminent; some minor details just had to be cleared with the Spanish. On failing to get hold of Valverde Gill at the hotel I went straight to Martinez and waited for him in the downstairs hallway, admiring the beautiful tiles from Seville; their blue, gold, brown and green pictures of olive groves, castles and Spanish ladies at bullfights extended all the way around the walls and up the stairs to the restaurant. Valverde Gill walked in with a strange smile on his face. 'Ola, Desmond! Why do you think I am late?' he asked. 'I had a visit at midday from a young third secretary of the Foreign Office. He told me in a very condescending way that I was free to return to Spain. I thanked him for the information, and asked if he would like to join me for a coffee, or a sherry. While we were having coffee the young brat told me that permission had only been granted on the condition that I was to be of good behaviour. As you can imagine, Desmond, I was rather taken aback, so I asked, on whose condition? "The Foreign Office's of course," replied the little bastard. So, what do you think of that, Desmond?'

I was rather speechless that someone from the Foreign Office could be that tactless and that anyone in the Foreign Office thought they were in a position to dictate anything to Valverde Gill. 'What a bloody nerve,' was all I could think of to say.

As we walked up the stairs to lunch, he told me of the vineyards and bodega he owned. He was concerned that the distillery might have been damaged in his absence. We had another marvellous lunch accompanied by a bottle of very good Rioja. He extended an invitation to myself and my family if we were ever in his area of Spain. I of course accepted, adding that I would only visit to taste his brandy not to see him. We laughed. His travel documents were already organised, so there wasn't much I could help him with, but I gave him the Madrid telephone number of David Thomson, then head of MI6 in Spain.

A few days later I escorted Valverde Gill to the airport and as we said goodbye gave him a tin of Fortnum and Mason's Earl Grey tea. He grinned and said, 'This must be vintage, like my brandy waiting in Spain.'

Hamilton Stokes's bad eyesight was not helped by the new neon lights in his office. I am glad to say I used an old Victorian desk lamp. He retired in 1945 to become secretary of the Dublin Yacht Club, and I was appointed G – liaison officer and administrator of the Iberian Peninsula in England).

As G I was responsible for the administration of the stations in the Iberian section, and all communications to and from these stations were initially channelled through me. For instance, a demand from the Air Ministry for more information on a foreign air force would be requested through the G Section.

The system worked as follows: the Air Ministry might have requested information on the parts of a new fighter plane which were being manufactured in Seville. I would send the request to the head of station in Madrid who would put a suitably placed agent onto the project. The agent would obtain a job at the place of manufacture as anything from teaboy – whatever his qualifications would allow. Some weeks later the agent would report back: 'The subject in question is under construction but there are teething problems of one sort or another. Further details will follow.' 'One sort or another' often meant quite serious problems; 'further details will follow' often meant there would be a delay before more information would arrive. Of course the agent's message would be much longer, but the head of station in Madrid would edit it, put it in the diplomatic bag and send it off to London. Everything, including this particular message, arriving from the Iberian section would be dispatched to me. I would then mark it for circulation to the Air Ministry, and if appropriate to the Foreign Office.

The report would then be digested by its recipients and returned to me marked with an A, B, C or D according to its importance, usually accompanied by a request for further information. This post-box system was the intelligence side of the G section.

Every six months, I and my colleagues in G section would evaluate each agent in collaboration with the recipient departments of his or her reports and the head of station supplying the reports.

With this promotion came an invitation to join the Seniors' Club. This consisted of a small den in the basement of 54 Broadway (head office) which opened at 5.30 pm. The atmosphere reminded me of the snakepit at Glenalmond at first, but I soon realised it was somewhat of a farce and rather boring; most of the conversations were about the shop, and about people being laid off due to cutbacks. After all, the war had been a tremendous adventure for most of us, and I suppose the older members found it hard to accept it was over, and would continually recount their stories. Without the war the main intrigues going on were the rather pathetic attempts of the members jockeying for promotion and postings abroad; consequently the Seniors' Club reminded me of a chickenhouse full of broody hens. Rowing and my family had become more important and fun than sitting around drinking and talking about spies, and who had done this and who was replacing who and where was so-and-so.

Christmas 1945–46 was a happy one. The house in Twickenham was looking marvellous thanks to all Betty's work. Rosanne was growing up fast and my son John Desmond was a terrific new addition. Oh, and there was Buzz as well. Buzz was a dangerous bull terrier who ate chickens and cats and guarded us very well.

Being the G meant visiting stations from time to time. In January 1946 I went to Madrid to see David Thomson, and meet Albert Todd (a short, tough Irishman commonly known as Patrick), his Basque wife Nina and one of his Basque cronies. I listened to Todd's reports about the goings-on in the north of Spain. I don't remember specifics, but I'm sure some of the reports must have been about the Basque problem which was just starting to get serious, though not yet a real threat to Spain.

The stations were working on the strength and activity of the Spanish Communist Party, the Basques, the monarchy and any opposition groups. Through these we were also monitoring General Franco's efforts to keep the peace and watching the direction he was taking now the war was over. The political strength was mostly monarchist, therefore army. The balancing tricks the Generalissimo played between the Falange (the fascist party), the Church and the army (monarchists) were dangerous from his point of view, but he apparently knew what he was doing. The Falange party, which had played an important part in the Civil War and post-war period, was starting to lose political fervour, favour and clout, now that it was on its own without the support of Hitler or Mussolini.

Besides meeting with agents there were the more tedious aspects of administration to be dealt with, such as personnel, supplies and finally budget! The latter had become a very gloomy prospect for SIS in early peacetime as the cold war had not really started.

Two days before I was due to return home David Thomson took Pat Todd and his crowd, Bill Milton and myself out to lunch. Bill Milton, a friend from my previous visit to Madrid, was now processing German, Italian and Japanese assets in Spain on behalf of the Allies. He was working very closely with his American counterpart to try and close down these assets. During the lunch at the Meson we talked about the problems we now faced as Europeans, and certainly as British people, since Britain was rapidly making drastic political decisions concerning Spain. The Meson was an ideal meeting place. The food and wine were invariably good, but more importantly, due to petrol rations the only clients able to frequent a place that far out of town were foreign diplomats, businessmen and Spanish VIPs.

On the drive back to Madrid David's car skidded on the icy road and crashed into a tree. I remember lying in the back hoping the car would not catch fire as there was no way in hell I could get out due to the pain in my back and leg. As the shock subsided we were relieved to realise none of us were dead. Luckily another patron of the Meson was not far behind. We were rushed to Madrid General Hospital where we were stitched, plastered, given hot tea and generally taken very good care of. David had hurt his jaw, Nina Todd had broken her collar bone, Pat had hurt a few ribs, Juan, Pat's Basque friend, had split his head and I had fractured my pelvis.

During my examination by the doctors my right leg was allowed to fall off the examination table, and I can still recall the excruciating pain. That same day I was transferred to the small British-American hospital in Calle Padilla, where

Matron Margery Hill OBE, God bless her and her superbly trained Spanish nurses, took care of their then sole inmate. Thankfully I received visits from my fellow wounded who laughed at my plaster straitjacket.

Three weeks later I was leaning on crutches at Northolt airport in Middlesex while an over-zealous customs officer went through all my luggage. When I was finally allowed through, Betty, the only person in the lounge, gave me a hug and said, 'So much for being a member of the Foreign Services and SIS,' chuckling and sympathising at the same time.

When the plaster was removed, my atrophied right buttock needed to be rebuilt, so I sat in the training tub at London Rowing Club for twelve days and rowed the right portion of my bum back into shape.

After five weeks of absence I returned to the office, limping badly and using my crutches more than necessary; besides winning me more sympathy, my limping act enabled me to receive extra petrol coupons. My G assistant, Paul Boggis Rolfe, who had held the fort very well in my absence, went along with this pretence of immobility most helpfully.

Charles DeSalis, now our Section IX man in Paris, and John Bruce Lockhart, head of station in Paris, had expressed a wish to keep a Polish ex-lawyer named Popowski on the payroll. Popowski was a Soviet expert having been the state procurator at Vilno, on the Soviet border.

After many trips to the Home Office and much deliberation on their part I eventually was able to secure his naturalisation papers. It became necessary for him to change his name, and I suggested he should have a name which would not surprise anyone, like Smith or Jones. We decided on Pope (after all, he had been known as Popi); a strong English name with literary connections. He said he would like his Christian name to be George. Papers in order, our Russian expert George Pope went back to Paris where he stayed for three busy and useful years.

In 1946 I met up with Hans Scherrer. Hans had been a German newspaper correspondent in Spain during the Civil War. When the Second World War broke out the Abwehr had employed him to operate as an agent in Lisbon. By 1943 he had become disillusioned with the Nazis and decided to defect. He supplied our Lisbon station with a lot of information on the Abwehr. At some point he felt he had been detected and asked to be evacuated. While our station was making a decision Hans's apartment was raided by his German employers. As they broke down his door, he climbed out of the window, shinned down the drainpipe and ran to an MI6 safety house that Gene Risso Gill had told him about.

After a few days, Ralph Jarvis gave Hans British travel documents and put him on the train to Seville where George Joseph (Antonio Joseph's brother) picked him up and drove him to Gibraltar. Donald Darling organised safe passage aboard a ship and Hans, one of the first German defectors, arrived in England. For the last part of the war I believe Hans acted as some sort of adviser on the Germans.

When I met him in 1946 he asked if I could organise for him to be sent to Spain, where he felt there was more opportunity for him as a journalist and his mother would like to buy a house. I agreed to help, and he agreed to pass on any information which could possibly be useful to us. After all, he did have a lot of Falange friends from Civil War days and would be able to mix with the German colonists arriving in Spain.

The latter part of 1946 consisted of office routine, speculative discussions about the Russians with their new outfit, the KGB, and the Americans with their new outfit, the CIA, and a lot of rowing. Under the guidance of Tom Langton, the club's captain, we pulled oars at the Henley Regatta. On October 2nd I became the father of my second daughter, Annette.

In May 1947 we sold the house in Strawberry Hill. We had decided the pollution in London was unbearable, and unhealthy for the children; besides Betty and I had a dream of becoming farmers. We therefore bought a small farm in Essex. Betty and I discussed my giving up SIS work altogether and putting on a pair of wellingtons to take up farming seriously. But in September, David Thomson had to resign as head of station in Madrid because one of his agents was found with Spanish War Office papers in their possession, which, as you can imagine, caused a lot of embarrassment. The office invited me to take up the position. This offer meant I had to come to a real decision about the farm; after much deliberation and heart-searching, I thought that farming would be an ideal family life.

'Yes,' replied Betty, 'but this promotion would be wonderful for you, and you do enjoy the work. Besides, my experience in the Land Army showed me how much capital one needs for farming.' We would lie in bed in the mornings, talking over our cups of tea, until eventually I realised how right she was and how much I did enjoy being in the Firm. Besides, living in Madrid would be fun and perhaps I could help relations between England and Spain with my knowledge and basic understanding of the Spanish people.

The position as head of MI6's Iberian section would allow me to influence many situations; at least that is what I believed and thought about as we prepared ourselves for the move.

13

Head of the Iberian Section

Before leaving for Madrid I received an invitation from 'C', Major General Sir Stewart Menzies, the chief of MI6. This was the third time I had been in to see him during my career. By us, the younger element in MI6, it was called the August Presence.

He was a shy, quiet man and displayed an aloofness which served him very well in maintaining a barrier around him. This barrier, whether created purposely or not, kept the crawling members (arse lickers) of the office at bay, and there were quite a few.

I knocked on his door. C invited me in and offered me a chair. 'Hello, Bristow,' he said in his armified, somewhat blustery, aristocratic English, 'how are your preparations coming along? I understand you have a farm and family to sort out. From what I have heard, the schools and that sort of thing are supposed to be good out there.' He carried on with his polite social chit-chat for a while, then got to the point.

'This business with one of Thomson's agents has made your initial task rather difficult. We are trying to decide on what cover posting to give you. At the moment we are trying to persuade the Foreign Office to have you as Second Secretary of Chancery. Whatever position it is, you are going to have to tread carefully at first.' He turned in his big Chesterfield armchair, pressed a button, and asked if I wanted coffee. A secretary brought it in.

Menzies continued. 'We are in a rapidly changing world, politically and economically, since the war ended. Basically it is becoming clear that Germany will slowly become our ally and the Russians our enemy. Spain remains somewhat of an enigma. We do not know what the majority of Spaniards really feel. There is still a strong Communist faction; and there are still a few Nazis running around. But, thank goodness, politically Spain is quiet at the moment. Even so, as far as some politicians are concerned there are unsavoury aspects to the present regime. You will be monitoring the Soviets as well as the Nazis. Do not forget that although the West is not an enemy of Russia, Russia claims it is, and Spain was the country where the Communists, aided by Russia, lost their first military effort. Stalin is still seething about General Franco, and although he is not in a position to attack Spain openly, he will certainly try to undermine Franco and most capitalistic ventures undertaken by the Spanish and anyone else in the Iberian sector. As I said, Franco, although politically unpopular with our more liberal politicians, has brought a degree of stability to Spain and hopefully will remain in power.' He paused and sipped his coffee. I sat back, listening intently, quite surprised at what I was hearing. He continued: 'I have a personal admiration for General Martinez-Campo and Vigon, despite their fraternising with the Germans during the war.'

This really surprised me as both these Generals, certainly Vigon, had very openly fraternised with the Germans. Perhaps Menzies knew something I didn't. Perhaps these Generals had used their friendship with the Germans actually to keep the Germans out of Spain. Maybe all is on record somewhere. Why Menzies should have any admiration for these men, if not for that reason, I have no idea.

'Anyway, Bristow,' he went on, 'I wish you luck. Give my regards to Alan Hilgarth when you bump into him. Anything you want to talk about directly with me, just do so.' We stood up and shook hands, and I thanked him. As a result of that chat, C took on a completely different hue for me. He had given me a very wide latitude, certainly much wider than the one I had formulated in my own mind, about my job in Spain. The chat definitely elated me.

Knowing that the farm would be well taken care of, and that the flight passages for the children had been booked, Betty and I packed the black Humber supplied by the office and set off to Madrid. We took a slight detour via Paris, where I met up with Charles DeSalis. We discussed how the department in Spain might help keep an eye on KGB activities in southern France, as well as local Communist Party movements. Before leaving Paris I received a telegram from HQ: 'There are problems on Franco-Spanish border at Irun and, with scarcity of petrol, delay your journey.' After a chat with Charles, whose agents in southern France implied the problems were not bad, I asked him to telegraph HQ to say, 'Pressing on regardless of problems!'

At the end of the first day we arrived in Tours and treated ourselves to a gourmet meal. The food in France was very different from in England, which was still on rations. The next day we drove across the border without any problems and made our way to San Sebastian. We stayed the night in a little hotel and made arrangements to have lunch with Ernest and Vy Copeland at Doit Ana (Dirty Anas, as Vy called it).

Ernest, the vice consul in San Sebastian, filled me in on the industrial and political situations around the area, which at that time were stable. The local fishing fleets were busy again and many small industries were re-establishing themselves. He was not too sure what was happening with the Basques, but he was more than happy to keep me updated. What with Ernest, and Pat Todd, the north of Spain was well covered. As we were saying goodbye he took me by the hand and wished me luck. 'Not an easy position to be in after the mishap with Thomson,' he said quietly.

After a gruelling drive through and around many road-work barriers, we arrived in Madrid and settled in to the Hotel Nacional where we stayed for three weeks – time to look around for a flat, find schools for the children, and for Betty to find her bearings while I settled in to the office. We looked in the shops and galleries and tried some of the restaurants. The Civil War scars were beginning to heal and an affluence was becoming apparent.

C and head office had succeeded in persuading the Foreign Office to give me the title of Second Secretary of Chancery as my cover posting. This meant I had a relatively plush office at the top of the very regal staircase in the Embassy. As head of MI6 I had a chauffeur and other perks unusual for a Second Secretary, which caused me a small problem of explanation. Not for long, however, as in those days it was not uncommon for Embassy people to be privately wealthy; I certainly was not, but perhaps people liked the idea that I was, and this seemed to be how they explained my extra perks.

The Iberian field section consisted of an ex-SOE chap named Kenneth Mills, who was the head of station in Gibraltar; Teddy Dunlop, our lady in Tangiers, a doctor's wife, and Henry Prior, our man in Lisbon. Barcelona was vacant, as an unfortunate accident had killed our man there just before I arrived. He had been watching his MG being unloaded from a ship when the cable snapped and he was crushed. Also, of course, there was Pat Todd in Bilbao.

Pat was rather a remarkable man. He recruited agents in northern Spain from about 1940 until about 1944. Many of his 'observers', as he liked to call them, were Basque nationalists and consequently very pro-British. One of his closest collaborators was Flavio Ajuriaguerra, the brother of Juan Ajuriaguerra, then head of the Basque nationalist movement. With the help of a Basque dockworker who had many fishermen friends, and a Spaniard who worked for a German typewriter company where all the local German agents were recruited, Pat and the British intelligence network were able to render most of the German operatives in the area useless.

While the watching of the German agents was going on Pat, who had recruited a group of Basques, organised the capture of a German merchant ship carrying iron ore. He contacted the navy in Gibraltar and informed them of the estimated time to rendezvous with the ship. He armed and briefed eight Basque volunteers, then with his wife watched from the wharf while the German boat was captured under the very noses of five or six other German vessels. When the pirates had tied up the German crew they set sail in a northerly direction. As soon as they weighed anchor the other German merchant ships, being part of the convoy, followed suit and sailed with them. The pirates waited until dark, when they turned around and set sail for Gibraltar.

With typical English gratitude, when the mission was successfully carried out the Basque pirates were made prisoners of war in England and left to rot. Fortunately Pat heard of their dilemma and created one hell of a stink with Admiral Limpney. The Admiral completely agreed with Pat and was able to persuade the government to hand over the £5000 they had promised to the pirates. On their release Pat heard that one disappeared and another joined the 8th Army and was killed in North Africa; he is not sure what happened to the other six.

Besides these escapades, Pat ran seventeen independent lines from northern Spain, across the Pyrenees and into France, one of which went as far as Paris. Some of these lines brought intelligence information out of France which was too bulky to be transmitted by wireless. Some of the lines transported wireless sets into France, and some transported money into France to help keep the Resistance going.

A wireless set was needed in Dax, and Pat was faced with the problem of disguising it. He found an illustrated pamphlet, written in German, advertising portable medical equipment and put it inside a suitcase which contained a transmitter. The medical diagrams were not unlike diagrams of the transmitter. At one stage of the journey it was strapped to the back of a motorcycle. The man riding the bike was stopped by a German control between St Jean Pied de Port and Dax. The control looked at the pamphlet and at the suit-case. After about five minutes, during which time the poor chap almost sh— in his pants, the officer in charge gave him a friendly tap on the shoulder and sent him on his way.

On a less amusing note, I will add that during some stay-behind preparations Pat organised, in case of a Ger-man invasion (very similar to the ones Brian and I pre-pared in southern Spain), some of his agents were shot by Germanophile Franco troops.

* * *

On our second Sunday in Madrid I took Betty for lunch at El Meson, and as we walked in I noticed Bill Milton with his secretary, sitting at a corner table in deep discussion. I ignored him, and hoped he would ignore me too. The place was full, and in Madrid no one knew who was watching who; and with David Thomson's cover being completely blown I was very nervous of my position.

The people interested in who was head of MI6 in Spain were: the Spanish secret police, the members of the Nazi ring who were shipping personnel off to South America, the Dutch, the French, the Russians of course, and the Americans.

My tasks were to monitor the political wranglings going on in the government, and to help Britain understand Spain's economic movements and requirements. In certain ways this coincided with the task of collecting and assessing information on German-owned assets: businesses, factories, boats, cars, trucks and real estate. This information would help me establish a monitoring system to watch the flow of Germans in and out of the country, and the number of Germans, especially Nazis, living in Spain.

I needed to find someone in a position to help me gather this information and update me as time went on; someone in direct contact with German affairs who would be willing to be a so-called agent for me. It had to be someone already working on and processing this type of information; someone I could swap information with, perhaps.

I decided to call Bill Milton, whom I had met briefly in Madrid in 1942, and again in January 1946, after my car accident. Bill had visited me in hospital almost every day, bearing grapes and the occasional bottle of vino. I knew he worked for the Ministry of Economic Warfare

189

(MEW), and had something to do with monitoring German businesses.

'Hello, Bill, Desmond here. I have something I need to talk to you about in private; could we meet for lunch at the Argentina restaurant – or perhaps you know somewhere else . . . that only Spaniards go to.'

'I'd be delighted, so long as you are paying. And yes, the Argentina is the best place for privacy. Since I know the manager I'll call and make a reservation. See you there at 1.30. Adios, amigo.'

I knew I had to be prepared to let Bill know who I was more or less. To take my mind off the subject, I got my secretary in and started some filing systems. I left at 1.00, having decided to walk, as walking enabled me to lose anyone who might follow more easily than if I was in my car. I walked out of the Embassy wearing my hat, which I used to enjoy wearing; somehow I felt as though it was a disguise.

I arrived at the restaurant a little early, sat at the bar and ordered a vino tinto. I felt a tap on my shoulder, turned, and saw no one. Then from behind I heard, 'Psssst.' I looked around again. 'Pssst – over here, chum.' There was Bill, at a table in the corner, a wide-brimmed hat pulled down over his eyes, signalling me by holding out his lapel which had a carnation in the buttonhole. As I arrived at the table he stood up very quickly and put his finger over his lips. 'Sssh, I'm going to check for bugs,' he said. 'Sit down, sit down.' I laughed as he slunk through the restaurant looking furtively around, whispered in the waiter's ear and went to the bathroom. He obviously ordered wine, as an expensive bottle was placed on the table. I was admiring his choice when he came back, laughing.

'Hello, chum, how are you? Ordered a good bottle since the Firm is obviously paying. How's Betty enjoying Madrid? When are the kids coming over from England?'

Bill was always smiling; he liked to have fun, and to make fun of almost everything that was serious. He had tremendous energy, as though he was always in a sort of frenzy. I must add, he was always very good at what he did, and very particular.

Before I could get a word in, he continued, 'I've guessed what this is about, I think. You are the Firm's new big chief here, and you need information on the Germans.'

'Good God!' I immediately stopped worrying how I was going to ask him for information, and marvelled at the speed and accuracy of his guesswork. 'How did you come to that conclusion?' I asked. I suppose it was not so surprising since he knew what I had been doing in Gibraltar, and had become a good friend when I was in the hospital.

Over a good lunch, Bill agreed to provide me with any information I required about the Germans and their affairs, as and when I needed, and as he came across details. During the course of my German witch hunt, he provided a breakdown of businesses, properties, schools, all their asset information and a who's who of every single German who had been in Spain, was in Spain, and wanted to come to Spain.

I then started thinking about other people I could contact to help me with the German question, and decided to make contact with Hans Scherrer (as secretly arranged). I picked him up in my car near the fountain of Retiro Park, and for the first few minutes we exchanged the usual pleasantries.

'How's the writing coming along?' I asked.

'Not very well really. Germany does not seem very interested in reading about Spain at the moment,' he replied.

Hans, on his arrival in Spain in 1946, had started writing articles for a few German publications.

'Have you re-established contact with any of your old Falange friends and Germans since you have been here?' I asked.

'Oh yes, quite a few of them, but as you must know my countrymen are keeping a very low profile.'

I suggested that we meet again the following week, when I would drive out to his house at Torrelodones, half an hour north-west of Madrid. He agreed, I drove around the block and dropped him off.

During that week I had a couple more enjoyable and informative meetings with Bill Milton, got my secretary to finish the new filing system, and read through the office records. While sorting through the records I decided to call Tommy Thom, the passport control officer, in for a meeting. I asked him to liaise with me as much as possible about any Germans or Russians applying for visas, or any other information he might feel relevant, but he seemed rather unwilling to co-operate one hundred per cent. I realised he was upset that he had not been made the new head of section. Fortunately there was an old friend of mine from Cambridge within the passport control offices, who was one of MI6's senior agents. Nevertheless this was a very unprofessional attitude for Tommy Thom to take, and at times it made life difficult. I made out a report which I sent back to London, but he was not withdrawn from Spain until about two years later.

*   *   *

It was early in the morning, frost was on the ground and the car windshield was all white. Having cleaned off the frosty patterns I headed off to Torrelodones. Madrid's very beautiful centre was becoming positively busy again, cafés were full of people eating churros and drinking hot chocolate before they started their daily routine. An increasing number of gasogeno-powered cars were running around, filling the streets with smoke, honking their horns. All this created a very different scene to the Madrid of 1946.

Gasogeno was an alternative fuel to petrol that produced a lot of smoke. Unfortunately, Spain being very low on petrol supplies and refusing to buy in quantitity, it was essential for people with the money to buy gasogeno-powered cars. The limited amount of petrol was mostly used by government vehicles; to get it, people in government, Spanish or foreign, had to have tokens and a plaque attached to the rear licence-plate with the letters PMM (Parque Mobil Ministero), which was jokingly referred to as Para Mi Mujer (for my wife).

The half-hour drive through the very beautiful country north-west of Madrid sped by. I was on my way to ask Hans to become an agent, my mind full of the possible connections he might have and how best to utilise them. At the same time I did not want Hans to jeopardise himself in any way. The Nazis were still a very nasty lot. I decided to codename him Arthur, and have specific places and times to meet, to reduce the amount of telephone contact.

His house was on the outskirts of Torrelodones. He lived with his widowed mother, an avid gardener, who had planted up the front with lots of roses. I remember well; when I knocked on the front door their alsatian dog barked and jumped up at me, making me step back straight into a pruned and prickly rosebush. As I recovered Hans came out.

'Sorry, Desmond, I should have tied him up. Are you all right?'

'Yes, yes,' I responded, making sure no thorn remained embedded in me.

'Please come in and meet my mother, then we'll go for a walk. By the way, my mother speaks quite good English; so be . . . you know.'

On our walk, Hans agreed to be my agent, codenamed Arthur. He emphasised how many people he knew in the Falange party, and how many of them were friends with German businessmen. Although he had no positive details he could give me at that first meeting, he made it clear he was aware of many Spanish-named companies, with Spanish personnel, that were either wholly owned by Germans, or run by Spanish-German partnerships. Hans was well liked by the German and Spanish Germanophile elements in Madrid; after all, he was one of the few journalists writing articles about the peninsula being read in Germany. He and I made very strict arrangements. We would lunch on Tuesdays at a small restaurant, always full of artists and musicians, as a public place to chat where he could give undetailed information. During lunch he would say whether it was necessary to meet again in more private circumstances, when he would give me dossiers and sometimes photographs of personnel and places. I told Hans about Bill Milton, and suggested we all lunch together the following Tuesday. I drove back to Madrid feeling quite elated.

Hans was to prove a very valuable source of information and enabled me to build up an intricate and detailed file on the movements and businesses of Germans and Spanish Germanophiles. After the first lunch he suggested we meet at Bill's flat that Friday, and from then on we had our private meetings at Bill's. This worked out very well since a lot of Hans's information was useful to Bill. In fact, I can safely say that Hans Scherrer helped MEW close down or confiscate many German assets which, without his help, they might never have detected.

In early 1948, wanting to appear a little interested in the duties of my cover position as Second Secretary, I made a trip with Brian Wallace, the Third Secretary, to Barcelona. I introduced myself to the consul general and familiarised myself with some of the staff. I seem to remember I made a point of making sure the Spanish knew I went on the trip. Not long after, HQ decided to send my old assistant of G Section days, Paul Boggis Rolfe, as our man in Barcelona. Why, I have no idea; he spoke no Spanish at all. Consequently he was not very useful and his stay was brief. Thankfully the post was taken over by my feluccing friend, Frederick Elder.

By September 1948 I had settled into a routine of liaison with the various heads of station and agents. Tommy Thom being not yet out of the country but basically out of the way, friction with passport control was over. The monitoring of German and any other foreign economic or political activity was now well oiled and had become routine. Assessing and analysing Spain and General Franco's policies was also becoming easier. Franco was not following a military policy; he was intent on rebuilding a very broken-up country. Even so, while he was encouraging foreign investments he was not prepared to sell out to anybody. Britain's policy towards Spain continued to be one of ostracism. We had withdrawn our ambassador in 1946 and our politicians continued with this policy. The French and Americans also had no ambassador, but the politicians of these countries did not hold back their larger companies from investing in Spain.

We, the Bristow family, had moved into a beautiful house two miles outside Madrid. The house, with its magnificent walled garden, had once belonged to the sister of the king of Spain. We had moved in around May or June, and not long after that I had my first personal experience with bugging devices.

In May, I had a suspicion that the Spanish were bugging the phones in the Embassy. The anti-bug man arrived from England with instructions to test not only the Embassy but also certain houses, including ours. A faulty bug was discovered on the phone line at the Embassy. In our house, he found one little microphone in the bedroom, and one on the phone line. The idea of my family's private life being invaded to that extent was upsetting for me, but more especially for Betty.

In mid-1948 I remember a stepping-up of agents reporting on the state of the political prisons and prisoners, whose welfare was increasingly becoming the concern of some leading politicians in Britain. Some trade union activists were also creating about the prison situation. The Foreign Office was under increasing pressure to look into the fate of some named prisoners and 'rattle the sabre' against the regime. Except in a few cases this was not diplomatically acceptable. Nevertheless Bernard Malley, our locally employed counsellor, often attended trials and visited the infamous prison at O'Cana, sixty kilometres south of Madrid, where most political prisoners were held. I decided that it would be good policy to accompany him on some of his visits, partly for cover, and partly to see for myself what was really going on.

Despite the apparent viciousness of some court sentences, the general atmosphere within the prison walls was very informal. Guards and prisoners had card games going, families were allowed to visit as often as they chose bringing food, blankets, vino, cigarettes and even the odd Marxist tract, which the guards also appeared to read. It was obvious to me that the leftwing politicians in England were looking for excuses to undermine Franco. No doubt our visits and British interest made life easier for the prisoners, many of whose sentences were extreme, but leftwing politicians used this to try and undermine the delicate stability Spain was experiencing for the first time in years. Maybe because of my Spanish upbringing, and my having seen widespread poverty and starvation before Franco arrived, I became frustrated with leftwing tittle-tattle. Did the people really want a revolution in Spain again?

I have been asked many times why the West allowed the Franco regime to continue in power. My answer is that the West was not in a position to initiate any real alternative, as such an undertaking could only have been achieved by military intervention resulting in loss of life. At the same time we were looking at the Soviet machinations with ever-increasing concern; Britain and the US were beginning to face up to the impending cold war, and to realise that to wage it we needed as many allies as we could muster.

One afternoon, as I was finishing up my analysis of information I had received from Hans, the security porter, Hilario, rang me on the intercom and told me in his Spanish-sounding English, 'Someone is here in reception who wants to see you, sir. He is an American, calling himself Ricardo.' Hilario sounded indignant.

I quickly folded my papers and descended the grand

Embassy staircase. My visitor came towards me with a big smile – yes, it was indeed Ricardo Sicre.

'Hey, Desmond, you look like the Duke himself standing on that staircase. So this is the British Embassy – regal but threadbare.' He looked down at the worn red carpet.

'What the hell are you doing here?' I asked. 'Come on up to my chamber.' I offered him a whisky. 'So what brings you to these parts?' I asked.

'I am working for an American set-up called Ryans. As you know, Betty Lucier and I got married, after we dropped into France. As you can see, she and I made it behind the German lines. She was an amazing radio operator, you know. Anyway, Cornelius Ryan is a friend of Betty's father and a big business man, who needed a rep in Barcelona, so out I came. I have just made a deal with the Japs and Spanish – Spanish rice for Japanese potash.' He looked around my big office, felt the solid oak of my desk, and commented, with a twinkle, 'You look as though you are rather important these days.'

'No, no, they have mistaken me for someone else, but since the whisky is free and I have this big desk and comfy chair, I thought I would wait for them to realise their blunder.'

Ryan Cornelius was a close associate of William Stevenson, better known as 'A Man Called Intrepid'. My guess was that Ricardo was working for the OSS (later the CIA). He flatly denied it when I made a joke about it.

'How important are you?' he asked. 'I mean, would you be able to find out if my name is on any wanted lists in Spain?'

'Yes, I can find out for you; but why on earth *would* you be on such a list? Have you been stealing apples?'

He explained that his father had been a doctor near Barcelona, and he, Ricardo, had fought for the Republicans as a boy, during the first six months of the Civil War. That was until he had witnessed the Communists line people up against a wall and shoot them, for no apparent reason, other than their not knowing whom to fight for. After that he deserted and was on the run. He met up with Robert Graves who assisted him with papers and put him on a boat bound for England. 'Where I worked as a barber in Great Bardfield, Essex; the shop was called the Barber of Seville.'

'My God! That is where Betty and I have a farm. What an amazing coincidence.' We talked about the little village of Great Bardfield, then I asked, 'Where are you living now, Ricardo?'

'Barcelona; but Betty and I are thinking of moving to Madrid.' He looked at his watch. 'I'm running late, don't forget to find out if I'm wanted or not.'

As he left I called after him, 'By the way, I am going to be in Barcelona next week, visiting my old pal Frederick Elder.'

'You'd better look us up while you are there. Adios.'

I called my contact at Spanish internal security, whose name I am not going to disclose. He told me the only information they had on a Ricardo Sicre was that he was born near Barcelona, the son of a Doctor Sicre who was now dead.

The following week, Betty and I drove to Barcelona. We had a marvellous dinner and get-together with Frederick and his wife Diana, Ricardo and his wife Betty. We stayed the night with Ricardo and Betty, since Frederick's flat was too small. I was able to tell Ricardo he was not on any Spanish wanted lists, for which information he was very grateful.

The next day I went to Frederick's office to talk about MI6 affairs. Frederick had been able to cultivate a relationship with a senior officer in the Spanish military security department, who was fascinating and very well informed on the subject of the Spanish Communist Party. The gentleman was a strong Anglophile, and later on in the relationship, and with very little persuasion, gave Frederick a long report – about twenty-five pages – on the Spanish Communist Party structure before the Civil War, and how it had operated during World War Two. Unfortunately it did not contain many names. I translated it into English and sent one copy to the Foreign Office and a copy to head office.

While in Barcelona I decided Betty and I must see the world-famous monastery on Montserrat, today the stage of one of the best choirs in the world. In those days Barcelona was a medium-sized port town with wonderful old Spanish houses. Fish salesmen would push their wheelbarrows along the cobblestones, yelling out the catch of the day.

During this trip, I decided my friendship with the FBI man in Spain, Joe Presley, could possibly raise suspicion against me. The Americans were never shy about their CIA or FBI members, consequently everybody who watched Joe would notice we saw a lot of each other and would realise I was involved with the British Secret Service.

Joe and I met two or three times a week exchanging information about Germans and other causes of concern for both our countries; there was never anything of great importance, but it was an open co-operation between an FBI man and an MI6 man. I had taken it upon myself to cultivate our friendship and therefore our flow of information, as we were on the same side. On our return to Madrid from Barcelona I invited Joe to join a small shooting syndicate which Bill Milton and a Rumanian had organised. We spent many an afternoon in the campo near Naval Casnero, one hour north of Madrid, shooting the odd rabbit or pheasant while we exchanged information.

For example, a German from a company in Bilbao had put in an application for an American visa. I was able to tell Joe that this man had had some very shady dealings during the war and seemed to be an avid Nazi. Thus Joe was able to save time and stop an unsavoury character getting to America. Joe was able to do the same for me, but both of us were more concerned with economic matters. I remember talking at great length with him about Otto Skorzeny, the commander of the German commando troops. His arrival in Madrid after his release from the war criminal trials was cause for concern. In fact Otto seemed to be quite a gentleman, and avoided association with Nazis in Madrid. Joe met him a few times, and Otto forwarded information about fellow Germans who were undesirable characters quite readily. He also gave Joe information about hidden German assets which Joe passed on to me.

The shooting trips were always fun; Betty and the children, Joe's wife Marjorie and their children would usually join us and we would have enormous picnics. Bill always had new stories and jokes about politics and funny things that happened at the MEW. Of course, the shoot enabled Bill, Joe and myself to have three-way swappings of information without constantly looking over our shoulders.

In the middle of 1949 Al Wallace arrived from Washington with his family and a few weeks after his arrival Joe and Marjorie held a July 4th celebration party. It was fun attending a celebration of a time of discord between our two countries, during a time when we had only recently become hard and fast allies. (World War Two brought England and America together in a very fundamental way. Unfortunately, in my opinion, England has never fully accepted or appreciated this fact. Our stubborn pride and unwillingness to accept we no longer are the empire we once were has held us back from taking advantage of many opportunities, certainly as far as America is concerned.)

At that party I met and became friendly with the very busy American military attaché Charlie Dasher. He was successfully securing military bases for the American air force (bases used heavily during the recent Gulf War), and the use of Spanish ports for the American navy.

During the party Al Wallace teasingly said to Joe, 'One of my boys reported seeing you driving down the Calle de Granada in Desmond's sleuthing car a few days ago.'

'Oh!' exclaimed Joe. 'I'm glad you CIA boys have nothing better to do than watch me.'

'Actually he wasn't, he was watching Desmond's car, wondering what MI6 could be doing outside the Spanish police department.'

Al was head of the CIA in Madrid, and he helped keep me abreast of some of the American economic activities in Spain, while I reported sadly on Britain's economic non-activity there. (I hope some of the members of SIS who happen to be reading this book are turning uncomfortably in their chairs. Although most of the information we exchanged is insignificant, just the fact that I maintained such an open rapport with our American friends was not ever known by head office in England, and would certainly not have been appreciated.)

*   *   *

At the end of the war the Spanish government had readily accepted the 'Safe Haven Report', and for the most part complied with the rules, although obviously, given the amount of involvement the Germans had had with Spain before the war, there was some prevarication on the part of certain ministers. Nevertheless, the Allied Commission responsible had completed many of the investigations by 1947. But it was clear that much of the prevarication was to buy time for many Spaniards to hide their German-linked assets, which left many outstanding and important questions to be answered by Bill Milton's, and partly by MI6's investigations.

My discussions with Bill centred on who had been what, and which Spaniards had played any role, sinister or not, on behalf of the Germans during the war. Firms like Bayer, the worldwide chemical company, had several Abwehr agents on their payroll. A very slippery customer named Jeronimo Yplano had worked on direct orders from the German naval attaché in Barcelona. Jeronimo was responsible for looking after a small fleet of boats (mostly fishing) that were owned by the German navy. The fleet was camouflaged under the name of Jesus Franqueza of Barcelona. The purpose of the fleet was to run supplies out to German submarines operating in that area of the Mediterranean. Many German aircraft such as Heinkels and Messerschmitts had either crashed, force-landed, or just plain disappeared. Investigations on these went on until 1950. Many ended up in the Spanish air force. As investigations took place we monitored the behaviour of the Spanish, even those who readily complied with the so-called rules.

Had it not been for Bill Milton's sagacity, experience and knowledge of Spaniards, negotiations on that whole touchy subject would more than likely have been pursued in a very acrimonious manner. Bill's respected toughness and honesty, and his ability to communicate openly with the Spanish, meant that even those who had their German assets frozen or confiscated recognised he always adjudicated fairly. God knows how many lucrative backhanders he might have taken, if he had not been straight as a die.

Bill helped me understand a part of Spain that I had not been at all familiar with. His pre-war experience as administrator for the iron mines of 'Whitehall Securities' (a City-based mining finance company) around Seron in Almeria, and before that in Vizeu in Portugal, gave him a knowledge of business practices in the Iberian Peninsula that made him a key figure for MEW both during and after the war.

From our discussions it became clear to me how important a role MEW had played in Spain. For example, the manner in which some essential supplies were obtained from Switzerland via Spain is fascinating. In 1942 the British commercial counsellor in Spain, named Lomax, purchased a Swiss design of a quick-firing cannon for our Spitfires and Hurricanes. He initially negotiated through a Swiss gentleman named Birkigt who worked in Barcelona. Due to the success of the initial negotiations, Lomax was able to secure financing from MEW and went to Switzerland and finalised the deal. The contract papers were sent to Spain, where they were handed to a visiting MP named Kendall, who flew back to England from Lisbon. Why they trusted an MP with the papers is beyond me. Kendall left the papers on the plane. Fortunately for him, and Britain, they were retrieved. MPs, even today, are apt to leave confidential papers in taxis, or wherever.

Another MEW operation was to obtain a heavy industry

lathe manufactured in Switzerland. Shipping was a problem, but MEW created a way around it. They blacklisted the Swiss company and made sure the list fell into the hands of the Germans, thus erasing any suspicion the enemy might have had of the goods being delivered from that company to Spain. The blacklisting enabled the lathe to be transported through occupied France into Spain, and then by boat back to England. A more amusing example of their shipping techniques concerns a special type of ball-bearing, needed for Britain's fighter planes, which was manufactured in Sweden and Switzerland. The diplomatic bag from these two countries to Madrid was often used to carry the valuable bearings; once in Madrid they would be transported, usually by train, to Gibraltar and from there shipped back to England. As you can imagine, the bag was quite heavy.

The way in which MEW operated, and the depth of their knowledge of German assets in Spain, made my task easier. For instance, we knew the Germans had some $100,000,000 of assets in Spain in 1945, which in comparison to Britain's or any other country's was an enormous amount.

14

Guy Burgess and Other Funny Things

As 1949 rolled on, the only matter that caused any real concern and needed careful monitoring was the question constantly being raised about Gibraltar. Spain's Communist Party, although vocal, was relatively ineffectual, and the Russians certainly had very little influence in Spain. Consequently, head office decided to reduce the network of the Iberian section.

Spanish politicians usually took hold of the question of Gibraltar only when they needed to create a rise of nationalism, and apart from this almost continuous 'hot potato', I agreed that we no longer needed more than a few agents in the field in Iberia. Teddy Dunlop, in Tangiers, continued to monitor the small skirmishes which were continually taking place amongst the Arabs, but she had never required large funds for her agents, and the way she ran her field was her own affair. Henry Prior, in Lisbon, monitored the Spanish Royal family living in exile at Estoril. Portugal had the odd Russian wandering around, and like every country in Europe was busy trying to increase its trade; but nothing ever happened to cause real concern.

I did a tour of the peninsula, going to see Pat Todd in Bilbao, Frederick Elder in Barcelona and Henry Prior in Lisbon. Teddy Dunlop came to see me. They all agreed with the decision to reduce the number of field agents, and started to decrease their networks.

Of course we maintained our most important and hard-working agents. In November I had a meeting with Hans Scherrer who, besides giving me information about the Falange, and a couple of German newspaper men, said he had heard something about the monarchists – that they were making noises; he felt it was nothing serious. I was leaving for Lisbon in a few days, and said I would check up on what the exiled king was up to. He asked if he could come with me, as he had left some documents and personal belongings in his old Lisbon apartment which he would like to collect. 'I don't see why not,' I replied. 'I'll organise some English papers for you to travel on.'

Lisbon was quiet, and instead of posing as a tourist as I had on my last visit, this time I was able actually to be one, taking Betty around the town. The secret police were not interested in spies; there were no spies to be interested in. Now, for Britain, the only political point of interest was the activity of, and around, the exiled Spanish monarch living in Estoril.

Hans collected his belongings from his old apartment, then took Betty shopping while I had my rendezvous with Henry Prior. I asked Henry what was going on with the monarchy as I had heard very small rumours in Madrid. 'Well,' he replied, 'Señor Gill Robles has just returned from Madrid where he had talks with various monarchist sympathisers, and all seem to be of pretty much the same opinion; that without outside help they are unable to do anything.'

'That's good, the last thing Spain can take at this moment is another revolution. Food is still in short supply for most people.' We talked for an hour or so, and I told him about the cutbacks in agents, which did not really affect him very much.

I went to join Hans and Betty for lunch at the Palace Hotel. Crossing the road in front of the hotel reminded me of the time I had been arrested with Klop; those weeks in 1944 with Klop, the secret police, the possible German agents and all the hustle and bustle had been two of the most thrilling weeks of my work in the SIS.

After lunch Hans went off to see some old acquaintances and I took Betty to see Estoril. The next morning we headed back to Madrid, via Salamanca. Hans wanted to call in at the Irish College where, during the Civil War, he, Kim Philby and other foreign journalists had taken shelter before moving on to Burgos.

At the College Hans, who knew the building well, led the way to a large door and knocked on it. There was no reply, so knocking again Hans pushed the door open to find the rector, Father McCabe, sitting in his chair and slumped over his large desk, breathing very heavily, a large bottle of brandy in one hand and a pistol in the other. He had obviously consumed over half the bottle and was lying on paperwork which looked like deeds of some kind. Hans went over to him, accidentally kicking over an empty brandy bottle. At the sound of the bottle rattling over the stone floor, Father McCabe stirred from his stupor, looked up at Hans through bloodshot eyes, and in a strong Irish accent said, 'Hans, Hans Scherrer, me boy, Father in Heaven and Saints preserve us, have yer come to help me fend off those Spanish bastards? They are trying to take me College away from me, lad.' He kept on and on about his College and how the Spanish bastards were going to take it away.

Betty made him coffee, while Hans and I walked him

around outside. It had surprised me how in his condition he had recognised Hans so quickly. But as he slowly recovered he kept repeating, 'I never forget a face yer know. Fancy old Hansy, a goddamed kraut, being the one to come to me rescue. God does work in mysterious ways, yer know. What was yer name again?'

'Desmond Bristow,' I replied. He then went into more surprised profanities as he slowly realised I was English and a Protestant. We sobered him up and persuaded him to come with us to Madrid and stay until I was able to organise his return to Ireland. On the journey back he kept on about the mysterious ways in which God worked. Looking up at the roof of the car, he would ask, 'What are Yer trying to do to me? First off he's a Protestant kraut, second off these other two are English Protestants. What are Yer thinking of, sending the likes of them to help me?'

It appeared that Father McCabe had been left in the College alone for years, and the Spanish prelates had threatened to take over the College. He had been sitting behind his desk, a bottle in one hand and a pistol in the other, for two days before we arrived, and had been quite prepared to shoot any of the Spanish representatives, had they gone near him.

The Irish legation refused to deal with the problem or even take care of Father McCabe, so on Betty's insistence he stayed with us until he was sober and I could organise his return to Ireland. Betty was incredible, and the Father was soon dried out, healthy, and good company for the children and for us. After ten days, the Armagh (the Irish Vatican) organised the Father's return.

Father McCabe was replaced by Father Ransome who in gratitude for our help offered us the use of a College house at Pendueles, in northern Spain, for our summer holidays. Father Ransome would join us for the three weeks' holiday and would be part of the family. The Bristow heretics enjoyed the Father's company as I know he enjoyed ours.

For the second summer at Pendueles, Father Ransome was accompanied by a young Polish priest who had been first interned with the Poles at Dachau, then a captain chaplain in the Polish army. He had initially come to Spain to serve God, but during one of our discussions he turned to Betty and me and said, 'I am returning to England next week.' Betty asked, 'Why? I thought you had decided to stay in Spain and were looking for a place to work?'

'Yes, that is true, but I have come to realise I do not fit in here. I claim to be a good Catholic Christian, but sadly see so very little connection between the Spanish Church and the teachings I have received, that I do not feel I could happily carry on my evangelical work in Spain . . . a so-called Catholic country. Ironically I think I'll be able to work better in England.' We had many more conversations about religion, politics, wine and food.

The last port of call on my tour around the peninsula was Gibraltar, which was uneventful. Betty and I enjoyed the company of Ken and Patricia Mills; I explained the need to cut back, and that several agents had to paid be off. (In most cases the paying off of agents simply meant them being 'laid off'. There was no British Agents' Union to argue for just reward! SIS was poor financially, as well as in personnel.

Shortly after my visit to Gibraltar, Ken phoned me in Madrid. 'Desmond, do you know a chap called Guy Burgess?' he asked.

'Yes, unfortunately I do know the little poof – not well, I might add. The little shit is a friend of Philby's and Tommy Harris's. God knows why they like him . . . Why do you ask?'

'He's here in Gib, claiming that he's a good friend of Philby, that he knows you and is personal assistant to Sir Hector McNeil, and has asked me to change money for him. When I said I would have to check with you first, he went on to explain that he was on very friendly terms with Guy Liddell [deputy director of MI5), and did I know Dick White . . . Again I told him I would have to check with you. Well, he continued rattling on, then he started asking questions, persistently, and generally behaved like an insidious little bastard. What really rocked me was the way he slanged off the Americans, and expressed great admiration for Mao Tse Tung. Tell me, what do I do?'

In a very exasperated tone, I replied, 'Fuck him! On second thoughts no, he'd probably enjoy that. Just chuck him out; even though he is in the FO.'

'Don't exchange any money or do anything . . . We must not get involved?' asked Ken.

'No bloody fear,' said I. And that was that . . . So I thought at the time.

The telephone conversation worried me. Guy Burgess, the man I had told Kim Philby I could not stand, way back in 1941. What was he doing in Gibraltar stirring up trouble? Why did he need to change money?

A week or two later, it must have been early January 1950, the telephone rang. It was Teddy Dunlop calling from Tangier. 'Hello, Desmond, I have a problem in the name of Guy Burgess. He's rude, keeps pestering me for money and generally behaving in an appalling fashion.' She sounded very irritated.

'Well, for a start don't give him a penny and keep him out of the office.'

'But Desmond, he knows everyone! How can I just have him kicked out?'

'I don't know,' I replied. 'Maybe he's an FO agent spying on us,' I added jokingly.

'Well, if that's the case he should not have gone around broadcasting the name of the Swiss diplomat who allowed the British to use the Swiss diplomatic bag to bring rare pieces of equipment and information out of Switzerland.' She continued with more horrifying news about Burgess. 'Also he should not have pinched Harry Dean's Arab bum boy. He has created one hell of a scandal and that alone has really fixed him in Tangier.' (Harry owned a famous bar in Tangier and was a roaring queer – but a very likeable chap, who was well known in the area and had a lot of powerful friends. Burgess had set the gays of Tangier alight, it seemed.)

Teddy was very concerned. The Tangier community was scandalised by the behaviour of this member of the British Foreign Service. I told Teddy to collaborate with Ken and send a report to head office. Ken sent his report to MI5, in which he boldly stated that Burgess should not be in the employ of the Foreign Office let alone be a personal assistant for a minister of the Crown. Teddy sent a report to me and I sent my report to head office (MI6) with a covering report to the Foreign Office. To the three of us, official reaction, as witnessed later, was very strange and illogical. In February 1950 Ken had to go to England on personal business; on arrival he was called to a meeting with Guy Liddell and Bernard Hill, MI5's legal adviser.

Here follows a précis of a tape-recording which Ken gave me shortly before his sad death, recounting this meeting.

Guy Liddell cross-questioned me on most of the contents of my report, inferring I possibly had motives for slandering Burgess. I told him not to be so ridiculous. His most reluctant attitude to forwarding my report about Burgess to the Foreign Office astounded me. Here was a member of the Foreign Office behaving in a mad, wild and totally irresponsible manner abroad, throwing names around with complete abandon. Bernard Hill interrupted my retort to Guy Liddell and pointed out that if Liddell was to refuse to support a trusted member of his own department in MI5 and refuse to pass on this information to the Foreign Office, then the Foreign Office should be advised not to accept any more MI5 reports. Besides, either Liddell trusted his representatives, in which case he must act upon their reports, or he did not trust his representatives and should have them investigated. When Bernard Hill finished his barrage on Liddell, I added that if Liddell did not accept what I had to say there were plenty of people in the Rock Hotel and in Gibraltar who would more than willingly provide statements pertaining to Burgess's wild, decadent and insidious behaviour.

Three days later I heard that the Foreign Office had reprimanded Burgess. Burgess had then immediately reported back to Liddell about his reprimand due to my report, and inferred to Liddell that I was running a currency racket . . . What a terrible individual he was.

When Ken gave me the tape, he and I discussed it – this was after Blunt had been exposed. We were agreed about Blunt; even just after Maclean and Burgess escaped we thought Blunt must have tipped them off.

During our discussion we talked about Roger Hollis, who I might add had become the head of MI5 and been knighted for his services. I felt that someone else must have been involved other than Blunt, during the Burgess Maclean affair, and I thought it was Hollis and I still do. My argument was based on a brief history about Hollis that had come my way, concerning his involvement with Agnes Smedley in 1936 when Hollis was working for British American Tobacco in China. Agnes Smedley was a known KGB agent and Communist supporter. They had casually met at a party in Shanghai. Not long after this meeting he returned to England, owing to tuberculosis. When he had recovered he became obsessive about joining the Secret Services and suc-ceeded by socialising with the right people at a tennis club.

Later in 1945, he was chosen by Philby to interrogate Igor Gouzenko, the Russian cipher expert who defected to Canada. Why did Philby suggest Hollis, and why did the conversation Hollis had with Gouzenko take only about twenty minutes? Cyril Mills should have been the person to have gone, since he had well-established connections within the Canadian police. Moreover, besides the fact that the interview Hollis had with Gouzenko should have lasted a lot longer, he dismissed the information he did receive as worthless. The Canadians and the Americans who acted upon the information they obtained from Gouzenko successfully arrested a number of Soviet spies.

Despite my fairly strong evidence, Ken never agreed with me about Hollis.

My own unanswered questions remain: what were the motives? What could Guy Liddell have been thinking? Blunt had been in Liddell's department earlier on; and now here was Liddell supporting Burgess, and basically trying to cover up his behaviour in Gibraltar and Tangier. Curiouser and curiouser!

In March 1950 I returned to England to attend a course, housed in an old turreted mansion in Hampshire. We carried out night landings in rubber boats, learned how to use explosives, and the destructive power of two gallons of petrol. We were receiving lessons on wartime special operations. Our instructor was a tough man, about the same age as I was, named Fernandez. He was expert, meticulous and a very able and amiable teacher. He had been a member of the diving group which so successfully breached the underwater barbed-wire entanglements laid by the Germans around the Normandy beaches. (I last saw him in 1987–88, when he was vice consul in Algeciras.)

I then went to London to talk with the heads of department who were receiving reports from my section. My last call was on David Footman, the receiver of some of my reports from Madrid. He was an old hand in SIS and the expert on the Balkan states. I arrived at his office in a mood of irritated curiosity; his assistant had told me that he had not forwarded my report on Spanish Communism to the Foreign Office.

'Hello, David, how are you getting along?' I asked.

'I am glad you have come, Desmond. I was just preparing a note asking you to explain why Pat Todd should be kept on; he seems very pro-Franco to me.'

I laughed. 'My God! David, out of all of us in my section, who less so?'

'I don't think he should be kept on,' said Footman. I disagreed entirely, and gave my reasons. I then asked, 'I was wondering if you knew why Section IX has not responded to my report on Spanish Communism?' He coughed, and shuffled uncomfortably in his chair. 'I did not feel it worthwhile or relevant, consequently I didn't send it to the Foreign Office.'

'How funny you should not find it relevant. In case you didn't realise it, I am attached to the Foreign Office via Chancery, and sent my report directly to them. As a result I have received several pointed follow-up questions which leads me to believe they found it very interesting.'

Footman's face dropped. Then in an attempt to side-step the issue he said, 'Oh, by the way, I do not think you or your colleagues should write reports about other colleagues.'

'What are you talking about, David?' Suddenly I realised he meant the Burgess affair, which made me really cross. 'Listen, Footman; one, Burgess is no colleague of mine or of any of us in SIS for that matter and therefore should be no colleague of yours; two, I think I shall go straight up to C and have him read my report, then we can discuss the subject again.'

'C is not here today,' replied Footman.

'How very fortunate for you, Footman,' I said angrily.

He continued, 'All I am trying to say, is that we must not act as if we are Gestapo!' I was dumbfounded by his comment. Feeling very angry I got up, walked out and slammed the door.

Why was Footman defending Burgess's behaviour? What

was it about that man that made so many people in responsible positions defend him, even like him? Perhaps it was his
theatrical gaiety, supported by his blue blood, which possibly
made him amusing and interestingly eccentric. I don't know
if it was any more sinister than that. When all hell broke loose
over Maclean's and Burgess's escape to Russia, Footman's
remarks echoed in my head. They echoed again, when Philby
defected in 1963. As for Guy Liddell and his involvement, he
certainly allowed Blunt into the Service. He knew Burgess
and Philby very well. This may have been nothing more than
homosexual friendship.

On my flight back to Madrid I mulled over Footman's
outrageous remarks about Pat Todd. Pat had done wonders
during the war for MEW, MI9, SIS and Section V. He was
producing good, clear reports on the Basques and their
aspirations, a subject the Foreign Office and SIS were very
interested in. The Bilbao consul had recently reported how
extremely helpful Pat Todd was. For someone like Footman
to be raising doubts about Pat was inconceivable. Was it just
economy?

One week after my return to Madrid, I called a general
meeting of Ken, Teddy, Pat, and Frederick Elder, who could
not attend. I reported on the Burgess affair, and Footman's
comments. We debated the situation – not in terms of moles
or double agents, we were still blissfully naïve on that topic! –
but as truly concerned members of the British Secret Service
and, for my part, as a member of the Foreign Service. At
the end of the meeting we decided to 'press on regardless'.
We were not in a position to take or recommend further action. We agreed to ignore Footman's remarks and

recommendations. We decided that in the unlikely event of any other employee of His Majesty's Government behaving in our territory in a comparably bad way, we would behave like the Gestapo again and file a report directly to C.

After the war British and Spanish representatives met twice a year to discuss their trade dealings. There was an ongoing wrangle between the two countries. Britain was invariably represented by a member of the Treasury, someone from the Board of Trade, our minister and of course the resident commercial counsellor of the Embassy. Spain was purchasing little from England and each year the balance grew in Spain's favour. We continually tried to persuade them to buy British cars, a difficult deal for them to accept, with petrol being rationed and their need for more essential items. But besides the question of cars, Spain was not playing the game.

I was asked to find out what their attitude was likely to be at the second meeting of 1949. On my asking a few pertinent questions, 'a friend' in the Ministry of Economics assured me that at long last they were planning on buying more cars. Added to which they wanted spares and castings for their newly electrified train, their pride and joy, the famous articulated 'Talgo'.

'What about buying more quality coal, such as anthracite?' I asked.

'I don't know about that; our mines in Asturias are producing large quantities of lower grade coal; I will have to check up about anthracite and the cleaner burning types,' he replied.

Our recently appointed commercial counsellor, Pelham (known as Pompous Pelham), was determined to make a name for himself. At a meeting a few days before the trade mission arrived, Pelham stated that, 'In the event of Spain prevaricating, I will pick up the phone in the middle of the meeting, call the Board of Trade and request them to stop all anthracite supplies to Spain.' The threat hung on the fact that anthracite was quite rare, and essential for firing sensitive chemical and engineering plants. All present, except me, agreed that this would be a good tactic. I tried pointing out that this seemed rather a puerile move, besides which the idea was to increase purchases of British goods, not lessen them. The meeting was broken up with Pelham sticking to his plan of action.

The day before the meeting a 'Spanish friend' from Galicia, educated at Fettes School in Scotland, came down to Madrid. He was in the coaling business and therefore interested in the forthcoming Anglo-Spanish agreement. He spoke perfect Spanish and English with a Scottish accent. We met at one of my favourite little tapas bars around the corner from the Embassy.

'Jock,' I said, 'Pelham is going to perform at tomorrow's meeting.'

'Perform! What do you mean, do monkey tricks?'

I told him of Pelham's plan.

'Desmond! For God's sake don't let him try to pull that schoolboy trick. I cannot believe someone in his position is capable of such stupid behaviour. It would be better for him if he did some monkey tricks, or swung on a trapeze.'

'Oh, he's quite capable of it. I don't think he will take any notice of me,' I said, knowing that Pelham did not approve of us MI6 chaps.

'Well, he is going to look a total idiot. We have already imported 200,000 tons more anthracite than our quota, and we have more on its way before the year is through . . . and believe me it will arrive. We have been trading with the mines in Cardiff for over eighty years – and the Welsh don't like being told what to do by the British Board of Trade.'

I called Pelham and explained how the quota had been exceeded already; but he took no notice, implying it was not true.

The meeting went ahead, Pelham pulled his trick. That afternoon I received a phone call from my friend in the Spanish ministry. 'Desmond,' he said, 'I'm curious as to who this Pelham chap is, and why the British have chosen such an idiot to be in his position? He must be very unaware of life. If we had not restrained ourselves the meeting would have become a total farce. You know we like the British, but this man . . . Well, anyway, we are now thinking of selling our surplus coal to Poland – but don't tell Pelham.' No more was said, and the coal and anthracite trade continued. Pelham later became HMG's ambassador in Tel Aviv.

15

Garbo: A Question of Resurrection

Tommy Harris was a frequent visitor to Madrid, and by 1950 was living most of the time in Camp de Mar, Majorca. He would come to Madrid to sell or exhibit his paintings, coloured glass, ceramics and etchings. He was a prolific artist, as well as dealing in others' works. I had been corresponding with Juan Pujol (Garbo) who was living in Caracas, Venezuela. I had suggested he join the only Venezuelan Eastern bloc society (the Czech Society) with the idea of gaining their trust. Obviously the idea was to find out about their interests in South America, but more importantly, once he was trusted by them I planned to have him transferred to Paris where he would try to infiltrate the Soviet subversive 'Juggernaut' operating in France.

I discussed my plan with Tommy, who was able to give me more insight into Pujol's character and abilities. At first Tommy thought it a very good idea, and said he would help in any way he could. I wrote a letter with my ideas to Pujol. When I heard back from Pujol, who expressed his willingness and wholehearted co-operation, I started negotiating with head office. Two or three weeks went by and Tommy, who in the meantime had been to Majorca, returned to Madrid. On this visit he was much less supportive, having discussed the whole idea with Philby. He did say that he had arranged for

Pujol to visit him in Majorca to discuss some other business, and would send him on to Madrid to see me.

Pujol visited, and we talked the idea over for a few days. He flew back to Caracas, leaving me with the impression that he was keen to go ahead; then head office sent me a message, with very little explanation, telling me to drop the plan. I telegraphed Pujol informing him the plan was aborted.

Some very strange things happened around Pujol, and he certainly was a most capable liar with very few morals. According to him, his wife, Aracelli Gonzalez, who had supported them all through the Civil War and had been by his side while he was playing Garbo, had deserted him and was living somewhere in Madrid. In 1980 Betty and I met up with Aracelli and after so many years we became good friends. She told us a very different story. In 1948, Pujol sent her and their two sons and daughter back to Madrid. After a year she realised that Pujol had deserted her and, by then completely broke, she managed to rent a house from an old friend, paying the rent and for food by taking in paying guests. I was even more shocked when she went on to tell us that she had called on passport control for help, and been refused. Why this matter was not referred to me at the time, I do not know. According to her, the person who refused to help her answered a description of David Thomson. Very curious . . .

How very insidious of Pujol to lie to me.

Anyway, in 1950 I was disappointed about Garbo not being resurrected; it rather took the wind out of my sails. Not long after, in about June of that year, I was in my office one evening trying to continue to think outwardly and sustain my counter-espionage instinct somehow, when the telephone rang. The duty lady on the Embassy switchboard said there was a gentleman on the phone wanting to speak to the military attaché's assistant urgently. I asked her to tell him he was out. In fact I was the only one in the Embassy at the time – why, I cannot recall.

Upon the gentleman's insistence I accepted the call, and an excited young man told me he was on the run from the police and had important information to report. I asked if he had been to the United States Embassy.

'No,' was his somewhat angry reply. 'I prefer this Embassy.'

I told him to call back the next morning as I had no charter to listen to him. He became very agitated and insistent, so I eventually agreed to meet him the next morning. He gave his name as José Ponce de Leon.

The following day, posing as the military attaché's assistant (there wasn't one in our Embassy), I interviewed José. He was shaggy, dirty and unshaven, and gave me a long and reasonably authentic-sounding story, which concerned a possible coup against Franco. I emphasised that the possible coup was of course of interest but that our interests had better not be misconstrued. I started to suspect he was a plant by the Spanish security service who were trying to discover who was head of MI6 in Madrid.

I sent him over to passport control, where he was given a little money and sent to a well known safe house which the Spanish secret police would have under surveillance. He spent one night there and disappeared the next morning.

1950 passed slowly. My work with Bill Milton was drawing to an end; of course we stayed close friends, shooting and going to guitar recitals by Segovia. Betty and I were doing quite a lot of diplomatic entertaining at home, some of which was fun, but too expensive, considering how little we received from the Foreign Office. In those days it was assumed that all diplomats had large private incomes, part of which could be spent on behalf of the country, maintaining liaison and social contact if nothing else.

Towards the end of the year rumours started to filter through about the appointment of an ambassador. It was time; the Spanish were starting to resent Britain's continued ostracism, and we in the Embassy were starting to resent the extra workload.

The Ambassador, Sir John Balfour, and his wife arrived early in 1951, and as is the custom a ceremony was held where the Ambassador was received by, and presented himself to the head of state, in this case General Franco. The ceremony was very grand. Franco wanted to show off some of the splendour of Spain. The streets of Madrid echoed with the sound of horses' hooves and carriage wheels; the pavements were filled with flag-waving, confetti-throwing people; chauffeur-driven cars bearing flags followed in procession; army uniforms and polished buttons, shining shoes and twinkling medals. I arrived at the royal palace, having chosen not to wear my medals; I wanted to draw as little attention to myself as possible. I suppose I felt my true line of work would be questioned if I pinned them on.

We were ushered to our places, we shuffled around and bowed our heads, and then there I was shaking hands with the Generalissimo, the man who had plunged Spain into the bloody Civil War; but under whose leadership Spain was recovering fast. His character had been smeared and attacked at every possible opportunity by liberals and socialists . . . Yes, it was Franco who had brought about the Civil War, but I knew what Spain had been suffering before: constant political upheaval, starvation, disease, and the isolation of many villages from the rest of the world, due to the lack of roads and communication. Spain had suffered from a total lack of central organisation – in short, chaos. Besides, in my opinion, if Franco had not started the War, Spain would not have survived much longer without some sort of revolution; and it was a virtual certainty that had the Republic continued, Germany would have walked into Spain after the fall of France. So there I was, shaking hands with the so-called butcher of Guernica.

The arrival of the Ambassador certainly warmed things up socially, with highbrow parties and social events. Economically our relationship did not change at all; Britain continued to maintain a critical and aloof attitude of superiority. France and Italy were winning out. The Renault car factory installation, and the marriage of Fiat to a Spanish company which produced Seat, resulted in an increasing number of cars being made in Spain which started to fill up the roads. The number of American bases and naval vessels docked was evidence of a military relationship co-relating to the cold war. The Americans were trying desperately to woo Franco with economic aid and always failing. In his words: 'Spain is not for sale to anyone.'

Because I knew the Spanish were fond of us Brits, and wanted to work with us more than with most others, I became frustrated as I watched so many opportunities for Britain fall into the hands of other countries purely because of our offhand arrogance.

As for MI6, we continued to monitor the political and economic jockeying, but for me and my colleagues, our enthusiasm was faltering. I would occasionally go over to passport control in Calle Montesquinza on the pretext that I needed to check up on information pertaining to some minor historical fact about relations between England and Spain. In reality I was liaising with my friend from Cambridge, the archivist who was working with a great many MI6 operations and was still one of the most successful agent operators in Madrid. We were able to converse in French if necessary, since she was trilingual like myself. (Her usual line of communication to me was via the small diplomatic bag that went from passport control over to the Embassy.)

My training for deception and undercover work had most definitely included routine; but I was never subjected to routine for any length of time, and unfortunately when I was, I became bored.

Not long after the arrival of the Ambassador, head office instructed me to meet a Mr Dowding and his colleague at the airport, explaining that he was the head of HM's customs investigation branch. I duly met the bright and friendly Mr Dowding, who explained that his department wished to arrive at a *modus vivendi* with the Spanish head of customs. A subsequent meeting between the two opened the door to a continuing relationship of free-flowing information. This apparently insignificant arrangement was to benefit not only me but MI6 in the future.

At the end of May, my life as a Secret Service man fell prey to doubt and misconceptions, as the news of Burgess's and Maclean's flight to the Soviet Union spread through the world. I became especially disturbed when I heard about the inefficiency of Dick White (MI5's director of counter-espionage) from internal sources. As soon as he heard about the flight of Burgess and Maclean, White had gone to Newhaven to follow their trail. On presenting his passport to immigration he was informed it was six months out of date; and they did not care who he was, he could not leave the country with an out-of-date passport. I was beginning to wonder about SIS.

My friend Kim Philby was then withdrawn from Washington due to demands from the CIA. Kim was suspected of informing Burgess and Maclean about the up-and-coming investigation of Maclean. I was stunned and shaken by what I was hearing through the service grapevine, and by what I was reading in the newspapers. Kim was politely forced to resign by Sir Stewart Menzies.

Trying to avoid thinking about Kim's possible treachery was virtually impossible. Joe Presley (FBI), Al Wallace (CIA), Bill Milton, Tommy Harris and all of us could not help speculating. In the autumn Kim was cross-questioned and found not guilty, despite the amount of circumstantial evidence found . . . Where was the flower with the petals; not to ask about being loved or not, but was he? Or wasn't he?

I wrote privately to head office saying the uncertainty was intolerable, and suggesting, 'Why not lock him up in a flat with two bottles of whisky and see if he confesses?' Needless to say I had no response. But I did receive a visit from a member of the London office, Mary Neigh. This was the first official visit in three years by a head office representative.

At first Mary Neigh was very guarded and asked a lot of questions. I remember being irritated by the officialness of her visit, in light of the fact that head office had hitherto left us alone in the Iberian section.

Perhaps I was under suspicion as well?

After she left I met with Al Wallace who informed me that

the CIA had been trying to warn Britain about a 'mole'. Al could not believe we had blundered so badly over Burgess and Maclean.

'Do you mean to say they escaped – or were allowed to escape?' Al asked. 'When you tell me that Dick White arrived with an out-of-date passport I have to think it was deliberate.'

'I don't know,' I replied rather despondently.

'Do you mean to say that it is possible for your lot, having orchestrated the D Day deception, suddenly to turn into an outfit not worthy of the Keystone Cops? Oh no! There must be more in it than that! And what about the guy who is being interrogated, or has just been interrogated – Philby? Is he in it too?'

'I hope not. Kim Philby is someone I consider quite a close friend . . . I just don't know,' I replied. 'I find it very hard to think about let alone believe. Burgess, well, the couple of times I have run across him I have, I can honestly say, despised him. He must have got to know that Maclean was a Soviet spy. Perhaps he saw some communication in Philby's office. After all he was living with Philby in Washington, much to poor Aileen Philby's horror.'

Accepting the drink Al offered, I continued. 'Listen, Al! Here I am in Madrid; all I can do is surmise what happened or why. All I can say is that no one seems to be saying anything definitive to anyone. I have been on the best of terms with Philby, and the office well knows that, but that does not mean to say I would be kept informed of any developments. In fact with him being interrogated and now thrown out I would say the opposite. It is all very confusing and I just do not know what to think. I simply hope head office knows what's going on and what it is doing.' We talked back and forth for a long time. Fortunately Joe Presley did not press me on the subject, and just left Al to quiz me.

I did trust head office to sort the mess out, so that things would settle down. Unfortunately this was not to be. The internal bush telegraph, the press and others continued to ask the same questions. It turned into a perennial cloud of doubt hanging over the present, the past and the future. I lived up to my Gemini birth sign. I did not want to believe that Philby was the Third Man, as MP Marcus Lipton had called him, yet I could not clear my head of nagging doubts, not least of which was his friendship with Burgess, which I never understood.

In early 1952 I received a message from head office advising me, 'Philby is due to arrive in Madrid on a contract for the *Observer*, and has been briefed not to have anything to do with you! We strongly advise you not to have any contact with him.' I did not know whether to laugh or cry. Philby and I were, as I thought, good friends; we had worked together during the war. He had been my boss and in many ways my teacher in the ways of espionage. For him to come to Madrid, and for me to pretend that I did not want to see him would have been ridiculous and could possibly have raised his suspicions. I telegraphed London saying that I was well aware of the circumstances, but if the situation arose I would see Philby.

It was a Tuesday at 2.30 pm; a tremendous thunderstorm was raging when the phone rang. 'Desmond.' I immediately recognised the voice.

'Hello, Kim. Where are you?'

'I'm at the Iberian bus t-t-terminal in the m-m-middle of M-madrid and I'm stuck. I was wondering if you might know of a small hotel.'

'Oh, don't worry, I'll come and fetch you and we'll see what we can sort out.' Confronted by him directly like that I could not bring myself to think of him as a Soviet agent.

I telephoned Bill Milton who lived near the city centre and organised to meet him after I had picked up Kim. In the event, Bill offered to put Kim up for that night, taking him next day to a small hotel in Calle Miguel Angel.

I warned Joe Presley and Al Wallace of Kim Philby's presence. We agreed to play the game with him as though nothing had happened. 'He might make a false move,' suggested Al.

Well, Kim was looking for journalistic leads so I introduced him to Sam Brewer of United Press and Bobby Papworth of Reuters. Through them Kim was able to meet all the Anglo-American journalists in Madrid, and become a member of the Journalists' Club.

Kim's friend Lady Frances Lindsay-Hogg arrived during his stay. They joined us on one of our picnics. Kim and I spoke very little about the Burgess and Maclean affair. He once reminded me of how I had never liked Burgess. 'How on earth do you remember that?' I asked. 'Oh, just one of those things.' Somehow we never discussed politics, or the weight of suspicion he was carrying on his shoulders.

He seemed to enjoy his months in Spain, and being a journalist. We gave a party for him when he left.

The big question mark remained. Despite his being cleared by the Prime Minister, Harold Macmillan, I could not make up my mind. Why should the Firm have found him a job in Spain? Was it to string him along? Was it to see who he made contact with? What was at the back of it all? By this time it was clear that Burgess and Maclean were guilty; was Kim, therefore? Or was he our double agent? Head office must know something that those of us in the field did not. This period of uncertainty had a most demoralising effect on many of us; it certainly did on me.

Surely Kim must have been working for us, and reported on Burgess and Maclean, so that he had posed as a journalist and come to Spain as a safe haven. But then, why the letter from head office? My imagination ran wild with questions. Had I been instructed not to see him to save me from being blown? Or to save him from arousing the Spanish seguridad's suspicion? Here was a journalist, in good standing with the Spanish authorities due to his correspondent work during the Civil War, in touch with a member of HM's Embassy – why? But then all foreign journalists were frequently in the company of diplomats.

His visit caused Bill, Joe, Al and I to talk about him more than ever, and made my mind more of a muddle than ever.

At times I felt like talking about him with anyone around who might have an opinion, but of course I did not. There was no bridle nor bit, however, on the mad galloping of my imagination. If Philby was a Soviet agent then all those who knew him at St Albans would fall under a cloud of doubt. Doubt was starting to plague me, though I was certain I personally had no real reason to worry. But the wrong fish can often get caught in a net. I realised that of the Iberian section I was closer to Kim than anyone. His only other close friend in that part of the world was Tommy Harris. I remember reminiscing with Tommy about the war days and wondering if it was possible that Kim, whom we had got drunk with, who had ridden so often on the back of my motorcycle, who had introduced the two of us, was really a Soviet spy.

That summer was our last holiday in northern Spain.

Speculation about Philby subsided.

In January 1953, head office started intimating that my days in Madrid were numbered, and I was soon to return to England. I was told so often that I was leaving, and then not leaving, that Betty and I must have attended six or seven farewell parties. Eventually head office was sure it had found my replacement and on April 1st we left Madrid.

Rosanne, our eldest daughter, flew back to England with Tommy and Hilda Harris making room in the car for Pepe, a friend's young servant who had decided he wanted to come to England with us. We packed as much as we could into our Austin; the rest of our belongings went by freight. John and Annette went in the back with Pepe; Betty and Dardo, the English setter, sat in the passenger area and I drove. For the first hour Betty and I discussed whether we had left anything behind, while John, Annette and Pepe played the irritating game of 'I-spy'. The family disputes and Dardo getting car sick must have made Pepe wonder why he had decided to come with us to England – or even why he had decided to go to England at all.

Our first stop was San Sebastian, where we had lobster, mussels, fresh sardines and a marvellous bottle of wine (or two) at a restaurant overlooking the moonlit Bay of Biscay. We stayed in a new high-rise hotel. In the morning we were awakened by Pepe, in a panic.

'Señor, señor,' he yelled, pounding on our door. Sleepily, Betty and I got out of bed, as Pepe rushed in explaining that Annette and John were climbing from their balcony onto the next in a daring attempt to surprise us. This would have been good fun, had our rooms not been a hundred feet above the road. I peered around the corner of the window just in time to see Annette land safely on the balcony next to ours. Betty yelled for them to stay where they were. I rushed out of the room and knocked up our sleepy neighbour.

'Excuse me, señor,' I said in Spanish. 'Our children are on your balcony and I would like to retrieve them before they attempt to climb onto ours.' With a look of horror he invited me in and opened the window fastenings as fast as he could. I grabbed Annette, who smiled broadly and said in Spanish, 'Good morning, Papa, how are you today? We were going to surprise you by climbing in your bedroom window while you were asleep.'

When she realised how upset we were, she kept explaining why they had attempted their death-defying act. Betty and I knew full well that John had persuaded Annette it would be a good idea, and the more she reasoned with us on their behalf the less upset Betty and I became. Of course her brother kept his mouth firmly shut, and looked as though he was about to burst into tears. After about half an hour we all calmed down, had breakfast and set off to Le Touquet. By the time we arrived, we were all laughing about the children's climbing exploits.

Le Touquet retained some of the grandeur of the days when it had been as important to tennis tournaments as Wimbledon. Because of the dog we had decided to fly the short route from Le Touquet to Lydd in Kent. A dog box was prepared, Dardo was immunised and we said goodbye to him, not to see his muddy paws in our home for six months, when he would emerge from rabies quarantine.

After five and a half years it was somewhat of a culture shock to be back at Hawkins Harvest, our small farm near Great

Bardfield in Essex. Betty and I could see a thousand and one alterations and repairs that needed to be done; our budget would cover about half of them. I had two weeks' leave in which to help Betty unpack, do some minor plumbing, electrical repairs and carpentry, and purchase an old jeep that had been in North Africa about the same time as I was. As we settled in, the change in environment and the physical labour helped me brainwash myself about Spain.

When my leave was up, I drove to Chelmsford station early on Monday morning and caught the train to Liverpool Street. It was time for me to report to head office and find out what they had in store for me.

I was invited to become the head of a newly formed section of MI6 which dealt with the very complicated problem of strategic trade. This obscure title referred to about one hundred items which the United States and Britain had decided must be prevented from reaching the Warsaw Pact countries. Priority goods on the list were copper in any shape or form, aluminium, diamonds and a host of accessories not available behind the Iron Curtain, especially electrical goods and embryonic electronic parts. This represented a great challenge, and I felt very enthusiastic about my new position.

That first journey home went very quickly as my mind was occupied with details of my new responsibilities, in the office and at home: ships full of copper during the weekdays, horses, cattle, chickens and pigs during the evenings and weekends. The clickety-clack of the train wheels put my mind in a condition for day-dreaming. The rich Essex countryside slipped past as condensation on the window clouded my vision: very green grass, full oak and chestnut trees, crops covering the gently undulating fields.

My day dream was about farming. Farmyards stood beside

the railway line, and I imagined our little farm: Betty collecting the eggs, the milking of the cows, the tractor-driving, and gymkhanas at the weekends.

I could not help wondering if Betty and I were not trying to do too much, as the new job was more exciting and responsible than I had expected. Getting out at Chelmsford with all the other commuters and walking to the car felt like fun on that first evening. The drive to Hawkins Harvest was beautiful. The narrow lanes around our house were lined with high banks and thick hedgerows, apple orchards, woods and little country cottages; in most places only one car could pass along them. In those days we were one of the few families that had a car; most others, who had lived in the area for years, had bicycles or old tractors. It was very romantic and a lot of hard work. Thank goodness Pepe had come with us; he was a great help to Betty in the garden and with the outbuildings.

16

Diamonds Are a Girl's Best Friend

For the next week Jack Sharp, my assistant, showed me how the office worked: he explained who gave what information in the offices down the hallway, the system for monitoring the strategically listed exports, and who were our representatives abroad, providing much of the information. I was now involved in the cold war.

The Bill of Lading had become ineffective as a means of monitoring the passage of goods, as ships often changed their route and destination while on the high seas. Before I headed this new department the Allies had established a shipping intervention programme using receivers. Each country was consigned a particular number of receiving companies, which would receive incoming goods that were on the strategic trade list. But without constant vigilance this method was full of holes, and goods continued to go behind the Iron Curtain. The office and the CIA set up agents in jobs that would enable us to monitor sea traffic as closely as possible. Once goods arrived in the country, customs officers would carry out random investigations on the receiving companies.

I will use Chile as an example since it produced copper, which was in very high demand behind the Iron Curtain. In Chile both the consul and the commercial counsellor worked for us and had a network of agents who passed on information about shipping. These agents usually worked in the import and export department, or in the shipping telegraph station. When the consul or commercial counsellor heard about a particular ship, carrying copper, which had been leaving for Oslo and then received instructions to redirect to Gdansk, they would send me details, often very explicit, perhaps even including the captain's name. I would then inform the naval intelligence department. The navy would follow the passage of the copper-carrying ship, and at a strategic point intercept it and redirect it to an English or French port. The cargo would usually be confiscated and put on the market, and the receiving company in Oslo would be investigated and blacklisted. We worked very closely with the CIA in our endeavours to monitor shipping and the developments of strategic trade.

During my second week, Jack and I needed the help of Britain's customs investigation branch. I called the head of that department, to discover that I was speaking to Mr Dowding, whom I had introduced to the Spanish customs authorities.

Jack came into my office with a telegram from the consul in Chile about a shipment of copper which was due to arrive in England. The copper had been bought by a well-known English trading house (whose name and major shareholders belong to a well-known aristocratic family). The consul's agent in the telegraph office picked up a message requesting the ship to change its final destination. Instead of Liverpool, the ship was ordered to go to Newcastle. This was strange; Liverpool, being on the Atlantic side of England, was the natural port for industrial goods arriving from the Americas. Also most copper-processing plants were in Manchester or

Preston, both of which are within easier access of Liverpool than Newcastle.

I called Mr Dowding, and explained the situation. Two or three weeks later Dowding called me back.

'Mr Bristow, the copper-carrying ship has apparently finished unloading its cargo, but the quantity in the warehouse is one quarter of the quantity you told me the ship was carrying. The receiving company's receipt, made out by the trading company, seems to be in order. They apparently were only expecting one quarter of the load. The captain has departure papers dated for tomorrow.'

'Has the ship taken on any cargo since its arrival?' I asked.

'Besides normal food rations and medical supplies for the crew, no it has not,' he replied. 'And the captain's papers are all in order, with export approved instructions issued by the trading company for him to deliver the remaining copper to Stockholm, so I'm unable to hold him or the ship.'

'Right you are, I'll take it from here, thanks. I'll talk to you soon, I expect.'

Jack called up his friend in the navy to find out if they had a ship in the northern part of the Channel, near Holland or Denmark. I called naval intelligence and informed them of the situation. While I was giving the details to naval intelligence, Jack was on the other phone taking details of naval vessels on manoeuvres near Denmark. Jack always took details of naval vessels in these situations as sometimes the officer at the other end of the phone was slow to react, or made a fuss. When that happened Jack and I would give the details of ships' positions and tell the liaison officer at the other end of the phone . . . to get on with it. It was quite amazing how some people reacted in these situations.

I'm sure they were fed up with war, and basically we were fighting a strategic goods war.

Back to the ship leaving Newcastle. Four days later it was stopped by the navy as it sailed passed Stockholm, quite obviously on its way to Gdansk. The ship was forced to return to England where it was impounded by customs. As a result of this the English trading company was blacklisted by us and carefully watched. Despite this, and restrictions placed upon the company, during my time as head of strategic trade, Jack and I stopped four or five more shipments, organised by the same trader, reaching the Eastern bloc.

While this copper escapade was going on, of course a lot of other trading movements were taking place. One involved the CIA, the American navy, and some classified electronic components being shipped to England. They were to do with fighter planes. I don't remember all the details, but as a result of the liaison between myself and the CIA man in London, we became friends. He shall remain anonymous, and during the next few paragraphs I refer to him as John X.

It happened around the time Tommy Harris had one of his parties, a big bash. Kim Philby was there, and Blunt, and a host of others; a very social gathering. Tommy wanted Kim to write a book about his being withdrawn from Washington and ousted from the Service, due to his knowing Burgess and Maclean. Up to that point, as far as we all knew, Kim had been very good as head of several departments and to all appearances a very successful operator, quite possibly due for the position of C.

The following Monday Kim and I had lunch. Though Kim was at a loose end, and broke, he told me that he did not think he would be able to write his book, and the more pressure Tommy put on him the less inclined he felt to put pen to paper. I felt sorry for him at the time and told him the book was a good idea. He changed the subject and asked after the family, and vaguely asked about the Firm. I walked back to the office feeling some doubt once again about everything to do with the Service.

Back in the office, I was pulled out of my gloomy mood. Jack told me that John X wanted to see me and it sounded rather urgent. I called John X and agreed to go to his office in the American Embassy in Grosvenor Square.

I hailed a cab, puzzled, because John X, normally a rather cool character, had sounded very concerned. At the Embassy, I showed my pass to the guard, and was escorted by another guard along the passage to the elevators and up to John X's floor. The floor number was marked with some cover name and I remember thinking how crazy for them to bother. Everybody knew the CIA was there.

John X offered me coffee, and gestured to one of his comfortable chairs. The CIA had large offices which looked and smelled wealthy and efficient compared to ours. His room was very comfortable, with Chesterfield chairs and couch. His bookshelves were full of American and English law books. Next to the picture of the President was a photograph of John at Harvard, receiving his graduation papers. The secretary brought in the coffee.

'So what's all this about?' I asked.

'Diamonds, Desmond; you know, a girl's best friend. Except these are industrial diamonds.' He went on to explain, in his mild American accent, 'I have received a message from Washington saying that they believe diamonds are reaching Poland and East Germany, obviously for their wire-making and metal-finishing factories.'

'So, how does that affect us?'

'My colleagues at home seem to have information which points the finger towards the Diamond Trading Company – you know, part of the De Beers set-up.' I knew very well the company he was referring to. I also knew that through the Diamond Trading Company (DTC), diamonds were then (as now) a very important contributor to Britain's balance of payments. It was essential that this highly regarded international business should not have its reputation tarnished. If it was indeed involved with marketing diamonds to the Eastern bloc, America would, as John X said, 'blacklist the company and stop importing. We are talking big bucks here, Desmond.'

Speaking my thoughts out loud I said, 'I cannot believe the Diamond Trading Company is involved, or even aware of any of its diamonds reaching behind the Iron Curtain. If they are indeed getting to Poland or East Germany, it must be through one of the Belgian buyers, in Antwerp.' We discussed various possibilities for the remainder of the afternoon.

On the train going home that evening I looked at the faces around me; I wondered if any of these men worked at DTC and if so, whether they knew of any Russian trade. No; they would be blissfully ignorant, I thought. I shuddered at the idea of the international scandal it would cause if indeed De Beers were trading with the Eastern bloc. And the financial blow to the City as a whole if the Americans stopped buying industrial diamonds would be terrible.

The next morning I called Peter Bowie, our liaison officer for all the internationaly operating companies, who I knew had contact with one of the directors of DTC. I asked Peter to get an up-to-date list of all the European diamond buyers. In the meantime Jack and I started checking through intercepts and telegrams to and from DTC and the buying companies in Belgium. We even looked into the possibility of getting the Belgian security services to tap certain Belgian buyers' phones, but it became too complicated and political.

It was refreshing working on strategic trade; it seemed as though it was one of the very few departments that was able to pull in the co-operation of all other departments without the normal back-stabbing and silly games. I suppose that's what comes of being in the department dealing with the physical elements of cold war.

After a month of reading through thousands of intercepts, and thoroughly investigating all the international trading companies and analysing information from many commercial counsellors and consuls, we found no evidence that any European company was involved in diamond smuggling to the Eastern bloc. What we did discover was an ancient diamond-trading trail going from West Africa via the Lebanon. A lot of the diamonds that went to India, and certainly Russia before the revolution, were bought and sold by Lebanese traders. We concluded that the diamonds reaching the Iron Curtain countries emanated from what we thought of as the illicit diamond trade centred mostly in Liberia and other West African countries, and still run by Lebanese traders.

Peter Bowie, Jack and I went for a celebration drink at the club. The three of us wondered where the CIA had received its information implicating DTC.

'You know, the CIA have a lot of chaps in West Africa and Lebanon,' Peter said thoughtfully. 'I wonder why they are not aware of the diamonds circulating in those areas, which are nothing to do with De Beers?'

'God only knows!' I exclaimed. 'I would imagine they are

too busy worrying about oil. Besides, aren't they under the
illusion that DTC is a world monopoly, and that all diamonds
go through their hands?'

'Yes, Desmond, and that has made business difficult for
DTC in America. But even so it surprises me that our
American friends seem so ignorant. When you go to see
John X, ask him about it.'

'I will. I'm seeing him tomorrow.'

Jack offered his cigarettes around. 'You know, what
puzzles me is where the Americans got their information from.'

After a few more drinks, and conversation that went
around and around the same subject, we came to the
conclusion that the KGB had possibly fed a CIA agent with
the rumour in order to tarnish the name of De Beers, thus
reducing American trade with the company, which would
indirectly have a very damaging effect on Britain.

The next day I convinced John X of DTC's innocence, and
that none of the European buyers were in any way involved.
I told him and showed evidence, some of it historical, about
the diamond business run by the Lebanese in West Africa.

It was true; the CIA had no idea, or at least John X
told me they had no idea, of the Lebanese traders. Quite
surprising really, since historically the Lebanese had been
trading in diamonds long before the DTC and so many of
the CIA chaps were history buffs.

He was as glad to hear the news as I was in giving it to
him. I broached the next subject with caution as it could have
been a bit touchy.

'John', I said, clearing my throat, 'Peter, Jack and myself
think it quite possible that the KGB fed misinformation to
one of your agents, perhaps in Poland. The idea would

obviously be to tarnish De Beers with your country, thus undermining the company's trade with the US which would potentially have the devastating effect on Britain we have already discussed.' Lighting a cigarette I continued, 'It means they know the identity of your agent.'

'Yes, Desmond, you could be right.' He thought for a moment, and exclaimed, 'My God! This could be very tricky. I'll have someone look into this idea of yours; you just never know.'

Whether his agent was exposed to the KGB I never found out, but I'm sure if there was a problem John sorted it out. This was the last exciting assignment I was involved in.

Although working on strategic trade was fascinating, there was no way in which this prophylactic exercise achieved more than fifty per cent success. It did, however, slow down the development of the war machine in Russia. Unfortunately this had no effect on Soviet espionage, subversion, disinformation or any other undermining tactics in which Russia and some of its reluctant allies were engaged.

Radio Moscow broadcast the Communist Party rules, and repeatedly slanged Imperialism, a practice at which Russia had become ruthlessly expert. Hypocritically it remained the masthead of their anti-democratic propaganda. Every time the subject was raised, or I read a newspaper article about the Communist Party or a Communist-organised strike, Burgess and Maclean would come to mind, and then, invariably, the uncertainty around Kim Philby.

We were witnessing Soviet Russia practising one of its basic commandments: 'The Communist Parties in the Imperialist countries must render systematic aid to the colonial revolutionary liberation movement of oppressed nationalities generally. The duty of rendering active support to the movements rests primarily upon the workers in the countries upon which the oppressed nations are economically, financially or politically dependent. The Communist Parties must openly recognise the right of colonies to separation and their right to carry on propaganda to this end aimed at independence of the colonies from the Imperialist state. They must recognise their right of armed defence against Imperialism and give active support to this defence by all means in their power. This policy must be adopted by the Communist Party in regard to all oppressed nations.'

This avalanche of directed subversion was what we in the West were up against. The cloud of political fall-out was as effective as the atomic bomb. It permeated the minds of a great percentage of academics, journalists and the so-called intelligentsia of Western Europe. It certainly affected our workforce, causing strikes and a strong rise in the political strength of leftwing unions.

America was also under verbal attack, and the fear this generated led to the McCarthy period of 'Reds under the bed'.

The slowing down of technical aid and supplies was initiated to put off the day when Soviet words of abuse might be turned into active weapons of war.

My Section, because it was actively achieving visible results, became the object of curiosity from other incumbents of 54 Broadway. Fortunately our two offices were at the end of a tortuous corridor at the back of the first floor which kept the less zealous away. One afternoon I returned to my office to find a chap dressed in naval uniform, khaki anorak and tilted naval cap standing in the doorway talking to Jack.

'Excuse me, but what are you doing here?' I asked. 'And what is your name?'

'I just thought I would come and have a look at the department that seems to be faring well against our Russian friends.' He edged into the office. I moved in front of him. 'I have just returned from Germany and heard several reports about your work.'

'Oh, really . . . What was your name again?'

'Blake, George Blake.'

'Well, George, unless you are here officially you can f— off, since we are very busy and don't really appreciate snoopers.'

He turned on his heel. 'Not very friendly, are you?'

'No, we are not, now get out of here,' I retorted angrily.

George Blake was arrested as a Soviet spy some years later, and managed to escape from prison so he could reside in Russia (lucky fellow).

My good friend Ken Mills was back in London working for MI5, and we lunched together regularly, when we would discuss work, Philby, Burgess, and the extraordinary behaviour of Liddell, but usually have a good laugh. We were both still shaken by the Burgess-Maclean affair. In early 1954 – I remember there was snow on the ground – he invited me to join him at his club for lunch. He wanted my opinion.

'I have been offered a job outside the Service and don't know what to do.' He explained that Sir Percy Sillitoe, his old boss, had been invited to take up a post with De Beers. 'Percy wants me to join him. The company is going to set up a security organisation in South Africa to cover its diamond and gold mining interests.'

Hearing the excitement in Ken's voice, and knowing how disillusioned he was with MI5, I told him to go for it, and he did.

I envied Ken a little, and again thought of leaving the Service. By April 1954 the strategic trade work had become more or less routine, and the list of goods and companies we were watching had been whittled down to ten or twenty. The main concern was in the atomic field and in electronic components, mostly manufactured by America. There was neither the workload nor the room left for both Jack and me; and Jack seemed to enjoy the routine, which I did not.

Head office got to hear of my dissatisfaction and, in an attempt to keep me on, asked if I would be interested in going to Buenos Aires as head of MI6 in South America. My cover position would have been passport control officer. I was dumbfounded; so far as we were concerned, passport control was all very well, but every country's security service was well aware that this was British Secret Service cover. Besides, I did not want another upheaval for the family, or to leave the farm. I refused their offer of Buenos Aires and informed them I was going to start looking around for other work.

In May, at one of our weekly lunches, I told Ken of my desire to leave. Two weeks later he invited me to have a chat with Percy Sillitoe at their office at St Andrew's House, High Holborn.

Percy and Ken told me about the diamond smuggling in Liberia and other parts of West Africa, and the problems it was creating for De Beers. They needed another person to join them and wondered if I was interested. Little did either of them realise how close the diamond smuggling game in West Africa had come to causing the possible collapse of the mighty financial empire of De Beers. At that time, neither Ken nor Percy knew that I had been dealing with diamonds and so-called smuggling.

I thought about their offer, and talked about it with Betty over the next few days. She reminded me of how unhappy I had been ever since Philby's retirement. Besides, I felt the climate in the Service was getting worse, not better. Everybody was suspicious of everybody else.

I accepted Sir Percy's offer. I said goodbye to Jack and a couple of the secretaries; all my pals had left the Service long before. I went up to Sinclair, Menzies' replacement as the Chief, and shook his hand.

I received a cheque for two thousand pounds as my pay-off.

In the late summer of 1954 I was still commuting on the train up and down to London. We were still farming; we had pigs, cows, an old Fordson tractor, horses. Pepe had married and moved to Chelmsford. The children were fit and well; Rosanne had been to a couple of schools – she just could not settle down. That was rather how I felt, I suppose, but I was now employed by De Beers and chasing diamond smugglers around . . . and I could feel myself settling down slowly into a much more normal life without the need of deception or secretiveness with family or friends.

17

Questioned by Peter Wright

For the next eighteen months Ken and I thoroughly investigated the illicit diamond trade in West Africa. This included the countries of Sierra Leone, Liberia and the Gold Coast. Sir Percy Sillitoe spent most of his time asleep, dreaming of the sweetshop in Eastbourne which he had purchased on his retirement as chief of MI5.

As I have already mentioned, the so-called illicit diamond trade was a well-established business, with many of the West African governments in the pockets of the Lebanese traders (smugglers). We had meetings with a few government representatives and tried pointing out that this business was paying no taxes to the government, but they were not interested. We were trying to break into a trade that had been established for at least three hundred years. As far as the governments were concerned, the smugglers may not have been paying taxes, but indirectly they were bringing money into the area; as indeed they were.

'After all,' said one Sierra Leone representative in his Eton-cum-Oxford accent, 'the diggers, as you call them, the people picking up or digging up the diamonds, are paid with foreign money and then they spend it in our shops or put it in our banks.'

The good-looking, well-educated, very black African was

right. What's more, policing frontiers against smuggling would be very costly, and virtually impossible due to the wide-open nature of the bushland and semi-desert. Consequently we gave up trying to convince the governments to illegalise the smuggling.

However we did suggest that De Beers set up a buying company with outpost buying houses to purchase diamonds directly from the diggers. We also suggested that the company should start buying from some of the larger smuggling organisations which would make it possible to infiltrate their influence over some of the government officials involved. When they asked how they would persuade smugglers to sell them their goods, we pointed out that selling to De Beers in Africa would save the Lebanese carriers the long, expensive and dangerous journey back home. De Beers took up our suggestion and shortly afterwards had a very successful business going in West Africa, with small buying houses spread around the diamond-producing areas.

Ken, Percy and myself were now out of a job. Ken returned to MI5, Percy retired to his sweetshop in Eastbourne, and I accepted Sir Philip Oppenheimer's offer to stay on with De Beers and head up a security and property department.

Later in 1956 I received a surprise phone call from Ken – a surprise because I had lost touch with him since our lives had taken different directions.

'Hey Des, how are you, old chap?' asked his familiar, well-educated, throaty voice.

I was looking at the plans of a new building which DTC were constructing. 'Very well, old boy, busy as a beaver; and you? How is the old Firm treating you?' I asked, realising how little I missed the SIS.

'I was wondering if you would like to meet for lunch at

my club – you do remember it's the Garrick?' he added sarcastically, rubbing in the fact that we had not met for a long time. 'By the way, hope you don't mind, old chum, but I'm bringing along a friend who wants to meet you, what with you knowing Philby and all that sort of thing. He is one of our new boffins, come here from Marconi's, got all sorts of new devices for listening in on people. Anyway he is fascinated by Philby and has implied on several occasions that he would like to meet you.'

'Sounds good. I'll see you there,' I replied. 'By the way, what's his name?'

'Peter, Peter Wright. You'll like him. Cheerio.'

The Garrick was always a lively club, full of distinguished academics, artists, actors, some famous lawyers and not too many businessmen. Ken and I ordered campari and soda; Peter said, 'I could do with a large gin and tonic, if that's OK.' I still remember his slightly odd pronunciation of 'tonic'.

After the initial social niceties, Ken told Peter about Guy Burgess's antics in Gibraltar and Tangier, and referred to Liddell's comments at the time. The conversation, quite naturally, centred around Burgess and Maclean; this was still a topic of interest and concern, drawing attention as it did to the crass inefficiency of MI5.

Peter asked me a lot of questions about Philby, and wondered if I had any insight into Philby's loyalties.

'I imagine you are concerned about Philby's relationship with that arch-bugger Burgess,' I said. 'I had lunch with Kim not long ago; he is still broke, starting to look scruffy, drinking a lot and looking for a job. . . . I just don't know how he ever tolerated Burgess. Certainly Burgess has put him in the shit. But who in hell tipped off Burgess, and who called off the watchers at Maclean's house over the weekend they disappeared? That is what I would like to know!'

'Well, from what I now know of office procedure, I just don't know who it might have been. It could have been Liddell himself,' said Peter, laughing.

'Do you think Philby had anything to do with Burgess being tipped off about Maclean?' I asked, perhaps hoping for a definite answer one way or the other.

Peter chuckled. 'As you know, Burgess lived with Philby for some time in Washington. It seems obvious the leak was via Philby, and surely it might have been done wittingly, but whether it was any more than a friend telling his friends they were about to get into a lot of trouble – no one knows. Your old Firm, Desmond, seems convinced of his innocence; at least that is the official line.'

'Yes, I know, but if they genuinely believe in his innocence, why virtually sack him? And if there is any doubt, why not investigate him more thoroughly? I know Kim had no difficulty in answering questions from Milmo; Kim is very bright. In a situation like that he would just put on his stutter . . . I mean, Peter, I have had many long chats with Kim when he never stuttered; other times, when it suited him, he stuttered so badly I had to stop listening.'

We talked about my new work while the waiter served us, then I continued. 'I was about to say about Philby – and indeed Burgess and Maclean, but for me more Kim, because I consider him a friend . . . quite a close friend – the whole affair has completely demoralised me as far as ever working for MI6 again is concerned. Let's face it, the Russians must know an awful lot about our whole set-up thanks to Burgess, and just having to wonder whether Kim Philby is or isn't, is paralysing. The whole thing is a joke and I am sure Moscow are laughing at us all.' I was on my high horse and letting out some of my frustration.

Peter put in, 'We in 5 do not believe Philby is innocent, and we are still trying to build a case. Our problem is not being able to find any real proof.'

'What is real proof, Peter?' I asked, bewildered. 'How can any of us who have had anything to do with espionage expect real proof by British law standards? Our whole existence is due to the fact that we operate (or operated) outside the law.'

'Yes, of course; but when it comes to trying to prove a person's guilt we have to have hard evidence,' said Ken, pointing out that I might well be under suspicion also. 'You have known Kim a long time, Des; you are great friends with Tommy Harris, and he was great friends with Burgess – still is with Kim. According to you, Blunt and Liddell are often at Harris's parties . . . and if there is one bugger I don't trust in all of this, it is Blunt.'

Peter looked at me out of the corner of his eye. We decided to change the subject as Ken and I were becoming a bit rattled, and as people filtered out of the club our voices carried further. Peter told me about his work for Marconi's before he joined MI5. We discovered we lived close to each other in Essex and decided that if we should meet on the train we would go out for a drink.

'Perhaps at the Queen Anne's Castle, the old pub near Great Leighs,' said Peter.

Back in the office, I felt very glad to be working for a company that cared for its members and was operating in a relatively sane area of the business world, instead of walking along mind-twisting hallways infested with the suspicious thinking of espionage and counter-espionage.

About two months later Peter and I did meet on the train, and went for a drink to the Queen Anne's Castle, where the low oak beams made it necessary for even me to duck; the smoky, noisy atmosphere and the smell of keg beer were intoxicating, and we could talk without fear of being overheard since the noise level was good and loud.

'Peter, I heard a few days ago from my Spanish tutor at Cambridge; he told me that someone, he thinks from the Service, has been asking him a lot of questions about my political views during the Civil War and if I had been a member of any of the Communist groups at Cambridge.'

'Well – were you?' he asked.

'No, most certainly not.' I went on to explain my views. We then talked about his investigations, how things were with the Americans and Mr Hoover, the Suez Canal crisis, and how Mr Hollis, the Director General, was coping.

Peter did not have much to say about Hollis. 'As for Hoover, Desmond, he is not a nice man in the least. He is paranoid about Communism, cannot and will not get over Maclean, thinks Philby should be in jail; but he is at least talking to us again.'

Peter and I met a few more times, when he would invariably ask more questions about Philby, and what I knew of Tommy Harris, and kept on about Philby's proposed book. I saw him not long after Philby had gone to Beirut. Tommy had reimbursed André Deutsch Ltd, the publishing company, the sum of £3000 – the advance Kim had received from them to write the book. When I told Peter this he remarked, with a twinkle in his eye, 'You do know them well, don't you, Desmond?'

I didn't see him again for some time.

*　　*　　*

By Christmas 1958 I had completely settled into my work in the normal world. Life at De Beers was both interesting and straightforward, and I was enjoying being who I was supposed to be, instead of always pretending. Santa Claus was my only secret identity. The Diamond Trading Company was growing by leaps and bounds; the buying office in West Africa was very successful, the new building was finished. Apart from my odd meetings with Ken and Peter my connection with the old Firm grew fainter and fainter.

The farm in Essex was coming along slowly. I had four stockings to fill that Christmas Eve, as our fourth child, William Tomas, had been born on October 29th 1955. His godfathers were Tommy Harris and Ken Mills. (Perhaps it is because he has two MI5 chaps as godparents, and me as his father, that he is writing this book with me now; an inherited interest.)

It has often been said to me, once a member of the Secret Service, always a member. One day in late January 1958 the telephone rang. It was Mary Neigh, the London representative who had come out to Madrid. Since our return to England, her family and ours had become friends, and I was expecting her to ask us to an after-Christmas party or something. Instead she asked if I would be prepared to undertake a mission for the old Firm which would last about a week, and would involve my going to Tangiers.

Rather taken aback, I said, 'It depends what it is.' Then, realising my duties lay elsewhere, I added, 'And whether the managing director here will give me clearance.'

The managing director, knowing about my previous occupation, readily agreed. The next day I telephoned Mary and suggested we meet somewhere away from the old Firm's offices as I did not want to be seen anywhere near them. I don't know why I even entertained the idea of working for them again. Looking back I'm not sure if it was not due to nostalgia as much as anything.

We met at a Chinese restaurant in Soho. She was early, as usual, and had already ordered for both of us by the time I arrived. The slow ting-tang chimes of Chinese music and the dull light of the Chinese lanterns created a very appropriate atmosphere.

Mary was very businesslike, and got straight to the point. She asked if I remembered a Moroccan sergeant whom I had harboured, and MI6 had taken on, while I was in Algiers. I certainly did. He had been recommended to me by Doudot for his initiative, *savoir-faire* and general reliability, along with his hatred of the Germans. I had last seen him when he had just volunteered for active service and was about to be parachuted into Italy behind German lines.

'So what is this to do with me now?' I asked.

'Well,' she replied, 'he is now the head of the newly formed Moroccan security service and he has contacted our agent in Tangiers (David Y), a newspaper correspondent – you know Teddy Dunlop resigned not long after you left Madrid? Anyway, our friend has spoken to David about you and has stated quite firmly that before establishing any kind of liaison with MI6 he wants to discuss the details with you.'

'How very flattering,' I answered. I must admit it was a bit of a thrill to be asked back in, especially knowing it was only going to last for a week. A quick in and out, as it were. She gave me a few more details, and I thought for a while.

'OK, providing you let me make my own travel arrangements and the company reimburses my expenses through an exterior account of theirs, I'll go.' I smiled and said, 'But this will be the one and only time.'

Maybe my condition about travel arrangements was paranoia on my part, but as I told her, 'All Firm travel outfits are blown.' That is certainly what I thought then, and whether they were or not, she agreed to my conditions.

The restaurant had filled up with tourists and when an American couple sat at the table next to us Mary reduced her voice to almost a whisper. 'You will meet David Furgueson, our head man in Rabat, at the bar of the Hotel Minza in Tangiers, where he will organise a room for you to stay and – '

I interrupted, wagged my finger at her and said loudly, 'No! I would rather organise my own hotel as well, thank you.'

'OK,' she said, looking a little put out. 'You will meet him at the Hotel Minza bar where he will brief you. I don't have the details with me . . . for obvious reasons.'

On the appointed day in March I found myself on the BOAC flight from Heathrow. I must confess it was exciting to be back in the world of secrets; it was like going on an exciting adventure, and maybe I overplayed the importance of it, but it was fun.

I arrived in the early evening; the sunset was creating a wonderful red glow in the rapidly disappearing heat haze coming off the desert sands. I was reminded of how very quickly the evenings became cold in that part of the world.

The last time I had been in North Africa was in the middle of the war, and things had changed a little. Tangiers airport had been modernised and seemed very busy, with hundreds of Arab families arriving and leaving. There were still one or two jeeps, now operating as taxis. I jumped in one and asked for my hotel. The streets were full of people wrapped up in bundles of clothes, walking around and shopping. Chickens, goats, cheese, fruit, vegetables, carpets, lamps, camels, all sorts of things were on the market considering how late in the day it was. And the air was thick; amazingly, the smell of the animals was completely overpowered by the strong scents of herbs and spices – vanilla, cinnamon, cumin, cillentro, mint, pepper – it was almost intoxicating.

I checked in at the little hotel I had chosen and decided to walk to the Minza. Besides thinking it would be quicker in such traffic, I thought it would give me a chance to feel part of the hustle and bustle, and get used to moving amongst the Arabs. Straight from London as I was, I could not help being conspicuous, and at every other corner a young man would come up and offer hash; men with trays of gold and silver trinkets tried everything to entice money out of my pocket, and carpet traders grabbed my sleeves. By the time I arrived at the Minza, I had learnt to spot the more aggressive traders, and had developed a sidestepping technique.

I walked through the beautifully tiled lobby of the Hotel Minza, with its arched windows and doorways, into the lounge bar with its sumptuous Persian carpets. Our man in Rabat, David Furgueson, was easy to recognise. He looked very much the English charmer, and was reading *The Times*. He obviously recognised me, as he got up when I entered and asked if I wanted a drink.

'Very much so,' I answered, feeling a little worn out by my walk. 'What the hell is going on here? It's not Ramadan is it?' I asked.

'Well, Desmond, as a matter of fact it is.'

'Oh God! I thought so. Even the airport was packed and the Arabs don't like to fly all that much . . . unless it's on a carpet of course,' I added somewhat sarcastically.

The French bartender, wearing a fez, nodded a greeting

of recognition to David. I guessed he must have been one of his agents.

David was younger than myself, well-tanned and tough-looking, and very charming. I had made a point of reading up on his background on the plane trip over. I can't say I liked him at that moment, I was annoyed that neither he nor anyone else in the Firm's office had thought about Ramadan.

This is the period in the Islamic calendar when Muslims are required to fast during the day; they then eat, and eat, and eat at night. It is a very family-orientated period, when an Arab meeting a European in a public place would be very noticeable, and it would be impossible to meet at his house. It would only be possible to meet at some unearthly hour of the night.

I put this over to David, letting him know I was none too pleased. He then informed me he had not been able to fix a time with the head of security, and hoped our Moroccan friend would be able to see me later that evening.

I had a short meeting with my old acquaintance, who was very glad to see me, as I was him. We talked about his appointment as head of security and what he wanted from me. When he explained his requirements I realised it would take more than a week to sort out all the details, especially liaising with London. I explained I only had a week; he explained apologetically that after that evening he would not be able to do anything for the month of Ramadan. I persuaded him to liaise with the head of station in Tangiers when the month was over.

The next morning I called David and asked him to organise my trip home. Three days later I landed at Heathrow feeling furious. What a waste of taxpayers' money. Could the Firm not get anything right? Fancy them not checking on the dates of Ramadan, and David Furgueson not establishing that I was available for only a limited time. I realised how glad I was not to be surrounded by their crass inefficiency any longer. It reminded me of how often agents had been sent into the field wearing English clothes with the labels still attached, and the agent in Algiers whom they were sending to Italy with an ID photograph showing him wearing a specifically English shirt. No wonder the Americans lost faith; so had I.

Poor Betty; when I got home I verbalised my outrage about the Firm to her; and I was angry. The next day I wrote a stinking letter informing head office of my opinion, and that under no circumstances would I ever do anything for them ever again. Whether they built up a successful relationship with the Moroccan security department or not, I don't know; I didn't care then and I still don't.

In September 1962 Peter Wright called me in my office, asking to meet me at Liverpool Street station one evening. I suggested that same evening by the shoe-repair shop next to platform 9. I arrived a little early and watched one or two of the remaining steam trains puff out of the station, and the commuters coming from the underground in their droves. The *Evening Standard* paperman yelled out the latest headlines: 'Read all about it.' I wondered what Peter Wright could want; he would not have called me after all this time just to have a chat for old times' sake – we did not know each other well enough.

It had not been a good year. I was fed up with commuting such a distance; the farm had become much harder work with very little financial reward; John, my eldest son, wanted to emigrate to Canada and become a Mountie, or sail to Australia. What the hell did someone from MI5 want with me now? I made up my mind before Peter arrived that I was not going to accept a job of any sort.

I saw him walking slowly over. He was easy to pick out as everyone around him was in a hurry. He looked older and worried.

'Hello, Desmond.' He sounded tired.

'Hello, Peter, you look as though you need a drink.'

'Yes, I do. Do you mind if we wait for the buffet train?'

'Fine by me.' I checked the time on the departure board. We had fifteen minutes. 'Let's have a quick snifter in the pub,' I suggested.

We chatted casually. Peter had moved to Thorpe Le Soken, near Frinton. We were looking for a house near Witham as the drive from the farm to Chelmsford station was too tiring, and the farm was too much work.

We were the first on the buffet train. Peter walked straight to the bar and bought a gin and tonic and a whisky and soda. We sat down. Peter took a swig on his gin, looked me straight in the face and said, 'Desmond, I need a full written report on everything you can remember about Philby, from the day you met him.' I looked at Peter and thought about what he was asking me to do.

'You must have found something new on him – or are your masters just creating a fuss again?'

'No, they are not. I am, though, and I have some information which confirms our worst suspicions; and it seems as though he is going to confess.'

'So what do you need a written report from me for?' Peter did not answer straight away. I felt my bubble of delusion about Philby burst completely. Well, at least all my questioning about him was over. Somehow I was not as angry about his deception as I might have been. I still vaguely wondered if he might be a double double agent (romantic folly). When Peter said what he said, I felt a tightening in my stomach.

'Well, it seems as though you are one of his close friends who was on the right side, and I am collecting every piece of information on him possible.'

I remember thinking, how convenient for the present-day office to have its old members to spy on. It annoyed me.

'Why the hell are you bothering with all this? The Secret Service is about as secret as the Eamonn Andrews Show, the office treats us all so badly. Why the hell did they re-employ Kim – just to get him to admit to being a bad boy so you can bring him home, smack his hand and make him stand in the corner with a dunce's hat on? Besides, I don't suppose you will bring him home. If those idiots Burgess and Maclean got away, I can't imagine 5 outsmarting Kim at this stage of the game.'

I realised it must have been Peter who had sent someone to question my old tutor at Cambridge about my political views. I wondered if he was still delving – even still suspicious that I might be involved with Philby – or if his investigations had made it clear I was not.

However, I agreed to write a report on Philby. Here it is, as close to the original as I can remember.

September 1962

Dear Peter,

The first time I met Kim Philby was at my initial interview with Felix Cowgill in 1941. Kim, a gentle-looking man with smiling eyes and an air of confidence, was wearing an old sports jacket with leather elbows. He sat behind Felix making notes, and only interrupted a few times to ask me to repeat myself. My first impression was of a man with quiet intellectual charm.

My second meeting with Kim Philby took place when he drove me up to St Albans. During this drive I realised he was in charge of organising the Iberian section of Section V of MI6. I immediately liked him and knew working with him was going to be fun and interesting. He had a spiritual tranquillity about him. He was very unassuming and modest.

From before I arrived and for a little time afterwards, Section V increased in numbers, as Philby gathered together a team of intellectual adventurers, all of us speaking at least two languages fluently. During my nine and a half months at St Albans we had many discussions and even arguments, but never any rows. Philby was an able 'chef d'orchestre'. I never witnessed him lose his temper. He and I would often go to the pub together, either on my motorcycle, in his car or on foot. My conversations with Kim were often about hypothetical political situations consisting of a lot of ifs and buts. Our families would always enter as a point of interest of health and well-being, and he would always encourage me to have them near me, certainly while I was at St Albans. He and his wife, Aileen, my wife and I would often have meals together. The evening sessions in the snakepit were usually called by Philby and terminated by him, unless members of other departments appeared. He was invariably the centre of the group, and even those from other departments found themselves drawn to his magnetic personality.

He had great admiration for Hugh Trevor-Roper, but the association was purely business. Hugh did not fall for his charm and remained aloof.

For the game of espionage and counter-espionage we could not have had a better teacher and leader; he guided the department with a careful, disciplined and nurturing warmth. We worked hard, long hours, enjoying every minute as our imaginations were allowed to flow and be expressed. I certainly feel the success of our department was largely due to Philby. He was very thorough and he himself worked harder than anyone.

As far as friends go, he was certainly one of my best friends at that time. We had some common ground: Cambridge, the fact that we were raised as expatriates, that our parents had lived abroad and sent us to England for our education. We both liked art, we both liked drinking and conversation, whether idle or constructive.

I can say without any doubt his best friend was and is Tommy Harris, whom Kim introduced me to at Christmas 1941, the same time I met Kim's mother. He spent a lot of time talking with Herbert Hart [MI5's ISOS specialist] and appeared to have a close relationship with him. A person Kim expressed admiration for was Tar Robertson.

I remember Kim having a certain conflict with Felix Cowgill. He wanted ISOS Ultra information to be shared with more departments, whereas Felix wanted to retain control. On the one hand, Felix was almost too possessive; but on the other hand, Kim often appeared to be quite prepared to pass on information freely and risk knowledge of ISOS reaching the Germans.

The Garbo situation. As far as our department was concerned, Philby made all the major decisions, as Cowgill would not make a move without him. Kim remained calm, slightly aloof and very much in control of every move.

From 1942–44 I was abroad as the Section V man in Gibraltar and then Algiers. From those two stations Philby seemed to be running the English end very well.

After the war Philby and I moved into different departments and only saw each other socially, usually at Tommy and Hilda Harris's rather decadent parties. Always a heavy drinker, he appeared to have started drinking excessively.

1947 I was stationed in Madrid and from then on my only contact with Kim was the occasional phone call and letter. Visits to Tommy and Hilda's house in Majorca, or their visits to Madrid, would often include a conversation or two about Kim.

After the flight of Burgess and Maclean he was posted to Madrid by the *Observer*. During his stay we saw a certain amount of each other despite my being warned not to by the office. We did not talk about their defection, or about Kim being asked to leave the Service; he always sidestepped the issue. I assumed at the time that he was very upset about the whole affair. I would say he was preoccupied. He was joined by Lady Frances Lindsay-Hogg, about whom he told me very little, other than that she was a friend from the Civil War days. With most of my friends, and with Philby in the past, we would have talked about Frances, about who she was, etc. He even avoided talking about Tommy and Hilda. He maintained a barrier I did not want to transgress.

On my return to London, again I met up with Kim at Tommy and Hilda's parties. When I left the Service he and I would have lunch together. It was during this period

I noticed a decline in his outward appearance, especially after his acquittal by Macmillan in 1955. To round off, Peter, I regard Kim Philby as a friend who has partially died, as far as I'm concerned. The suspicion about his loyalties has created so much doubt in my mind about him as a friend, but more doubt about the abilities of my past employers, that I find it hard and somewhat painful to think about him in a clear, positive fashion. Whether your present investigations prove he is a Soviet agent or not, the fact that he has shaken the very foundation of the Secret Service in the way he has is partly his doing and partly the doing of the Services themselves.

Yours sincerely

Desmond Bristow

Now, with the privilege of hindsight, it is easy for me to see suspicious acts and searching words in conversations, but to say I was truly suspicious of Kim at the time would be a lie.

Perhaps I should have been angry with him for coming to see me in Madrid after he had been let off the hook, and was still under suspicion, but it was, and still is, very difficult to contemplate one's good friend being a traitor whether for a worthy cause (in his eyes) or not.

At Christmas 1962–63 Betty and I received a card from Beirut. The picture on the front was of three bedouins heading East. The message read simply, 'Have a Happy Christmas and a Happy New Year. May not see you for a while. Love, Kim'. It was his way of telling me he was the third man.

*   *   *

I wrote my report. Philby defected. We moved house to Rivenhall, near Witham, and Peter and I became regular train-travelling companions. On the train, and in the pub near the station in Witham, Peter started to confide in me much of the contents of his book. I remember he was scared and felt very lonely.

One evening we were at our usual table in the buffet carriage. A cricket match was in progress on the playing fields of Brentwood School, and I commented that it must have been a good game to have lasted so late into the evening. We were talking about Harold Wilson and the unions, when Peter sat forward in his chair and indicated that he wanted to say something quietly in my ear. 'Desmond, I am at the point where I cannot talk to anybody in the office and I only trust a couple of my colleagues. It is quite awful, but I am convinced there is still a mole in MI5 and I do not know what to do about it.'

Not quite sure what to say, or why Peter was suddenly using me as his father confessor, I replied, 'Peter, when I left MI6 I thought the whole outfit was full of moles and as it turned out I was not far wrong.' I was of course joking, trying to make light of what he had said. There were many loyal people still working for MI6 when I left, but I did not really want to talk about them or the Service very much. 'Do you not think one gets to the stage when one starts to suffer from mole mania?'

I do not want to repeat the contents of *Spycatcher*, but over the next year or so Peter confided in me about many of the suspicions he disclosed in the book. He convinced me that Sir Roger Hollis was definitely a Russian mole, and I convinced him that Liddell, if not actively a Russian mole, had certainly helped the cause by defending Burgess and Blunt, and that it was Liddell who had brought Blunt out of retirement from the Service to check all of Burgess's personal belongings.

Cyril Mills has accused Peter Wright of being a traitor and a liar; perhaps that means that Mills himself had something to hide, or perhaps he was ashamed of having been duped by the Russian moles, or of having lied about his own accomplishments connected with Garbo. Whatever Mills's motive, there is no conceivable way in which Peter has ever betrayed his country. My feeling is that the security service or the politicians betrayed him, as they betrayed many loyal employees through sheer lack of compassion or understanding. Perhaps the politicians were so ashamed of the way in which the government has ignored information and advice from people such as Peter Wright that they tried to create a block, and paid dearly for it.

My last meeting with Peter was in 1988 when Betty and I were visiting our eldest son and his family in Australia. I called from my son's house just outside Melbourne and arranged to visit Peter. He seemed very hesitant at first. Undaunted by his reserve, Betty, John and I, after a wonderful drive through Tasmania, arrived in Cygnet, where I telephoned Peter again.

He still seemed hesitant, but agreed to see us. I don't know if he thought I had come to check up on him, or whether he was embarrassed by his living conditions. We arrived at a shack which consisted of three rooms covered with tin sheet roofing, sheltered by gum trees. The surrounding fields were very waterlogged, which was marvellous for the mosquitoes, not for the Wrights. The floors were filthy dirty, the kitchen was in chaos and quite obviously every penny went into the horses. Once over his initial surprise at seeing me and

Betty again, Peter relaxed and showed us the stables. 'The horses have been our saviour from financial ruin, would you believe?'

He explained how the area was infested with deadly poisonous tiger snakes, and how when walking outside one always had to wear wellington boots to avoid being bitten.

The case against him still seems very strange to me. I cannot see why *Spycatcher* was so disturbing to Maggie Thatcher and the government. OK, Hollis was knighted, but so was Blunt, and that is their fault, not Wright's. Peter, on his retirement, received a pension of £2000 per annum.

As we were saying goodbye I remembered the time Peter had come to me with tears in his eyes. 'Desmond, I simply cannot afford the Welsh farm; the office have cheated me on my pension,' he had told me. I had been slightly incredulous.

'Yes. Like a fool I took their word for it, and did not insist on a contract; and they have cheated me, and I cannot live on £2000 a year.'

When we left Peter's shack we decided to spend another day exploring Tasmania, and we learnt about the terrible massacre of the Aboriginals on the island. The following day we took off from the little airport, and as I looked down on the sumptuous green of Tasmania, my last conversation with Peter ran through my mind; I thought about some of the amazing achievements of England, and Englishmen, and how far the Empire had once stretched, and some of the atrocities committed to further it. Peter had had no part in such dishonourable deeds. He had served his country in the field of espionage. Yet he would have been better off betraying his country, confessing, and being granted immunity like Sir Anthony Blunt; or defecting and running to

Russia. Instead he had worked conscientiously, and applied himself wholeheartedly to the security of the country, to end up living in a shack surrounded by snakes because the government had reneged on his pension. What a terrible and sad truth about my country. Peter Wright is not the only person who has been treated like a disposable piece of human rubbish by the security services.

I went over in my mind once again the whole affair which led to Peter Wright's investigations of the Service as head of the Fluency committee, starting with the defection of Maclean and Burgess. Why were the people watching Maclean taken off duty, allowing the two of them to escape to Russia? Why did Dick White arrive at their port of departure with an out-of-date passport? My conclusion is that the government did not want to deal with two traitors publicly; it might have led to a hanging and have caused a great deal of friction with the Soviet Union. I feel sure the same applies to the inadequate cross-examinations and investigations of Kim Philby, which came to the public conclusion of insubstantial evidence. The government just hoped he would run for the skirts of mother Russia sooner than he did.

18

Tommy Harris

Anyone who has read anything about Tommy Harris before will realise there are many questions about him which are and will probably remain unanswered. It is true to say that I knew Tommy Harris well; on the other hand, there is part of him I perhaps knew then, and know now, but did not and do not want to believe.

He was a romantic figure, often referred to as Jesus Christ because he looked like the paintings. He was an explorer with his mind and with art. These days, living in Spain, I will often smell the smoke of black tobacco cigarettes, which reminds me of him. With the number of his pictures hanging on our walls, and the pieces of furniture he gave us scattered through our house, few days go by when he does not enter our thoughts and conversations. Yes, I am saying he has a permanent presence in our house. He was perhaps one of the most complete human beings I have ever known; he was capable of tremendous displays of generosity, giving friends wonderful gifts, yet at times he could be very intolerant, especially towards his wife Hilda. He had a penetrating imagination and a far-reaching intellect. His soft, soulful eyes would suddenly take on a wild look when he had a bright idea, and would retain a certain wild, glazed look when he was painting or sculpting.

Some of the following details were written by Anthony Blunt in the foreword to the catalogue of the Lefevre Gallery when they held an exhibition of Tommy's work in 1954. The foreword is long and perhaps over-detailed, but gives an in-depth account of his background.

Tomas Harris was born in 1908, in London, whither his English father Lionel and his Spanish mother Enriqueta had returned after many years in Spain. During their life in Spain Lionel and Enriqueta had accumulated a great deal of knowledge and artifacts of Spanish furniture, ceramics, tapestries, jewellery, lace and paintings. On returning to London the Harrises opened a gallery in the rich and fashionable Conduit Street, Mayfair, enabling the public and connoisseurs to admire and buy Spanish works of art, ranging from the fifteenth up to the nineteenth century, never seen before in England. Royalty and dignitaries became regular visitors to the Spanish Art Gallery. Tommy, growing up in this world of art and beautiful things, showed his artistic talent at a very early age. He was fourteen and a half when he won a Trevelyan-Goodall Scholarship to the Slade School of Art (at that time the most important art school in England). When he had completed his course at the Slade he spent a year at the British Academy in Rome, where he developed an interest in Goya and El Greco. In 1930 his career as an artist was interrupted by his decision to enter his father's firm, but while working there he continued to paint, and used his opportunities to enlarge and deepen his knowledge of the great artists of the past, particularly Goya and El Greco. In the business, he very quickly showed an uncanny talent for dealing in antique furniture and paintings.

During the Civil War Tommy made numerous trips to northern Spain where he purchased many paintings and pieces of antique furniture and jewellery from Spanish refugees. He liaised from time to time with a Russian art dealer supposedly practising the same trade. On one such trip he apparently met Philby, I believe in Burgos, and I have heard tales of Tommy acting as a courier for Kim, taking *Times* correspondence to France.

In 1937, Tommy and his father decided to hold an exhibition of their own large Goya collection, to raise money for the Spanish Red Cross who were helping victims of the Civil War. The exhibition was opened by Tommy's friend, the art historian Anthony Blunt. The exhibition, a resounding success, instantly aroused great interest in Goya, up till then generally ignored in England.

At the outbreak of World War Two Tommy and Hilda were recruited by Burgess as cook and housekeeper for Section D of MI5, which was later disbanded and made into SOE.

When Section D was disbanded Tommy was kept on and moved to B Section of MI5; a surprising jump, except that Blunt was Liddell's assistant at the time. Tommy was more than capable of the work intellectually, but had Blunt not introduced him to Liddell (who was a sucker for artists and art connoisseurs), Liddell would have been unaware of Tommy's potential. By 1941 Tommy was in a position to recommend Philby as head of the Iberian section of Section V.

Tommy, well established in B Section, in the bowels of MI5, later became case officer to Juan Pujol (otherwise known as Garbo). The success with which Garbo was built up over the years prior to D Day is certainly due in part to Juan Pujol (Garbo), but it owes much more to the penetrating imagination of Tomas Harris.

I had witnessed the way in which Tommy started his initial correspondence with the Germans. After the war was over, Tommy would sometimes talk about the fun he and Garbo had had creating fictitious characters dotted around various parts of the world. He explained that the real problem had been convincing the Germans that their imaginary characters existed; once the Germans showed their belief, the fun was in the making up of stories to send to the Abwehr – rather like writing a play for an already captive audience. Cyril Mills has been heard to claim that he was responsible for bringing Garbo into England, and acted as his case officer. Cowgill and Philby were responsible for bringing Garbo into England. I interviewed Garbo under the administrative eye of Mills, but as the latter could speak no language except English he was sent to Canada as a liaison officer with the Mounties and from time to time acted as an agent for Garbo.

Anyone who has read about the exploits of Garbo will be well aware of Tommy's contribution. I remember him receiving the OBE, and after the ceremony telling me about his interview with General Eisenhower. 'At the end of our talk, Desmond, the General leant across his very large and very ugly desk and said to me' – Tommy mimicked Eisenhower's accent – "You know, Mr Harris, your work with Mr Pujol most probably amounts to the equivalent of a whole army division; you have saved a lot of lives, Mr Harris." The General stood up, put out his hand, and said, "I thank you, Mr Harris. I thank you very much."'

Many people have suggested Tommy was a Russian agent; and from the point of view of a Soviet spy set-up he was in an ideal situation. There was Blunt as Liddell's personal secretary, Philby as head of Iberian Section V –

and Tommy as head of the Iberian section of MI5, and then as a case officer of the world's most successful wartime deception agent.

During and after the war, the parties chez Harris were the congregating ground for Blunt, Burgess, Philby and, to a lesser extent, Maclean.

After the war Tommy wrote a report containing a very detailed account of his work with Garbo. He showed me his copy just before handing it over to Liddell. According to someone who was searching through the files for a copy of this report, it is now missing; or maybe MI5 are reluctant to reveal its contents for some strange reason; or Liddell misplaced it; perhaps he sent it to the Russians. Or perhaps Tommy never submitted it to Liddell.

I have been told that Tommy managed to persuade Blunt to authenticate fake paintings, which would relate to something Aracelli (Juan Pujol's wife) told Betty and me during a conversation in 1986. She said that shortly after the war Juan and Tommy started up a fake painting business in Caracas. They had sold several fakes when their business was cut short by a Venezuelan art expert, who discovered one or two of the forgeries in a famous collection. So it would seem Blunt was indeed persuaded by Tommy to authenticate the fakes. My question is whether it was for money, or perhaps as a favour to a Soviet agent colleague?

Another nagging question, and I have many about Tommy, which concerns Aracelli, goes back to 1947 when I became head of station in Madrid. Aracelli returned to Madrid and was expecting Juan Pujol to follow her but after six months she realised she had been abandoned. According to Aracelli, Tommy would sometimes see her and help her out financially; when he stopped helping her, she rented a house from friends and in turn rented out rooms to support herself. Juan Pujol had sold off all her jewellery ˉand belongings to finance himself. Why did Tommy never tell me about this situation, I ask myself. He would have known that I would have helped Aracelli; he would also have known I would have contacted Pujol about her. There was definitely a conspiratory aspect to the post-war Pujol-Harris relationship.

I was blissfully unaware of this during my time as MI6 man on the Iberian Peninsula, and Betty and I spent some wonderful weekends at Tommy and Hilda's retreat house at Camp de Mar, near Palma in Majorca. And back in England we went to most of the parties at their wonderful house at 1 Logan Place. Of course Blunt and Philby were at several of these, and it was at one of these parties that Tommy had publicly suggested Kim should write a book about his achievements and work for the Services, and about his withdrawal from Washington and early retirement because of his friendship with Guy Burgess. It was Tommy who secured the contract to publish with André Deutsch Ltd on Kim's behalf, and Tommy who, after a year of trying to persuade Kim to write the book, reimbursed the £3000 advance. Why, I wonder? Perhaps it was Russian money.

As I have said, Betty and I invited Tommy to be our fourth child's godfather. We had some marvellous times with Tommy and Hilda.

In the late autumn of 1958, on a Sunday evening after one of their big Saturday-night, near-Christmas parties, Hilda, Betty, Tommy and I were about to sit down to scrambled eggs. Tommy had gone to the kitchen for a serving spoon when the door buzzer buzzed – they had a security system with a camera at the door and an intercom. Tommy pressed the enter button and walked into the dining room. As soon as Tommy sat down there was a knock on the kitchen door, which Tommy had left open, and a voice said, 'Hello, I'm back for Christmas.'

Much to our surprise Kim Philby walked into the dining room. We had not seen Kim for some time. His wife Aileen had recently died under very strange circumstances; it had even been suggested that he might have murdered her, or had her killed. He was rather taken aback to see Betty and me, and started backing out of the room, apologising that he could not stay as he was catching a train to Oxford. It was very obvious that he had needed to talk to Tommy. Late that evening, after we had all retired to bed, the telephone rang and Tommy had a very long conversation. The next morning Betty asked Hilda who the late call was from. 'Oh, Kim.' She sounded irritated. 'He often calls but I never know what about.'

Not long after the New Year we went to a party with Tommy and Hilda. We drove back with them to Logan Place, and had just got out of the car when they started to argue. By the time we had reached the house they were yelling and screaming at each other. Hilda walked into the kitchen and poured herself a drink. Tommy followed, only to have a plate thrown at him. Tommy started to yell in such a fashion that Betty and I began to feel nervous for their safety. Hilda began crying hysterically and came rushing out of the kitchen and into the living room. Betty followed and tried to comfort her. I went in and asked Tommy if he was all right. There were a couple of broken plates on the kitchen floor. Tommy was sitting on a stool, running his hands through his hair. 'Oh Christ, Desmond, I am sorry about this.'

Betty convinced me that, if we could possibly persuade

them to, they should come with us to Essex instead of staying in London for the weekend. Tommy accepted. He walked over and put his hand on my shoulder. 'Can Betty take Hilly to the car, and I'll collect a few belongings. Could you pour me a scotch?'

I asked no questions, and on the drive I think Betty and I talked about the cows.

The next morning Betty asked Hilda why they had suddenly started to argue. Hilda explained that it happened a lot, and if the argument wasn't about the book on Goya that Tommy was working on, then it was about Philby.

Tommy and Hilda started to spend much more time in Majorca, only coming over to London occasionally to shop, or when Tommy wanted to sell a painting. Consequently we saw very little of them between then and the fateful day in 1964 when Tommy crashed his car and died.

The day after the accident Betty answered the telephone to a very distraught Hilda. 'Betty, Tommy is dead, he killed himself in a car accident yesterday.'

Betty, in a state of semi-shock, asked if he had been alone, and Hilda explained that she had been in the car with him and felt it was her fault, and so on and so on. Poor Hilda. I agreed to fly out and help her however I could. On my arrival I retrieved the smashed-up car from Spanish customs. Hilda was very upset at the sight of the car and that evening she told me the whole story. 'Oh, Desmond! What have I done?' she said. I poured her a large brandy and asked, 'What do you mean? For God's sake tell me what happened, Hilly.'

'Tommy and I went to Palma, he had a meeting with his antique dealer, Señor Acosta. After the meeting Tommy wanted to take some of his latest ceramics to the ceramista to be fired. I went off to do some shopping while he went to see Acosta. We agreed to meet down by the little port. I finished shopping so I went and sat down outside the port restaurant to wait for him. When Tommy arrived he seemed in a tetchy mood. We had a couple of drinks and then an argument ensued; don't ask me what about, I haven't a clue; most probably I was angry with him for being late.'

Her hands were shaking so much she spilt some brandy on the floor. She took a deep breath and continued. 'Well . . . we set off, and Tommy drove like hell, and the more I asked him to be careful the faster he went, until we crossed a small humpback bridge, the car left the ground, he lost control, we skidded into a tree and I was thrown out. When I came to he was still in the car, not moving or breathing or anything. I can't believe it.' She took another large sip of brandy, and wiped the tears off her face. She rocked back and forth in her chair. 'Why, Desmond? Why?'

I did not know what to say. I am not very good in that sort of situation; besides, it was a bit of a shock for me. Sniffing hard, she continued, 'He was killed instantly. As you can see, I received a few bumps and bruises on my face and arm.' She burst into tears. Unable to restrain my own emotions I walked over, took her in my arms and joined her.

The next day I checked with the police report and every-thing tallied. Tommy's untimely death at the age of fifty-five deprived the world of perhaps the foremost post-war Goya specialist, and a very talented artist. I quote from an article written by Enrique Lafuente Ferrari (the director of the Museum of Modern Art in Madrid) in 1957. 'Expressionism seems to be the most exact definition of his work. But there is nothing about his draughtsmanship to suggest his

Spanish blood. The penetrating precision of his lines suggests something of intellectual torment which certainly is very little Spanish. Some affinity with Grunewald, Van Gogh and Münch seems to proclaim itself in the analytical, bold annotations which Harris uses to give his forms perspective. There was already something of this quality in his Malaga landscapes. Since then his style has deepened its own qualities, gaining in sureness and fire – *a frigid intellectual fire.*'

I don't know if Tomas Harris worked for the Russians or not; all I can say is that I find it hard to believe that a man with his talents, his intellect and his imagination would not have known of Philby's, Blunt's and Burgess's activities. For myself I also find it hard to believe that he actively participated: knowing Tommy, he was more than likely just amused to know he had friends working for the opposite side. My wife Betty, on the other hand, feels very strongly that he did work for the Russians; she also admits it was more than likely for the amusement value. Perhaps I was too personally involved with him, and I admit I was very fond of him, to see or want to see the evidence. Even now, with the evidence in front of me, I want there to be an explanation of his innocence.

Could this be how we all felt at the time of the defections, besides feeling like complete fools? Now, as I finish writing this book, I realise why writing it has been a long process for me; for at the end one very important friend was a traitor and another very important friend may also have been a traitor.

As I sit here with my son Bill reflecting happily for the most part, but sadly as far as the behaviour of those in authority is concerned, I realise that the investigations of Philby, which went on for ten years, and the prolonged investigations of most of the others, and the whole case against Peter Wright served the politicians not the country.

Of course, Philby was allowed to escape. Perhaps he was even encouraged. To have brought him back to England and convicted him as a traitor would have been even more embarrassing; and when they convicted him, could they really have hanged him? The press would have had a field day.

I have never seriously thought of life as a Secret Service man as anything but normal, but as Bill points out it is by no means what most people do or even think of doing. In writing this book and having had very lengthy discussions about the politics we played in the Services as opposed to the politics diplomats or politicians played, I realise he is right. As head of the Iberian section, on many occasions I witnessed some terrible diplomatic blunders. Following these blunders, one of my Spanish friends in Government would contact me to talk about the situation. They wanted me to try and rectify when all I could do was pacify and help keep relationships friendly. The work has frustrated me greatly when I think of how much talent Britain truly had, and still has, and how many countries used to respect us. It was soul destroying during the years following the war, witnessing one stupid mistake made after another.

On my retirement from MI6 in 1954 I had regrets about leaving. I rapidly had to 'brainwash' myself of the job, the environment and most of the people. Fortunately, being at home with a young family, a small farm and the animals to attend to, this was not difficult; and Madrid, Gibraltar, Algiers and the 54 Broadway buildings were cast into the oblivion of my subconscious mind. The various jobs and countries I had served in had given me wide experience and some wonderful adventures. Most colleagues and some bosses were amiable, and co-operative. As in any other business, there were those who were objectionable, but for the latter part of my career I was able to pick out those with whom to associate, whether for social or professional reasons. Some stayed friends after I left.

Joining the great big world outside was intimidating, but the transit was helped by working with my old friend Ken Mills, the friendliness and sense of humour of the Diamond Trading directors and the clear welcome I received from almost all in that enterprise.

It was not long before I realised how happy I was to be out of the undercover world of espionage and counter-espionage work in peacetime. The sheer façade to be constantly maintained; not being able to chat about my day's work with my wife and family or friends had been highly frustrating. Chinks in my self-discipline might have manifested themselves at awkward moments, with consequences which might have jeopardised one situation or another – especially after all the doubts surrounding Kim at that time. If I had remained in the Service and therefore been a part of it when he finally ran to Moscow, God knows what effect it might have had on me.

Looking back and remembering Peter Wright's remark: 'Desmond, you do know them all!' I wonder whether the moles, in an indirect way, helped break down the fear which Soviet Russia had of the West and the West had of the Soviets. Could some of their activities and a few drops of their revelations have led to *glasnost*, and the wall coming down?

All this considered, despite my own 'brainwashing devices', being involved in that work has kept my mind very active. Frequently, discussions in our household are about world political behaviour. Of course, during the Peter Wright case the conversation was heated, and I was very upset by the pathetic behaviour of the Government from beginning to end. When discussions are not about politics, they are about the garden or a new terrace or wall for the house, or some new business venture I am involved in; and very often about art and wine.

Now the book is over and finished I will talk less about politics. As for the years of governmental investigations and the soul-destroying moments, here is a little Churchillian-type quote which I think sums it up: 'Never was so much time wasted by so many people keeping non-secrets secret from their own people' – Tapwater.

Index